Deprivation and Compensatory Education: A Consideration

Helen E. Rees / Smith College

HOUGHTON MIFFLIN COMPANY • BOSTON
New York • Atlanta • Geneva, Ill. • Dallas • Palo Alto

Dedicated to
John E. H. Blackie, M.A. (Cantab.)
Companion of the Order of the Bath
Her Britannic Majesty's
Chief Inspector of Primary Schools, 1958–1966

CONTENTS

EDITOR'S INTRODUCTION

There is no doubt today that American society has at long last recognized the problems of its impoverished and underdeveloped members—those referred to variously as "the disadvantaged," "the deprived," or "the culturally disadvantaged" or "culturally deprived." The emerging recognition of these problems is bringing with it a realization that the situation cannot remain dormant, that we cannot wait for time to solve the problems. Furthermore, the acuteness of the situation demands not only immediate action, but intelligent action. Many efforts of local, state, and national bodies are sporadic, impulsive, and temporary. Most of them are, to use a time-worn phrase, "too little and too late."

The programs to alleviate and rectify the problems have evolved under differing approaches and differing philosophies, and it is, therefore, very difficult for most of us to understand their many ramifications. What are such programs as Head Start, the Peace Corps, VISTA, the National Teachers Corps, Upward Bound, the Job Corps, Adult Basic Education, Tutorial programs? What are the programs under "Title VI" of the Elementary and Secondary Education Act? What efforts are being made by local urban school districts? by rural school districts?

In DEPRIVATION AND COMPENSATORY EDUCATION, Helen Rees has brought together a mass of information on the programs and projects aimed at providing help for disadvantaged children and adults. Individuals engaging in or planning to engage in programs for the poor and depressed segments of society will find between the covers of this one book an up-to-date discussion and description of current philosophies and programs.

Samuel A. Kirk

PREFACE

At a time such as this when the key word is *change* and all of us are faced with the intermingling of opposite ideologies such as independence and interdependence, affluence and poverty, value and challenge, stability and mobility, all of it bringing forth torrents of words from all directions, one hesitates to add more words. It seems to take the occasion of an unforeseen happy and enriching experience and the added encouragement of those involved to give one the courage to take pen in hand and add further expressions of thought.

I express appreciation to Dr. James D. Koerner and to Mr. John E. H. Blackie for making possible my sharing of ideas on Compensatory Education for the Deprived with representative School Inspectors of Great Britain in the beautiful setting at Dartington College of Arts at Totnes in Devon, England, during the summer of 1966.

My appreciation also goes to Dr. Samuel Kirk and Mr. William MacDonald for the encouragement to expand the ideas presented at the summer Conference. And all of us who are deeply interested and concerned about the plight of the children and youth of the special one third of our nation recognize and value the extensive work and research being done in the field of deprivation and compensatory education. These furnish the sound basis for experimentation in educational thought and planning with the hope of finding the appropriate attitudes, the communication of understanding, and the door of opportunity that can be opened in order to reach these people and help them discover their own worth as human beings.

Special thanks are indeed due to the following, whose time, encouragement, and assistance have made this book possible: Elizabeth Robinton, Elsie Koester, Alice Campbell, Evelyn Cannon, Kay Thompson, Dave Wharton, Jerome Peterson, David McElwain, Linda Filadoro, and Megan Andruss.

H.E.R.

"Individual freedom and effectiveness and the progress of the society require the development of every citizen's rational powers. Among the many important purposes of American schools the fostering of that development must be central.

"Man has already transformed his world by using his mind. As he expands the application of rational methods to problems old and new, and as people in growing numbers are enabled to contribute to such endeavors, man will increase his ability to understand, to act, and to alter his environment. Where these developments will lead cannot be foretold.

"Man has before him the possibility of a new level of greatness, a new realization of human dignity and effectiveness. The instrument which will realize this possibility is that kind of education which frees the mind and enables it to contribute to a full and worthy life. To achieve this goal is the high hope of the nation and the central challenge to its schools."

Educational Policies Commission, *The Central Purpose of American Education* (Washington: National Education Association, 1965), p. 21.

Introduction

The growing concern for compensatory education expressed in books and educational journals makes it clear that the time has come to give this subject careful consideration. Some tentative conclusions can be drawn concerning the progress that has been made and where it has brought all of those deeply concerned with the problem. The time for evaluating the efforts of the past is also the time for raising questions that may determine the direction of the steps we still have to take.

The most serious challenge yet to face education in the United States is that of meeting the needs of the deprived child and the deprived youth within our own society. We are only recently discovering the ramifications, and the depth, of the problem. A realistic look at our cities and rural areas, our schools and the education they provide, the quality of communication among groups, and the conditions that we have generally accepted as adequate for living and learning shows that it will not be a simple task to give back to this country the "equal" education that we extol and that for too long we have assumed was in operation. In the process of disenthralling ourselves we find that we must now determine what we mean by *education* as well as determining the effects of the total environment, human relationships, the interaction of ideas, the meeting of the needs of all human beings, and aiding each person to discover and to cope within his environment.

General references to books and articles are indicated in the text by numbers within parentheses. These refer to numbers in the Bibliography at the end of the book. In some instances page numbers are also given; for example, (10:15–35). Raised numbers indicate specific references given at the end of each chapter, which are not included in the Bibliography.

Even before these meanings can be determined we find ourselves faced with a series of questions. At first they appear unrelated, but as one considers them there appears to be a thread which, if followed, may lead to a possible approach. Is compensatory education necessary? Why are we wasting not only human effort and human potentiality, but also human personality? How should the school as a social institution face the challenge of the world of change? What should be the real concerns of education and what should be today's educational promise? Must children be abused and exploited while we take time to experiment with the educational system? Is there room for both pride and prejudice in the schools we should plan for tomorrow? Should we educate for a Great Society? What is it important to learn? Should we revise our ideas of equal educational opportunity and education for excellence, and, if so, what will be the new definitions of *equal* and *excellence*? Are we ready to answer the question that has been put before us many times before — education for what?

These questions remain unanswered. Answers are being offered, but the true answers can come only through proof within the schools and special educational programs, and within the unquestionable success of those individuals partaking of the total educational program, regardless of age, class, race, level of ability, or level of potentiality.

Can we accept the following statement of the outcomes of a liberal education for each and every person?

> The liberally-educated man is articulate, both in speech and writing. He has a feel for language, a respect for clarity and directness of expression, and a knowledge of some language other than his own. He is at home in the world of quantity, number, and measurement. He thinks rationally, logically, objectively, and knows the difference between fact and opinion. When the occasion demands, however, his thought is imaginative, and creative rather than logical. He is perceptive, sensitive to form, and affected by beauty. His mind is flexible and adaptable, curious and independent. He knows a good deal about the world of nature, the world of man, about the culture of which he is a part, but he is never merely "well-informed." He can use what he knows, with judgment and discrimination. He thinks of his business or profession, his family life, and his avocations as parts of a larger whole, parts of a purpose which he has made his own. Whether making a professional or a personal decision, he acts with maturity, balance, and perspective, which come ultimately from his knowledge of other persons, other problems, other times and places.[1]

Can we agree with Paul Woodring? He states:

> In a society of free men, the proper aim of education is to prepare the individual to make wise decisions. *All else is but contributory.*
>
> The educated man is one who can choose between good and bad, between truth and falsehood, between the beautiful and the ugly, between the worthwhile and the trivial. His education will enable him to make ethical decisions, political decisions, decisions within the home and on the job. It will enable him to choose a good book, a good painting, or a good piece of music. It will enable him to make the many decisions necessary in planning a good life and conducting it properly.[2]

In seeking the words with which to present the ideas of a far more satisfactory approach to the problem of total education, we must remember that none of this effort will be effective if we forget the learner, the child. "Each child is an important part of our lives. We merely help to shape his future, ultimately, he will determine ours." (396:2)

There is a frame of reference here, however, that must serve to orient us as we give consideration to the best education for each learner. This is the society in which we are living. This is the society in which the child and youth are living. This society is beset with problems to solve, changes to make. The changes are social, economic and educational in nature. These are the problems of prejudice, discrimination, segregation, slum housing, unequal pay, hunger, disease, unrest, violence, destruction of property, incitement, militant leadership, refutation of values, responsibilities, and laws, and the refusal to work or to teach while arbitration of conditions of work and pay is in progress. These problems must be resolved; changes must be brought about. Is this possible? Not all of the problems are conditions of poverty. The solution of each of these problems is essential to ensuring the successful changing of the attitudes of our society and the renewing of our educational system. Can our country rise to the tremendous tasks at hand or must we accept the conclusion stated by a recognized, elected spokesman: ". . . the Great Society has become a sick society. . . . Our country is being weakened by a grotesque inversion of priorities, the effects of which are becoming clear to more and more Americans—in Congress, the press and the country at large."[3]

Until such time as our educational system is reconstructed to be able to meet the needs of every individual regardless of background and condition, some form of education for the deprived child and the deprived youth, deprived because of the social, economic, and educational condition of poverty, is necessary. Recognizing that poverty is at the root of the many forms of deprivation, let us consider education for the deprived child and deprived youth within the framework of what we may hopefully call social, economic, cultural, and educational change. Compensatory education within this framework must be far more than "adequate," for it must demand a richness, a depth, and a breadth in the everyday learning and living experiences of each and every child, youth, and adult. Differences for different persons may be a matter of degree depending upon the needs and potentialities of these persons, but at no time can it be allowed that the accepted educational pattern is to be of different quality for different persons or different groups. Can we meet this challenge?

In considering compensatory education we cannot limit the thinking and the planning to the young child; nor can we single out the deprived adolescent or the deprived adult. Poverty strikes with equal force at the heart of every age. Any new approach to education must be carefully planned for the span of human life: the health and welfare of the infant, the young child's first exciting steps in learning, the growing child's seriousness of purpose in learning the tools for living, the adolescent's readjustment to life within the setting of obtainable goals, the young adult's flexible re-education in the light of change, and the satisfactions that come to the mature and aging adult from appropriate labor, good human relationships, and active participation within the rich cultural world.

To be considered here will be terse statements of some of the thinking concerning basic facts essential to better understanding, of some of the knowledge we have gained in identifying those deprived through poverty, of some of the steps taken by the more formal social institution, the school, of the role that government appears to be playing in the solution of more immediate problems, and of the values of some of the objective efforts of programs that give evidence of advance toward the goals set. It is hoped that there will be detected within these statements not only description but tentative evaluations and indications for further steps along the way. It would be difficult to give recognition to all who have contributed, but through the representation given, major elements of progress are expressed.

It is well to keep in mind that there are always those who are successfully doing that which the majority is still seeking, and have for themselves the inner satisfaction of work well done.

REFERENCES

[1] McGeorge Bundy, *et al., General Education in School and College* (Cambridge: Harvard University Press, 1952), pp. 19–20.

[2] Paul Woodring, *A Fourth of a Nation* (New York: McGraw-Hill Book Company, Inc., 1957), p. 111.

[3] J. W. Fulbright, "The Great Society Is a Sick Society," *The New York Times Magazine* (August 20, 1967), pp. 30, 92–93.

The Essential Background of Understanding

All persons concerned with the current problems in education are aware of the enormity of the task of undertaking to present a comprehensive statement of the essential background of understanding, even when confined to the problems of deprivation and compensatory education, for the very words used to describe the true condition seem to limit its seriousness. One needs to see the situation through the eyes of the anthropologist, the historian, the sociologist, the psychologist, and the educator. Then, through the aggregate of these observations, he can endeavor to understand the condition of poverty as it affects the social institution of education. This list of those concerned should also include the representatives of government at the federal, state, and local levels, the social workers, and, of course, the teachers who have lived with the children of poverty within the school itself. They have all become "experts," and are ready and willing to express their impressions, their theories, and their recommendations for quick solutions. Perhaps we need to look to the behavioral scientists, who have been carrying on considerable research, and to recognize that our greatest hope lies in close cooperation between them and the educator who is concerned with the total picture of the developmental study approach to human beings. He sees education as a long-term process, and can translate the research into material for that most important process of teaching and learning, thus giving stability and meaning to the changes that must come about.

At the outset we should review the current terminology and

definition used to identify those we call "deprived." Tribute should be paid to those in the field of health, who have opened our eyes to some of the conditions that exist, even before we look at social theories concerning the deprived and their place in society and consider the factor of cultural difference. We shall then look at the social, economic, and educational aspects of the current situation that have bearing on our further deliberation on the child and youth within deprived situations and on the school and the educational process we envision for them.

Terminology and Definition

Within the current literature the following terms are used most commonly to describe the children and youth being discussed here: culturally disadvantaged or culturally deprived, socially disadvantaged or socially deprived, and educationally disadvantaged or educationally deprived. In many instances it appears obvious that these terms are interchanged for variety of language rather than distinction in basic meaning. It is indeed true that if a child is disadvantaged or deprived, he is so in the cultural, social, and educational areas. Deprived people are found where opportunities in these areas are small or nonexistent.

The question arises whether or not the terms "disadvantaged" and "deprived" can be used interchangeably. *Disadvantaged* has a less ominous sound and raises hope for finding one's way out of the condition of poverty. It gives one the feeling that for the time being conditions are not good, but it may be only a matter of time, opportunity, or even effort until those to whom the label is attached may rise above the present situation. *Deprived* gives one a sense of unwilling loss, a loss that may extend over a long period of time, hence having more of an aura of hopelessness, of defeat, and even of desolation among many who seemingly are almost within reach of much. Unfortunately this is what we are facing. In a discussion limited to those who are in a position to need compensatory education there is no doubt that "deprived" is more fitting. Again, both words denote lack of economic status, but the term "deprived" means a loss over a longer period of time of the type of economic status necessary to provide even the essential and basic cultural, social, and educational advantages. It is the deprived child and deprived youth that we must help, for it appears to be the nature of the situation that hopelessness and desolation over a still longer period of time tend to breed even greater hopelessness and desolation, and it is this which our country cannot afford. Care should also be taken in adding any type of descriptive word to the term "deprived," such as "culturally" or "socially" or "educationally," to define that word clearly. Even the most severely deprived child is living within some type of culture. He is living within some form of social interaction and, in the same light, he is absorbing some form of education as he interacts with his own environment, no matter how meager. This same thinking also applies to the term "deprived" as related to geographic location. It is true that we find the majority of deprived children and deprived youth living within what we commonly call slums or depressed areas. The acuteness of the poverty, however, may cause a family or a small group to be on the move even within the limits of a large urban area so that as this basic problem continues we find that what was once a rather permanently located slum is now fluid and very much dependent upon the waves of mobility of its people. All of these sections are not only depressing for those of us on the outside but depressing and discouraging for those on the inside, and it is the desire to be in a better situation that is responsible for some of the mobility.

In considering poverty as the basis of deprivation it will be well to keep in mind that there are many kinds of poverty, and that the term can be used in connection with individuals and their families, but not, accurately, with large groups. Every effort should be made to see that the terms "poor" and "deprived" do not become labels to be hung around the necks of the children and the youth who are in no way responsible for the conditions in which they find themselves. The label belongs on the conditions, which must be corrected in order that those within can develop as unique human beings, with potential to be tapped and with opportunities to contribute positively not only to their narrow situation, but to the wider community. And the correction of poverty does not mean the providing of money to guarantee minimum requirements still within the poverty range, but the providing of a plan for the release of the people so that they may become the types of citizens desired in our democracy, not just by the middle class, but by all.

The problem of poverty in this country, as some would see it, is stated thus by the Task Force on Economic Growth and Opportunity:

> Poverty in America is of a far different order from poverty in most of
> the rest of the world and from the kind of poverty that most history
> has recorded. The United States has no mass "culture" of poverty.
> That is, Americans as a society do not believe that it is their fate to
> be poor, that poverty is inevitable. On the contrary, one of our prob-
> lems is a desire to become part of the "culture" of the non-poor and
> the frustrations that result from being unable to do so.[1]

There is evidence within the literature that there is not as yet
agreement on the use of terminology or on the definition of those
terms which are generally used. This lack of agreement does not
necessarily indicate confusion of thinking or divergence of ideas, but
rather is evidence that the many people who seek some form of
solution are still in the process of using a variety of approaches and
a variety of patterns of thought. This is a healthy sign.

James E. Russell gives a strong statement of the problem:

> There is at present a cancer eating at the heart of our nation. Whether
> we can cure it or not only the future will tell. It is not a problem of
> segregation or desegregation, of employment or unemployment, of race
> relations; it is not even a question of human justice, although it in-
> volves all those problems. It is the problem of our own underde-
> veloped people. We have called them "disadvantaged Americans."
> They are referred to also as the culturally deprived. Sometimes I wish
> that we could use the term "neolithic," for it fits. (131:35)

Frank Riessman comments upon two of the commonly used terms:

> A word is necessary about the term "culturally deprived." While
> lower socio-economic groups lack many of the advantages (and dis-
> advantages) of middle-class culture, we do not think it is appropriate
> to describe them as "culturally deprived." As we shall see, they pos-
> sess a culture of their own, with many positive characteristics that
> have developed out of coping with a difficult environment. The term
> "culturally deprived" refers to those aspects of middle-class culture—
> such as education, books, formal language—from which these groups
> have not benefited. However, because it is the term in current usage,
> we will use "culturally deprived" interchangeably with "educationally
> deprived" to refer to the members of lower socio-economic groups
> who have had limited access to education. (124:3)

For a period of time it was considered more appropriate to use
the term "socially deprived." But this term has not been inclusive
enough to take into account all of the forms of deprivation; nor has
it seemed to include finer distinctions for which some have been
searching. Martin Deutsch, of the Institute for Developmental

Studies, gives his explanation in view of this search for the more basic definition:

> We are dealing with a situation that really could be called "stimulus deprivation." Particularly is there a restriction in the variety of stimulation available to the child who comes from a slum atmosphere.
>
> Stimulus deprivation would be an aspect of the total deprivation complex that I would like to refer to. It doesn't have anything to do with culture, per se. It has something to do with the relevance of value systems of certain subcultural groups for the major group within our society and for the demands of middle-class society for certain kinds of learning.[2]

It is still necessary, therefore, to be arbitrary in the choice of the term one uses. In the present context we shall refer to those needing compensatory education as *deprived*, deprivation meaning without those broad essentials necessary for a higher level of living. The deprived child and the deprived youth will be those who have need for assistance in striving for, achieving, and using the social, economic, cultural, and educational opportunities that, through personal interaction, should give to each the chance for self-realization, the use of ability and potential, and active participation in a society of which he proves worthy. Compensatory education will mean the several aspects of a broad education translated into appropriate and enriching experiences which in turn will take each individual step by step toward this goal.

Identification of the Deprived

In order to determine as clearly as possible the setting in which we find the deprived child and the deprived youth it is necessary to ask an important question: Who are the deprived? According to Crow, Murray and Smythe (31:2–20) studies have been carried on for some time concerning the effects of poverty, endeavoring to identify the characteristics that would seem to be both the factors causing poverty and deprivation and the bases on which to work for improvement of conditions. The mobility of people and the constantly changing economic conditions of the whole country as well as within certain sections of the country make it possible and imperative to continue with the studies and to gain new information.

It is generally accepted that we find conditions of poverty and evidences of general deprivation when we locate families or small groups living, on low incomes and with high percentages of unemployment, in poor housing with poor sanitary conditions and inadequate living space. The atmosphere among these groups tends to be one of discouragement. There is lack of effort and little use of abilities, no understanding of what education might do, and, finally, willingness to take one's share of the doles offered and acceptance of the low level of living allowed by such doles. Inevitably these groupings include many aged, sick, and disabled people, who find themselves unable to rise above their meager surroundings. We find these groups among farm workers, in the cities, in certain geographic regions, and, too often, among what we call the minority groups.

Much of the discussion at the present time is concerned with those in the inner cities or the ghettoes, the negative aspects of which are publicized far too much. It is important to remember that it is those who have migrated from the rural South to the cities who are finding their rural ways of living incompatible with inner-city life. Also, American cities are changing rapidly. The migration of the middle class to the suburbs is leaving the major part of the city itself to these of the poverty class who have migrated from rural areas.

According to Pettigrew, the massive migration of the Negroes from the South, beginning in 1915, continues to the large urban centers. Between 1950 and 1960 more than half a million moved to the Northeast, half a million to the Midwest, and a third of a million to the western states. From 1940 to 1960 the non-white percentages in New York City and Philadelphia more than doubled, and they tripled in Chicago, Los Angeles, and Detroit.[3] Even in these larger cities there is little demand for unskilled labor and meager skills together with the southern dialect stand in the way of obtaining what employment is available. There is need among this group for retraining and further education.

Also, from the hill country of the South, the whites who have failed to make a living for their families there must move to areas where some form of labor is in demand. These Appalachian Mountain whites have found that economic growth has come to a standstill, that their farms are too small, and that they are no longer needed in the fields or the coal mines. These people, like the Negroes, bring with them very few skills and find few job opportunities as they move.

The number of migrants from Puerto Rico is increasing rapidly and constantly. They form another minority group in the city and, although figures do not remain static, it is known that in New York

City alone approximately 16 percent of the total population are Puerto Ricans. Like the other two groups, they are finding that they cannot locate work; this particular group of people is now moving westward. In some western cities they are finding means of becoming self-supporting and have been somewhat successful in making adjustments to their new surroundings. These are a proud people who are not yet willing to settle for the poorest of existences.

In the Southwest, the Mexican-Americans continue to live in the slum atmospheres they have known for so long. The work they undertake is seasonal and they are finding that greater mobility is necessary. These migrants are working their way toward the East, and as they do they discover that both their skin color and their language are handicaps (31).

In some 25 states are found the poorest Americans, the Indians. It is estimated that there are approximately 380,000 Indians living in or near the federal reservations. The conditions of squalor, substandard housing, and high incidence of disease are now a concern of those endeavoring to include them in the poverty program to a greater degree. A few tribes are now able to improve their living conditions through the good use of funds in the more productive areas. It is estimated, however, that only half of the work force, some 50,000, are currently employed.[4]

In addition to these specific groups with their own peculiar conditions of poverty, there are the poor of every locality, too many of them willing to accept the little that life offers. They share with the migrants the lack of appreciation for the value of education. Most of them in fact are filled with loneliness and hopelessness, and have little concern for themselves or their children and little desire to be part of the larger American society. All of these people are to some degree alienated from their communities and even from those who might be of help to them. There are those who are unaware of the availability of welfare assistance, unaware of the help at hand in case of illness, and seemingly unconcerned about the future of the children in their midst. Two questions arise: How have we permitted this situation to develop? Who should take the responsibility for eradicating this grave social illness?

How much do the American people know about the conditions that exist not too far from them? How many Americans are aware of the conditions under which young children are living and that create within deprived youth the dissatisfaction, the misunderstanding, and the hatred of life as it is? We glibly talk of the Great

Society and even of the role that education should play, but what is the average American's concept of such a Society? We speak of urbanization and urban renewal, the great advances in technology, the fact that both space and time have diminished in dimension and as a result we are more and more dependent upon each other, and, with the discussion of the growth in population, we calmly claim the affluent society as the goal for everyone. Are we thinking of the smallness of the world in terms of other lands or are we thinking of those people just thirty miles away down by the river? When we speak of man's great advances in the world of science and technology, do we translate them in terms of providing more jobs for the unemployed or even food for those who need it? It would be interesting to take a poll of the middle and upper classes to determine if the books they have read recently include books like those by Michael Harrington,[5] Jack Weller,[6] Steve Allen,[7] and Piri Thomas.[8] It would be a hopeful sign if any such books should reach the best-seller lists in our country.

Contributions of Public Health

All of us are becoming more fully aware of the necessity of good health for good living and good learning. At the same time, we are being made aware of the severity of the health problems among the deprived. It is most fortunate that the social institutions of this country include one group that has made strides in understanding the deprived. Public health personnel have led others in becoming acquainted with the deprived, learning about them, and taking some definite steps in helping them. They are providing us with scientific information gained from the results of excellent studies of poverty, and they have met with success in setting up programs for meeting the needs of the children as well as working with the parents in this area.

At the present time public health officials are striving to narrow the gap between the services they offer and the use of these services. They propose to do this by organizing public health and medical programs for low-income and minority groups in such places and in such ways that the programs can be desired and their structure understood by those in need. This will mean that through a process of health education the aspiration and expectation levels of the deprived in relation to these health and medical programs are raised.

Public health workers are endeavoring also to stress the importance of both quality and quantity of medical services, with equality in both for all citizens, whoever or wherever they may be, and particularly for the low-income groups, the ethnic minorities, and those still remaining in the rural areas. One of the problems that these workers have found is also met by other persons studying low-income groups. This is the very strong impact of ethnocentrism and ethnic exclusivity, the attitudes that tend to bind people of the same background or the same belief together within an area. These attitudes are evidenced in people's desire to remain with those with whom they have grown up, with those who hold to the same religion, or even with those whose families have known their families over a long period of time. Such desires are indications of the search for security, and they may point out the fear of meeting new people who live differently and observe different cultural practices. (467) Preserving the old ways of doing things, of course, stands in the way of establishing new knowledge and new understanding. This is particularly serious in relation to health problems. There are obvious important parallels to this in relation to education and intergroup living, and they are having a marked effect upon the attitudes of the children.

Suchman makes the following statement concerning the public health worker's point of view about a deprived person:

> He needs to be stimulated to make productive use of his own cultural tradition and norms in ways that are familiar to him and yet in keeping with positive medical and social goals, and to be informed and educated about necessary bureaucratic structures and procedures so that he feels more at home among them, and is more able to make intelligent decisions and evaluations about them as a medical consumer. (467:1733)

An interesting observation was made recently concerning an emphasis that occurred about 55 years ago on poverty and its causes as they were linked with ill health, family disorganization, and the attendant miseries. It was felt at that time that the condition of poverty and its consequences could be prevented or controlled. The question that is presently raised is whether, even if we are successful at this time, there will be a need for re-emphasis on these same problems again in the year 2015? These are the introductory ideas in excellent articles presented by Dr. George James, who fully discusses the question of poverty as an obstacle to health in our cities, and by Dr. Robert Straus, who gives a carefully prepared statement of poverty as an obstacle to health in our rural areas.[9] Dr. James concludes his article with the somber thought that if we in America, the land that has much, cannot deal with poverty in both cities and rural areas, there is little hope for the much larger numbers of the poor in other parts of the world. Dr. Straus leaves us with the thought that a consideration of the several aspects of health cannot be separated from a similar consideration of the aspects of the economy and education within our country.

Still another approach to poverty that has developed through the cooperation of the State Welfare Departments and Public Health Departments is the establishment of day care for children, or Day Care Centers. Federal funds are now available to the various states for these centers, but we see here also the necessity for joint effort, for evidence must be made available of the cooperative planning of health agencies, schools, and welfare organizations within the community in order to secure these funds. These Day Care Centers or Day Nurseries serve children from age two and, in many cases, in large groups. Their purpose is to offer a developmental program that will provide for and promote each child's physical, emotional, social, and intellectual growth. Particular attention is given to the child's nutritional needs, for nutrition, development, and learning are interdependent. Among the health services provided are visual and auditory screening, tuberculin testing, and clinical tests to detect the beginnings of possible future difficulties such as high blood pressure, postural defects, and anemia. This program has been particularly successful because, by the provision of services for the child, the parents are helped to understand his development and to anticipate the possible hazards that might occur in his normal development as he investigates the world around him. Thus the need for parental care and parental supervision is emphasized. The emotional health of the child is also given considerable attention. The parents in turn are helped to deal with such problems as excessive fears, discipline situations, and rivalry, and to understand a child's need to be with other children in order to have the opportunity to express himself emotionally and learn to live with others.[10]

The very revealing studies that are being made from the health point of view concerning migrant workers will be taken up in a later section, in a discussion of perhaps the most serious of deprived conditions.

It should prove most interesting, within the next few years, to watch the progress that can be made with the public assuming responsibility, with the support of the federal government, in caring for those who are ill and those who are in need of medical assistance in the lower-income brackets. If one fifth to one third of our population is now considered to be within this bracket, and if cities such as New York[11] report that poverty is the number three cause of death, efforts to educate can have little effect. A hungry child or a sick child cannot learn as he should. Our first responsibility is to cure the basic ills of the poor. Indeed, all areas of society must join together to work hand in hand for this cure, which is basic for all of us.

One is encouraged by the recent announcement appearing in a scientific journal:

> By 1 June the Office of Economic Opportunity (OEO) had made grants totaling more than $30 million for a score of comprehensive health projects, including six rural projects approved within the last few months. Neighborhood health centers are operating in Denver . . ., Boston, New York, and several other cities. Now Tufts University School of Medicine, which is operating the Columbia Point project in Boston, will undertake a similar venture in the Mississippi community of Mound Bayou, an all-Negro town in Bolivar County, at the heart of the cotton-growing delta region . . . serving the poor of a 400-square-mile area with a population of about 14,000. . . .
>
> A steady increase in the number of neighborhood health centers, urban and rural, is contemplated.[12]

Health has proved to be a factor in the rioting situations along with poverty. One of the resultant and forward steps taken in Watts recently was the opening of a new medical clinic. Each such step is an important one.

Social Theory

Within the many discussions and efforts to theorize about society, particularly as one reaches the point of good perspective on what has gone on before, the consistent recognizable thread that runs throughout is change. Change is the key word in the fascinating study of man within his environment through the centuries. It is change that has characterized the ideas of man and influenced him as he has organized and reorganized the various institutions of living. (131)

Various social organizations rise and fall, various movements are stirred and decline, but the ideas remain, and later generations are allowed the benefits of the past. From the distant past we learn the value of critical thinking, of ethical behavior, and of inductive reasoning. These ideals can be identified easily with those groups or "civilizations" that rose and fell in their turn. One cannot help but wonder what ideas will survive the changes within the current social movements of this country wh₂ ₚ₃ distance permits a more objective look.

One can trace back easily to the beginnings of the slum areas, through the period when it was thought that poverty was here to stay. There were even those who endeavored to set up the condition of poverty as a virtue, but this so-called "virtue" has become a blight of ignorance, of disease, of ugliness, of dirt, and finally of hopelessness. The greatest harm of all is what it is doing and has done through the years to the children of the poor. It is here that we cannot help but wonder if history will repeat itself. This statement by Daniel Thompson causes us to give serious thought:

> Our nation will begin to decline in strength and nobility of purpose, and could eventually fall, unless we take care to conserve and develop our most precious, and altogether indispensable, resource—the youth of this nation. (91:2)

Thompson makes this statement on the basis of Toynbee's conclusion that practically all of the early civilizations that fell did so because their youth did not possess the ". . . high ideals, the basic values, the fundamental skills, and the nobility of purpose which, in the first place, brought their nations to greatness." (91:2)

In any discussion of social theory, one thinks of the division into social classes. Allison Davis (32) considers three kinds of divisions: (1) social classes, (2) the ethnic or foreign-born groups, and (3) the color-castes. In his discussion he points out the possibility in this country that a person from one social class or from an ethnic or foreign-born group can, through education where he learns acceptable behavior of a higher level, move and live within that level, while, particularly in the southern states, those in the color-caste are allowed little or no status movement out of the group into which they were born. Recently we have seen some slight evidence of certain individuals' being able to move from a color-caste, but these are still rare instances. It would appear that the tendency toward moving from a lower class to a middle or upper class may have lessened a bit in the last few years because of the more acute awareness of differences by the public. Davis does recognize that those within the slum group have very little opportunity to learn the behavior necessary to move. Since those in the middle class tend to describe the behavior of the slum group as shiftless or unmotivated and delinquent because of some publicized examples, a stigma is attached to this group that makes it difficult for those who are motivated, who are willing to cooperate, and who wish to work, to find their way out.

While Davis recognizes the three classes, upper, middle, and lower, there were those in the popular press who changed the wording to the "haves" and the "have-nots." Very recently, and again by the press, three new classes are being described: (1) "the power structure" or "the establishment," (2) "the disadvantaged," "the culturally deprived," or "the poor," and (3) "the rat-racers" or the "middle class."[13] It will be interesting to watch for the trend in name-calling in the next few years, particularly to see whether the middle class has a chance for survival in that type of publicity.

Even though we do not have the perspective for judgment on the changes that are taking place all around us, it is well to note some of the indications in order to be aware of the types of changes that our children and youth are facing and will be facing. Perhaps the most important to note is that there has been a change in the tempo of change itself. This has become so rapid that all of us are forced to live with the feeling that we do not know what will happen tomorrow. This means that educational planning must include a type of attitude that accepts change as a part of day-to-day living. For now everyday life is a problem not of adapting to change but rather of discovering the ways in which to make use of it. This indicates for education not the absorption of knowledge but a way of discovering knowledge, not the learning of facts that are needed for today alone, but learning how to learn for what one may face tomorrow. Foremost, education should take on a newer look. More and more it should be accepted that there is no end to education, but that living becomes a constant process of re-education in the light of what currently is new.

Another major change which is upon us is the sudden widening of the horizons and hence the widening and deepening of the problems that are to be faced. Regardless of our politics or patriotism, we find ourselves citizens of a small world in which the decisions of a country far away may have almost immediate effects upon our thinking and our solutions to the problems we face here. Along with this change has come a new vocabulary. We talk of survival, the division of power because of the vastness of the knowledge we have, and the need for information to come from many rather than from a few. Our communication systems have brought us far more knowledge with which to cope than we have had on issues before. The problem of judgment is a much more serious one. We receive information about peoples we have never been concerned with before, and we are finding difficulty in keeping our attitudes apace with our knowledge. All of this has an undermining effect on those aspects of living that in the past we have felt were stable.

We still feel the need for a set of values, but we are asking what kind of values. Our belief in respect for human life must change to respect for each human life. Technology, along with better understanding of man, is forcing us to recognize that man has a higher potential, should have higher aspirations, and must be given greater opportunities than we have ever before realized. Through this recognition we now see poverty and deprivation in relation to what might be. We are recognizing that the conditions of poverty and the conditions of deprivation cannot be sealed off in the present world — certainly not in our own country, for the atmospheres created by these conditions permeate the total environment. Our country is the poorer because of our poor and our country is becoming deprived because of our deprived people, particularly our deprived children and youth, who form the outlook for tomorrow.

Cultural Differences

How important are the cultural differences that we find among groups of deprived people? It has been too readily assumed that these differences would dissolve in the discovery of similarities as these groups learned to live in their new environments, share common experiences, and build friendships. Actually, in the intermingling of various subcultures there has been little opportunity for people to know each other well enough to find similarities or even to discover the areas in which common experience might prevail. With the stirring within the great "melting pot," one by one the various ingredients are rising to the surface, each one still with its own characteristics. This is indicative of the depth of the subculture traditions, the importance of the individual values that have grown out of these traditions, and the strength of the attitudes built through the years as each group has had to cope with the conditions of life as it has found them.

"Cultural pluralism," a term meaning the coexistence of the several cultures, reminds us of the very history of our country and the positive contributions that the several cultures have made to our heritage. It should never take on the meaning of "live and let live." The sheer isolation implied in this meaning soon destroys the "let live," a fact well proven.

"Culture" is usually defined by the anthropologist and the sociologist as the total way of life of a people. It is the social bequest that each individual acquires from his group. This specific culture becomes the framework for the structuring of his life's activities. It is a force within the life of the individual that determines the pattern of his behavior, a very personal force that is transmitted from parent to child, a force far more powerful than the social grouping previously discussed. It takes more than the changing of environment and the mere intermingling of subcultures to bring about a change in the personal culture of the individual, for in his culture are his values, his attitudes, and his beliefs concerning the basic aspects of living. The sociologist and the educator must go beyond the study of class to the study of personal culture to find an approach to understanding the deprived people.

Riessman paints a vivid picture of some of the more outstanding characteristics of the culture of the deprived individual:

> He is traditional, "old fashioned" in many ways, patriarchal, super-stitious, somewhat religious, . . . reads ineffectively, is poorly in-formed . . . has definite, intense convictions . . . feels alienated . . . is not individualistic, introspective, self-oriented, or concerned with self-expression . . . holds the world, rather than himself, responsible for his misfortunes . . . prefers jobs that promise security to those that entail risk . . . is not class conscious . . . is not interested in politics . . . is strongly anti-communist . . . sets great store by his family and his personal comforts . . . likes excitement . . . is pragmatic and anti-intellectual. (124:26–28)

It is important to know these broad general characteristics in order to deal with these people. However, we must keep constantly in mind that among the deprived, as within any group, there are individual differences. And it is the individual who is important to us. We must also recognize the effect of change upon the cultural picture of the individual. The direct influence of the environment on his behavior and personality has been weakened by the element of mobility as the family structure has been weakened by the demands of urbanization. The several social agencies, including education, have the problem of counteracting the effects of change in order to prevent human deterioration within these groups. Expectations are increasing with the changes taking place, and a balance of control must be established between these expectations and reality as it exists in new situations and even within change itself.

One of our deepest concerns should be to prevent the formation of the concept of a culture of poverty within this country. The acceptance of the idea allocates to poverty a permanent position within the social order. It is assumed that the deprived must always be with us, that it is futile to go to the root of poverty and attempt to remove it, and that the children and youth shall not only inherit this culture but be responsible for maintaining it. We must take the responsibility for making possible a positive change in the cultural pattern of values and loyalties for every group. The excitement of discovery in the explosion of knowledge now taking place must carry to every group. Every individual must have a share in the so-called "cultural boom" as technology increases efficiency and man is given a new opportunity for enriched living and the continuing of education toward his own betterment in the leisure time provided. Everyone must share in the new enthusiasm evidenced for reading, music, art, and the performing arts. It is the responsibility of education to take a new form and open the doors of the cultural renaissance to all people. The freedom of each individual is implicit in our new knowledge and in the new opportunities for creativity and active self-expression. Each adult, each youth, and each child must have the privilege of discovering the answer to the question: Who am I? He must also know the answer to the question: What am I uniquely capable of doing?

These two questions imply a positive outlook rather than a negative one. It is essential to each individual that as he answers the first question, he sets forth the positive characteristics that make him a unique person. He must see his culture as a positive one even though it be a meager one, and it is on the *positive* aspects of his culture that he must build toward greater self-realization. His answer to the second question also implies a positive point of view, for his sheer uniqueness is identified through his personal, *positive* qualities. His own capabilities, though sometimes only at the potential stage, must be realized by him as valuable and also basic to his improvement.

It is here that we question the school's responsibility and capability

of accepting and improving the culture of a particular people. Thus
far care has been taken to emphasize that the school as a formal
social institution, though very important, is only a part of what we
must plan for and conceive in the way of the total educational
process. It is the culture of the people taught, the culture within
the environment where change is to take place, that serves as the
basis for evaluation and planning of educational philosophy, educational programs, and the curriculum itself. Neither education nor
the school as its instrument can progress far in the improvement of
values, in training for better methods of coping with situations, in
the improvement of basic behavior patterns, and in increasing aspirations and setting higher ideals unless it starts with the realization
that there already exists a culture containing at least the beginnings
of these various goals. The world changes and the culture must
change with it, and the educator will do well to recognize this statement by Margaret Mead: ". . . no one will live all his life in the
world into which he was born, and no one will die in the world in
which he worked in his maturity."[14]

Social, Economic, and Educational Considerations

John Hersey aptly states the point of view taken in this section:

> We are dealing here with the healing of generations yet the urgency
> is of an hour to hour order. One who wants to change a . . . system
> must have the time sense of a geologist.[15]

There is a point at which enough time has elapsed that certain
events and occasions appear to take shape, form, and proportion and
become a part of our almost immediate history. At the same time
there are those very current happenings that are indeed considerations but must be stated in terms of their importance for continued
observation, for weighing and reweighing of their influence on past
and future events, because their place in the final form of our total
social structure is still undetermined.

When the White House Conference on Education met in Washington in July, 1965, we saw evidences of a trend toward an understanding that education is a problem for those other than educators.
Those attending the Conference did include representatives of university, school, and educational association groups, but also included
were representatives of major foundations, government, industry,
the general public, and the press.[16] Here indeed is precedent for

clear-cut cooperation between educators and leaders in our society.

It would appear that there will be changes in the long disputed extent of federal involvement in education. It is evident that there must be a national focus on this problem because of the on-going social and technological changes affecting the country as a whole. Education has become the business of the United States, and the effects of this broadened interest and involvement bear watching.

Thus we find that social, economic, and educational problems are being considered as closely related and closely interdependent. Indications are that these current national problems henceforth will be viewed from several angles but at the same time considered together so that the solutions will be the results of joint effort and will be expressed in terms of a complex betterment of society.

In education alone, interest and effort are being extended to provide programs for the very young child and at the same time to consider the adolescent, particularly the adolescent dropout. We are beginning to hear of the possibilities of basic education for the deprived adult as well. (95) It is not possible to leave out the social and economic phases of the programs being designed if the needs of these older groups are to be met.

In considering the plight of the disadvantaged or deprived person, it is necessary to see what is happening to him as a result of the new programs for urban renewal, increased welfare, social medicine, and the problem of mobility. It is true that some progress has been made in the cooperation of the various agencies dealing with the deprived. But there is room for improvement here as long as the deprived person can make the statement that "welfare keeps you where you are, but urban renewal keeps you moving." We have not yet faced the issue of the problems we are constantly creating in our hurry to improve the structure of our cities, to clear away the slums, and to introduce beautification in order to make the city attractive as a place to live once again. The deprived are moved from the slums, but we fail to provide better housing for them and they are forced to move to other areas, many times far worse than those being cleared. In newer efforts, better living areas are being built to replace former slums, but the deprived often cannot afford to take up residence in this cleaner, more attractive community. (89:25)

Since the funding of education has become everybody's business, more and more evidence has been made available concerning the importance of the educational process to successful living. We find that in many of the cities more than 50 percent of the school children are from what we have termed deprived areas, recognizing, of course, that deprivation can be expressed in degrees of seriousness. It is being pointed out that as these children reach the upper grade levels a large percentage of them are retarded anywhere from one to three or four years in the basic skills, particularly reading. (242:232) This retardation shows up not only in the academic field but also in the social. Such facts have led us to discover the too-high percentage of these same children who are gradually alienated from the school and its educational program, many of them leaving before the completion of any type of accepted formal school program. This is sometimes explained by the need for the financial assistance of an adolescent by his family, but more often it appears that dropping out of school is due to inability to adapt further to its demands or to continue in the competition for success in school experiences. Have we in this country become willing to accept the fact that the quality of education depends upon the level of affluence within the society that we have slowly but surely developed layer by layer? Are we willing to educate the deprived so that he may continue his deprivation, and educate the children of the affluent society so that they may continue to increase their social status and their economic security?

Together with this apparent failure in American education, the teaching materials that are now being used in our schools have come under scrutiny. We find that ethnic groups of people who have played a very active role in the development of this country are being ignored by historians as they write the texts that will provide American children and youth with the basic concepts and attitudes concerning their country. As our historical heritage is pictured to young minds, it would appear that great care has been taken to omit the contributions made by the American Negro, as if assuming that he played little if any part. No doubt the omission of other groups will be found as studies are made to determine what emphases seem to be "fitting" to present to the American children.[17]

Recent efforts by many groups and by some communities to eradicate the social ill of prejudice have, because of a lack of planning and recognition of the problems involved, created in the general public an awareness of the *differences* of peoples — differences in cultures, living conditions, and attitudes — resulting in a greater gap in understanding. There is seldom a mention of similarities or of the truly basic facts that have created the situations leading to deprivation. An example of this is the difference in pay given to a white man as compared with that given to a Negro doing exactly the same work. (138:237) Such facts are seldom brought to public attention. Hence the public, through lack of knowledge and interest, places the blame for deprivation on the deprived and assigns the labels so frequently heard. But even knowledge and interest are not enough.

If this country is to work towards the solution of the combined social, economic, and educational problems that it faces, it must deal with this very strong destructive force that we have called prejudice. It may be true that we are now admitting to the existence of this evil in our country, but we must face the fact that prejudice has a strong hold here. The appalling fact is that within a short period of time prejudice has become widely spread within an environment supposedly created for the freedom of all people and for the recognition of human rights. We dare not assume that solution of only one aspect of the problem of deprivation, such as the economic, will erase it from our midst. And we must recognize that the only way in which a social illness can be eradicated is through a cure that substitutes for it a healthy condition. What does this demand?

Harrington gives this picture of the impact, the depth of prejudice:

> If all the discriminatory laws in the United States were immediately repealed, race would still remain as one of the most pressing moral and political problems in the nation. . . . There would still be a vast, silent, and automatic system directed against men and women of color. . . . To be equal, the Negro requires something much more profound than a way "into" the society; he needs a transformation of some of the basic institutions of the society . . . being born a Negro . . . [is] the most profound disability that the United States imposes upon a citizen. (64:72–73)

Silberman states that "Nothing less than a radical reconstruction of American society is required if the Negro is to be able to take his rightful place in American life . . . man cannot deny the humanity of his fellow man without destroying his own." (138:10, 16) Pettigrew, through a review of research studies, cites the following problem of the Negro resulting from our discriminatory practices:

> . . . impairment of human relatedness . . . impairment of the individual's acceptance and understanding of himself . . . the resulting confusion of self-identity and lowering of self-esteem . . . a generalized

perception of the world as a hostile, threatening place . . . family disorganization.[18]

Perhaps the most encouraging sign thus far is that the people whom we have termed "deprived" are showing evidence of no longer being willing to be poor and to accept a permanent lesser station in life. They are rising with a determination far stronger than that exerted by those outside who would correct the conditions that have placed these people in the deprived group. We have reached the point in our history where we are going to need to answer the questions put to us by the deprived and the alienated. (138) These people have had as a good example the change of status that has occurred among the working class. Also, there is every evidence that, with our present approach to economic and social growth, we are creating a situation in which those who have much are gaining even more. Seeing this, the deprived people themselves are beginning to fight against their hunger, disease, and ignorance, and to seek a share in economic security. As yet they have been given little support and little constructive help.

As the deprived struggle for higher levels of social status and a higher economic level, it is essential that we provide for them and for their children the type of education that will permit them to become the people they desire to be, an education preparing them for the social interaction, the intercommunication, the self-realization, and the self-actualization that they are now glimpsing as their goals.

Basic to this strong drive for improvement that is developing on the part of the deprived peoples is their use of the term "freedom." It is not only the deprived who have lost their freedom in this country, or perhaps we should say who have never realized their freedom; this loss is extending to other groups. There is less freedom to choose living quarters at a cost we would consider reasonable, less freedom to find various types of work without being handicapped by lack of experience or training, or by belonging to the wrong group. We are slowly losing the freedom to travel because of costs. Freedom that was an everyday expectancy is being destroyed by fear for one's safety on the highway, on the city streets, and even in the home. The increase in crime, the increase in lack of respect for authority, the increase in the waste of land, and the pollution of the water and the air have all decreased the spirit of freedom as well as the actual experience of freedom. With the increase of leisure time, the cultural boom in this country seemingly would provide a fine opportunity for people to share in cultural activities. But many people find the cost beyond reach and find also that, even with the present average education provided for them, they do not possess the background of understanding, appreciation, or skills for participation in these activities. It seems strange that a nation that began with a diversity of people who set out to live and work cooperatively to build a society of freedom, now, with this diversity of culture, of interest, and the same basic inherent desire for cooperative living, cannot continue to build and improve upon this society.

Can priorities be determined here? What is basic, except as it affects the individual — the adult or the child? For example, what does *freedom* mean to the deprived — more specifically, to the American Negro?

> . . . a complete casting off of the inferior role of "Negro"; it means the cessation of all of the disabilities traditionally placed upon black skin by American society. It means the stilling of self-hatred. Freedom also means an end to claims of white superiority, to dire poverty, to the social conditions permitting inflated rates of disease and inadequate medical care, low intelligence test scores, and heightened crime rates. Freedom means, in short, the right to participate fully in American society with the dollars and dignity of other Americans.[19]

It is not yet possible to look at the newer undertaking of integration, and specifically the desegregation of education, with enough perspective to evaluate its importance. This cannot be a time of watchful waiting without action. The watchful waiting must include the gathering of evidence for evaluation and judgments, and the determining of whether or not with the solution of this situation any improvement occurs in the educational process itself. It is not surprising that we find Negro parents, such as those in Boston's Roxbury area, urging to have their children sent by bus to better schools in other areas, even in the face of their strong desire that the schools within their own communities be improved. The problem is not the desire to mix groups or rub elbows with those of a different social status. It is a problem of the true meaning of equality of educational offerings — equipping each child to live equally according to his ability and his potential in his own world and the larger world. Nor can education alone totally solve this problem, even by providing such equality. Along with the improvement of education must go the improvement of living conditions and working conditions and the establishment of a security making it possible to release each individual to become himself.

Once again it is shown that the welfare, social service, and educational agencies must work hand in hand with those responsible for housing and for community rebuilding, and all must rely upon the sharing of information and share the single goal of meeting the needs of those for whom and with whom they are planning and working. Some communities have been able to organize such programs. Those which are being implemented successfully have shown that they demand from each person the practicing in everyday living of a respect for humanity, which in turn means respect for every individual in the situation.

We are now faced with the most serious of all facts: the person who cannot respect others, the deprived person who is subjected to prejudice, the youth involved in the ever increasing crime activity, and the citizen who refuses to accept his responsibility are all products of the education that we have developed and provided as free and equal to all people. This education supposedly has kept pace with the newer knowledge and newer methods of teaching. We have assumed that the teacher preparation programs have provided our schools with well trained, well educated teachers to transmit heritage and knowledge and to teach in the manner accepted by those in authority in our schools. The learner as a person has apparently been forgotten. Are not the following statements true? We have failed to help the learner to discover that self-respect and respect for others are the means of cooperative living. He has not learned that there is a place for independence and a place for working under authority. He has not learned that respect for others includes respect for others' property. Nor has he gained through the educational program a set of values that would guide both his behavior and his judgment in times of choice.

The latest excitement or sense of urgency that persists for further curriculum revision in the light of the continuing explosion of knowledge holds little hope. Looking carefully at the new forms of school organization, one discovers that the second-grade teacher supposedly can no longer master in an up-to-date manner all of the knowledge necessary for the seven-year-old to learn. These labors must be divided among several teachers, who become specialists in information. Secondary education is following closely on the heels of elementary education, and the reforms are many here. They appear in the fields of mathematics, the sciences, foreign languages, and most recently English and the social studies. The reforms call for learning more, faster, more efficiently. Here also the subject matter teacher must be an expert. But what is being done for the bewildered, excitable, lean and lanky adolescent?

It is most important that the new developments in curriculum be watched and studied. The term "curriculum" has a new meaning, and the method of presentation, with the emphasis upon student discovery, has much in its favor. It is true that the learners coming up through these changes appear to be advanced both in information gained and in ways of gaining this information. This is felt at the college level, for it is forcing curriculum revision here also to keep up-to-date with the increase in knowledge generally and with that of the students. Pressure is being exerted to do away with prescribed academic requirements; the student is given credit for having the ability and the maturity to pattern his own higher education, to be independent, to know what he needs to learn, and to set about learning it in the way he learns best. But where has he learned to make these decisions? One must ask where the student is in all of this, the student who is first and foremost a person learning to live in a world of change, still seeking guidance in channeling his interests and his abilities that are coming to the fore, and still hoping to find what we call *value*, which can serve as a steadying force in the upheaval of academic reform.

The educational system now includes the adult as a student. There is considerable interest not only in adult education and parent education as we have known them but in continuing education and programs of retraining and re-education. Changes are occurring in these programs and the adults, as learners or relearners, are groping toward a form of education and skill training that will prepare them for the jobs of which they know nothing at the present time. These are the jobs that will be waiting for them 10 years from now. Personal experience has taught them the importance of keeping pace with change, but they are asking how this can be done and how one prepares for the future. There is considerable discussion concerning the differences in the learning of the various social groupings at all age levels, but as yet there is no proof that there is an actual difference in the learning process itself, as is noted in the later discussion on learning problems. Meaningful learning should include much more than knowledge and much more than the discovery of ways of learning. The learner himself is yet to be discovered.

Again, *change* is the key word. Change has forced mobility of ideas and of values. The search for personal identity has become a search for refuge from uncertainty and indecision. It is hoped that as the total span of change occurs a refuge can be found by our youth on a solid base where each one has the time to find himself. It may yet be the child of today who leads us to this.

We are suddenly faced with the outward expression of this desire for change, with the need for expression of positive changes that must be recognized, and with the need for the expression of failure to bring about change because of apathy, lack of concern, and prejudice.

Our knowledge of each crucial situation is clouded by the emotional stirring—serious, damaging, and death-dealing at times—that is created by the few. Yet the many are blamed, even those who are hurt.

Are we willing to learn, even from disruption and violence, that all people are human beings worthy of dignity and fair shares in the business of living? Even those who have taken part in the urban riots are willing to admit that they took the wrong course and are providing good leadership in the reconstruction. Responsibility grows from the opportunity to make a choice. What choice will have to be put to all of us in order to make us choose to be responsible committed citizens?

Success is coming to those of the minority groups. In the arts, sports, government, business, and social institutions there are those now at the top who can reach down to help others move up. These groups must help themselves. Education and society are failing them as long as there are people who become educated but must still live in slums and work at menial tasks.

At no time in our history has living from day to day demanded more patience—patience to deal with education so that integration will prevail in the best schools, the slum schools; patience to know that good learning can come only through a meaningful education for each person, not in a temporary "crash" program; patience to direct the funds for improved education, housing, training, and employment to those in need, not to those who direct; patience to know that rioting and striking lead only to lack of confidence and failure in commitment. The development of human resources is our greatest task. Law, order, and mutual respect are basic to its accomplishment. Patience will flourish with progress, not with promises unfulfilled. Progress must come through good leadership, not through money alone. The time for backlash—black or white—has gone. It must be replaced by concerted, honest effort for good for all.

32 · *Deprivation and Compensatory Education*

Which group will gain the respect from all first? Education is a mighty tool and the pattern of need is emerging.

These are considerations of the current trends around us that seem to be carrying us forward, but through sound judgment must be evaluated as soon as distance permits perspective and a sense of proportion allows us to put the pieces into place. It may be that the deprived people themselves, through sheer lack of the fundamentals for living, can point out the important elements in the struggle we are endeavoring to resolve.

> To be a reactionary or a crusading liberal requires neither talent nor discipline. . . . No person ever teaches another person anything. Men of creativity, sensitivity, and intellectual curiosity merely exemplify ideas or insights or techniques that they have come to respect. . . . There are no teachers. There are only learned men and novices who wish to become such. Poets, artists, and wise men can at best merely demonstrate what they have learned or created. . . . No society will long endure, at least as a leader, unless it learns how to cultivate quality in considerable quantity. There is no option. . . .[20]

REFERENCES

[1] Task Force on Economic Growth and Opportunity, *The Concept of Poverty* (Washington, D.C.: Chamber of Commerce of the United States, 1965), p. 5.

[2] Martin Deutsch, "Some Elements in Compensatory Education," from a revision of a talk given in Sausalito, California, 1963 (Institute for Developmental Studies, School of Education, New York University), p. 2, mimeographed.

[3] Thomas F. Pettigrew, *A Profile of the Negro American* (Princeton: D. Van Nostrand Company, 1964), p. 180.

[4] "For the Indian: Squalor in the Great Society," *The New York Times*, September 13, 1966.

[5] Michael M. Harrington, *The Other America: Poverty in the United States* (New York: The Macmillan Company, 1962).

[6] Jack E. Weller, *Yesterday's People: Life in Contemporary Appalachia* (Lexington: University of Kentucky Press, 1966).

[7] Steve Allen, *The Ground Is Our Table* (Garden City, New York: Doubleday and Company, Inc., 1966).

[8] Piri Thomas, *Down These Mean Streets* (New York: Alfred A. Knopf, Inc., 1967).

⁹ George James, "Poverty As an Obstacle to Health Progress in Our Cities," and Robert Straus, "Poverty As an Obstacle to Health Progress in Our Rural Areas," *American Journal of Public Health*, 55 (November, 1965), pp. 1757–1779.

¹⁰ "Day Care for Children," *Currents in Public Health*, 4:1 (January, 1964) (Ross Laboratories, Columbus, Ohio); "Health Care of the Pre-school Child," *Currents in Public Health*, 5:4 (April, 1965) (Ross Laboratories, Columbus, Ohio).

¹¹ Reported by Dr. Arthur Bushel, acting New York City Health Commissioner, in *The New York Times*, April 26, 1966.

¹² Luther J. Carter, "Rural Health: OEO Launches Bold Mississippi Project," *Science*, 156 (16 June 1967), p. 1466.

¹³ See *The Boston Sunday Herald*, April 17, 1966, p. 80.

¹⁴ Margaret Mead, "Thinking Ahead: Why Is Education Obsolete?" *Harvard Business Review*, 36 (November–December, 1958), p. 34.

¹⁵ John Hersey, "Our Romance with Poverty," *American Scholar*, 33 (Fall, 1964), p. 530.

¹⁶ Reported in *National Association of Independent Schools Bulletin*, 4 (September, 1965), p. 1.

¹⁷ "Integrating the Texts," *Newsweek*, March 7, 1966, pp. 93–94.

¹⁸ Thomas F. Pettigrew, *A Profile of the Negro American* (Princeton: D. Van Nostrand Company, 1964), pp. 5–26.

¹⁹ Pettigrew, p. 201.

²⁰ Most Reverend James P. Shannon, "The Challenge of the Creative Teacher," *Education Age* (January–February, 1966), pp. 12–13.

6 Gene James, "Inequities in Obtaining Health Process in One Culture and Role of Status, Powers As in Obtaining Health Process in One Human Group," American Journal of Public Health, 65 (September 1975), pp. 1037-1070.

7 See "Care for Children's Concerns in Public Health 37 (January 1968), [Rise] Incorporates Community Action," "Health Care of the Urban Child: Contexts in Public Health," 58 (April 1968), (Box La-bortion), Columbus (Ohio).

8 Margaret H. Th. Within Public Action, New York City Health Commissioner, in The New York Times, April 20 1980.

9 Luther J. Carter, "Rural Health: OEO Launches Bold Mississippi Project," Science 150, (16 June 1967) p. 1466-a.

10 The Boston Sunday Herald, April 17, 1966, p. 80.

11 George A. Miller, "Thinking Ahead, Where is Education Headed," Harvard Business Review, 36 (November-December 1958), p. 4.

12 John Haag, "One Romance with Poverty," American Scholar, 35 (Fall 1966) p. 356.

13 Reported in National Association of Independent School Bulletin, 4 (September 1964) p. 1.

14 Interpreting the Tests, Newsweek, March 7, 1966, pp. 95-99.

15 Thomas F. Pettigrew, A Profile of the Negro American (Princeton, D. Van Nostrand Company, 1964), pp. [xxxx].

16 Pettigrew, [xxx].

17 Most Reverend James P. Shannon, "The Challenge of the Creative Teacher," Education Age (January-February 1966), pp. 12-15.

II

The Deprived Child and
the Deprived Youth

Nature intends that children shall be children before they are men. If we insist on reversing this order we shall have fruit early indeed, but unripe and tasteless, and liable to early decay; we shall have young savants and old children. Childhood has its own methods of seeing, thinking, feeling. . . . (129:52)

Consideration of the deprived child and the deprived youth thus far has been in the context of his social group, and from the viewpoint of the varied social, economic, and educational problems that are facing us at the present time. It has been pointed out that this child is called deprived because as he grows up he lacks what most people would consider essentials for living and for learning. The emphasis has been upon the fact that though he is deprived he is still a human person and should be respected as such. As we consider him here we should take seriously the warning given by Rousseau and see him first as a young child, secondly, as he grows through the middle years into preadolescence, then as an adolescent growing into adulthood. Whether he is in school, playing in the street, dealing with adults, working for a few pennies, lounging on the street corner with his gang, or joining the crowd in his expression of fear and hate, something should be done for him to allow him to be a child before he is pushed into the mold of a man's thought and action. He should have time to think, to see, and to feel as a child.

As we endeavor to determine some of the common characteristics and basic needs of the deprived child and youth we should keep in mind that the child we are analyzing is more than the mere sum of these characteristics and the satisfaction of individual needs. We should look at him as a whole person, reacting in totality and suffering in totality, and remember that his image of himself becomes that of himself as a person. One of our goals for him goes beyond mere self-discovery to the establishment of a positive self-concept, which we recognize as essential for good learning. Little do we realize what we are asking of him now in his present atmosphere of deprivation when we ask that he look at himself in a positive manner and think well of himself. Dr. Robert Coles gives a very clear illustration of this thought:

> Ruby and Jimmy and all the boys and girls I have known these past years have learned to identify themselves, somewhat, by their skin color. . . . What they have learned about their skin has been only the beginning of what they will learn. Yet, when they finally know what color they possess and what color they lack, they know something about their future. As one little Negro girl in Mississippi said after she had drawn a picture of herself: "That's me, and the Lord made me, but I must always remember that He did it, and it's His idea. So when I draw the Lord He'll be a real big man. He has to be to explain about the way things are."[1]

This child has been created by the society that we have permitted to develop in this country, and we are responsible for the attitudes he has had to form in order to provide for himself some manner of defense. This child has been ignored, mistreated, and exploited, but, rather than dwell upon these points and the resultant characteristics found in his behavior and thought patterns, we would do well to ask if, through this neglect, this country has not lost a major source of manpower, of creative thinking, and of a vast range of talents? Are there many of these children? Riessman (124) states that in 1950 it was estimated that in 14 of our largest cities one child out of every ten was deprived, and that by 1960 the figure was thought to be one in three. One must keep in mind here that the trend in rapid migration to urban centers would account for some of this increase. Riessman predicts that by 1970 there may be one deprived child in every two in school in these same cities. This, of course, does not include those still within the rural areas and those out of school. It is far too easy to limit our thinking to the deprived children in the inner cities, for these are the ones who are receiving the attention at present. When we speak of the deprived child and youth we must remind ourselves that these are the children of the Negroes in the rural South and in the northern cities. They are the children of Puerto Rican heritage who have come into the North, the Midwest, and the West. They include white children in the rural South and in the southern mountains, as well as many whose families have ventured north and into the central states. They are the children of the rural Mexicans who are migrating into our western and middle-western states and of the rural Spanish-Americans who remain in the southwestern states. And they are the children of the American Indians in some 25 states. A great many of these children are disadvantaged or deprived, but not all. We must also remember that deprived children do not come from these groups exclusively.

Characteristics and Basic Needs

In our endeavor to know the deprived child and the deprived youth, it is important to be aware of some of the characteristics and needs they seem to have in common, as observed in their behavior patterns. These are vividly described in terms of the conditions of poverty and deprivation by Silberman (138), Strom (143), Harrington (64), and Greene and Ryan (58). Contributions to our understanding have also come from the studies and research carried on at the Institute of Developmental Studies by John (332) and Martin Deutsch (245). (See listing of further studies on pages 251–252.)

Some of these deprived children are physically different from the ones whom we usually think of as typical school children. Undernourishment often results in their being undersized. There are those who are chronically fatigued and show a listlessness due to the lack of both food and sleep. Many show signs of certain physical defects already present or incipient, such as heart ailments and anemia.

These children show a lack of social experience in everyday interaction with their peers and with the adults in their environments. We must remember that many of them have come with their families from isolated rural areas, a fact that in itself encourages lack of communication. When they are brought to the cities and placed in groups with other children, their response seems to be one of aggression and hyperactivity. Although in many cases their physical skills have been developed, they still cannot use these skills in a controlled situation and their behavior evidences a seeming lack of coordination, for they must react with the only behavior they know. They have learned to run and to jump, to strike out, and to yell. This remains their social pattern until they have the opportunity both to observe and to learn a more acceptable manner of interacting.

Deprived children give the appearance of being afraid of new situations and of the people concerned. Even when they respond through action and by yelling it is often done in fear. They have not learned to verbalize, so their actions often speak loudly of the feelings deep inside. When we discuss the child and his family within the home we will see the source of the fear that he so readily displays.

Although deprived children have learned a vocabulary, and certain speech patterns of those around them in their homes and their communities, they suffer from the effects of the social discrimination that limits intercommunication. In the deprived home there is very little to talk about, the parents have little to say to the children except to give short commands, and the discouraged atmosphere in which they live tends to give a tone of defeat or belligerence to the words that are spoken.

The children live in a world of fantasy, but a fantasy far different from that experienced by a typical child. They have little to base fantasy on except for the experiences of everyday life, what they see, and what they hear as they listen to adult discussions, much of which they do not understand. Their fantasy is their imaginative depicting of a life they would like to live, but, with their meager experience, this can take on a weird connotation.

All children vividly reflect the world they live in. The deprived child, whom we too often think of as being in isolation, also feels the tensions and the stress of today's world in addition to the handicaps that are the direct result of the depressing atmosphere in which he lives from day to day. He feels the need even more for routines, for some structure or organization within his life, and he is aware of the lack of it, as are many other children where the tendency is to give them more freedom and to assume too early that they have the abilities within them to carry out and build their own structures. Today's children are allowed far more freedom in speaking, in expressing opinions, and in questioning the reasons for rules and regulations. This freedom, which is, of course, experienced by the deprived child, adds still another burden for him. He is often left with little help in learning to control his thoughts, his reactions, his behavior, and his words. Permissiveness, which is at best upsetting even to the child who feels sure of his safety and security in his home, is far worse for the deprived child, who does not feel this.

He is left puzzled, resentful, and lost. Every child needs and craves a form of guidance and direction, ample examples of behavior he should emulate, explanations for the why, the how, and the when to determine the proper behavior that he himself wants to be his own.

One of the characteristics of the deprived child, so generally discussed that it has become a hindrance to our understanding of him, is his apparent slowness. Even though he starts with a minimum of experience in the early years and there are some resultant differences between his ability to cope with learning situations and that shown by middle-class children, it is pointed out that this gap in ability becomes wider as he goes through his school years. There are those who would say that the lack of intellectual growth and development in the very early years preconditions this child to failure later on. There is no doubt that any child is more sensitive to environmental influences when he is young. But we have been responsible for helping the deprived child to build a defense against this environment as he grows older, which in turn encourages him to protect himself against its increasing demands. With this defense, the damage to him caused by his circumstances may be less in the later years. But is this what we want for this child, a behavior of fear and a response of reduced reaction to any environment in which he finds himself, negative or positive?

The question of this child's apparent slowness should not be left completely with the discussion of his language and learning problems. There are those broad aspects in his life that clearly explain this particular characteristic. It is important for every person who works with him to have a full knowledge of some of these aspects that may explain a characteristic that must not be misunderstood nor misinterpreted. Every deprived child and every deprived youth deserves to be considered as a distinct individual in his own world, including his school. If he has been severely deprived of the very basic experiences of life usually afforded the young child of the middle class, he should, regardless of his age, have the opportunities to begin at the point where deprivation started, with the simple experiences followed by a sense of success, with pressures removed, with the element of competition omitted. Any program planned for him should be one of a building of life experiences step by step and bound together with personal success, with encouragement, and with the feeling that he himself is most important. These experiences must begin with opportunities to *see*, to *feel*, and to *do* on the simplest of levels. He needs to become acquainted with all of the common objects another child takes for granted, learning to say their names, learning what they do, finding their meaning for him, and being proud of what he is learning. He should learn to speak clearly, at first with a simple word or two, for he is accustomed to hearing single words. He needs to discover the excitement of looking at a picture and identifying something familiar in it. He needs the opportunity of taking home this excitement of learning and of sharing it with his family. Few people can fail to catch a spark of enthusiasm from a happy child.

To help the deprived child one needs to find the point at which he has lost his sense of curiosity and his sense of wonder, for he must rediscover them if he is to be encouraged to learn more and more. Let him take time to look, to watch for certain happenings, to listen, and to think through what he does see and hear without having to ask a question or be able to give a sentence about his thoughts. Learning for him should be a carefully guided rediscovery of the simple, familiar things around him, correction of his misconceptions, learning proper terminology, rediscovering differences in color, shape, size, and sound, and rediscovering people. Why do we insist that a child is dull or is a slow learner because he cannot name colors properly at so many years and so many months of age? Let us take advantage of the newer approaches to learning, particularly that of discovery, and actually give it the true test by permitting a deprived child at his own rate, in his own way, to discover and rediscover his world, without a time limit, and with a mind that is free to assimilate what he experiences in this discovery from day to day.

Ample time is essential as the child learns much through his senses and gradually begins to see relationships, to see that people work together and enjoy doing things together, and to see that life is made up of experiences that can be pleasant. Some children will learn more rapidly than others, for there are differences in motivation, aspiration, and even in reactions among these children just as within any group of children. The older child needs help not only to go back to the beginning to gain the missing experience without loss of face, but also to break down misconceptions and poor attitudes that deter his thinking and acceptance of new ideas. He should discover that wonderment can be greater for him because he is older and it can be even more spectacular as he becomes more able to absorb what can happen to him. All of this, of course, is orientation, but it should be an orientation to his life through slow but sure stimulation, through a widening of horizons, through meeting with success in the simple things he learns to do, avoiding failure, depression, negative attitudes, and particularly the feeling that he is not competent to learn. It is only by this approach that we may discover his abilities and his potentialities. Only by knowing these can anyone build a program of guidance and further education for him. All of this demands of those who work with the deprived child enthusiasm and a sense of wonderment that they can share the excitement of each new experience with him. In turn, the child becomes aware that there is someone who cares, knows how he feels, and stands by ready to help him take the next step. Is there any reason why this cannot be termed the educational process?

It is through a positive interpretation of the characteristics of this child that his needs can be discovered. He has the basic needs for nourishing food, appropriate clothing, and shelter, but he is forced to accept his environment as it is. Hence, one of his greatest needs is to learn that the way in which he accepts it and himself determines his ability to grow, to learn, and to mature to the level of his potential. *He must be important to himself.* Through knowing his own abilities he may not only appreciate them but use them. He should discover what he is able to do physically, how he can control his strength, how he can use the various parts of his body and at the same time operate as a unit. It is through thought that he can control his physical actions and develop the finer skills. It is through thinking that he will realize the importance of certain forms of behavior and that it is he, himself, who must channel his strength and his energy.

He should learn that part of his physical equipment are the senses — that he can find enjoyment in the feeling of shapes, size and texture of objects and materials, and that it is through taste and smell that he can recognize and enjoy foods. He needs help in learning to listen; he needs help to see, and to have a purpose behind looking. All of this brings about the wonder of self-discovery.

He needs to learn that he has feelings, many of which are strong, and that these feelings frequently supersede thinking and direct his activity. He can be helped in learning to balance his feelings and his thinking, using both to channel his energy and his desires.

He will also learn, as he interrelates with others, to see them as persons and that they consider him as a person. He needs help in learning that others may tend to think of him as he thinks of himself, for it is he who gives to them the picture of himself. He will understand that other persons have the same drives for behavior, many of the same feelings, and much of the same ability to react and demonstrate their thoughts in terms of behavior. These discoveries open the door to the possible ways of interacting and communicating with others. The child begins to see for himself the importance of speech, of shared activities and shared excitement in learning and in accomplishment, and that life is a process of giving and of taking, and of mutual respect.

It has been indicated that the deprived child requires help in fulfilling his needs. Lack of support, of personal interest, and of help at hand will too often negate satisfactory fulfillment and destroy the child's self-picture. He becomes dull, listless, distrustful, cares little for himself or for others, and finds that he is a problem to himself, to his family, and to society as a whole.

Not all children from the poorest areas become dropouts from school. Children in a deprived area who live with those who appreciate them and their capabilities, encourage them to grow beyond their present environment, love them and want them, and give them the support that is esssential to maintain positive self-concepts do find success in learning. They are capable of being successful in their experiences and in coping with their environments. When much is expected of them by someone whom they respect, they in turn will set their goals to meet these expectations. This is true for every child and every youth, but it would appear that it is the deprived who make the greatest use of what they have and react most positively to the love and support that many others seem to take for granted. Parents and teachers play exceedingly important roles in the lives of their children.

Much of what has been said here can apply to the young adolescent in the secondary school. Unfortunately he has had the time to establish strong defenses against attempts to help him make a better adjustment to his environment. A number of the negative characteristics of deprived children have taken a firm hold. He presents a picture of low achievement and tends to be overage and to have a high failure rate. As a result of a long period of poor motivation, he has reading difficulties as well as learning problems in other areas. He has little knowledge of what is ahead for him, and his parents have little conception of any schooling past the secondary level. Because of parental lack of interest in his education his attendance at school is poor, and because of the lack of any particular vocational aspiration he begins to look forward to the time when he will be permitted to drop out. He uses a community language and has developed an unsatisfactory self-concept, for he sees himself as a failure and in his own defense has no desire to learn. This kind of failure is no indication of a lack of ability on the part of this youth. He has had no goals and hence has formed no purpose on which his learning might have been focused. His sense of failure and his poor self-concept will permit him to be satisfied with any type of unskilled labor, for he feels that if he gets a job of any kind he will be lucky. He has reached the point where he will appear defiant to offers of help because he feels it is too late for him. It is indeed too late if his negative attitude, which is so deeply rooted, persists.

This adolescent is living in an environment that engenders self-hatred and feelings of inferiority. Yet our society as a whole still does not permit the freedom of assertion of self-love, self-respect, or humanness either psychologically or physically. For the Negro, slavery within the white world still exists with its atmosphere of subservience. This adolescent finds it difficult in this setting to reconstruct his self-picture, to replace frustration with constructive self-assertion. Only as the deep-seated discriminatory attitudes of our society are uprooted and replaced with understanding, acceptance of each other as equal, and a desire to share with all in the daily business of living, can he find the opportunity to build his positive self-image, first in a pride in being black, then in a pride in being an American, physically and psychologically.[2]

This youth is a product of our social and educational systems. There seems to be too little concern on the part of the school that he leaves even to make a last effort to hold him. His antagonistic attitude does not help the atmosphere for others in the school. It is at this point that a false expectation is set up for him. Society generally is not surprised that this dropout becomes a juvenile delinquent. However, although a very high percentage of juvenile delinquents are school dropouts, not all dropouts are delinquents.[3]

One cannot help wondering what might have been in store for this adolescent, living under the same environmental conditions, if his parents had had a favorable attitude towards formal learning, had shown an interest in his school work, and had encouraged him to seek help in the setting of realistic goals for himself, not only while at school, but for the years following. If his negative attitudes had been positive ones, he might have been motivated to learn. Success in reading would have opened the doors to success in the other subjects. His speech would improve, for he would be willing to use the school language rather than the community language. With the support of his family and his school he would have had a better picture of himself and those around him also would have seen him as a learner rather than a nonlearner. There would have been evidences of his potentialities and his level of intelligence that were never glimpsed as he gradually became a dropout. When would it have been necessary for these positive forces to begin working on this adolescent to have saved him from the dropout class and put him in the graduating class?

The dropout is not a problem for one small segment of the educational organization. It is true that the secondary schools cannot handle or solve the problem alone, but we must not go to the other extreme and say that a child who fails in reading in the first grade is earmarked as a potential dropout. Statements are seen in the literature that dropouts can be detected early. (44:61–64) Unfortunately there are teachers who year after year permit a child to continue on the way to becoming a dropout because he is earmarked by them as dull, disinterested, troublesome, and even hopeless. Help can be given at every age. Parents can be reached at any point, even though it take persistence. Self-concepts can be changed and motivation encouraged if the child is given some purpose. Success can be the end result of learning experiences instead of failure. The parents of the deprived child and the deprived youth must be challenged with their responsibility. In turn, the school must accept the challenge of its responsibility. We might ask what has happened to the education that Horace Mann defined as ". . . the great equalizer of the conditions of men . . . the balance wheel of the social machinery."

The Home and the Parents

In much of the available literature, and certainly in the tone of the comments made here thus far, considerable blame for the condition of the deprived child and youth is placed upon the home as an unfavorable environment and upon the attitudes of the parents, particularly as they are basic to the attitudes of the child in relation to his schooling. Nevertheless, there are certain facets in any consideration of the home and the family of this child that are of a positive significance. To the deprived child his family is most important, and this feeling must not be destroyed. The family are the people with whom he communicates, and to whom he goes for safety. The family may be made up of the parents, or possibly only one parent, and usually other adults too, for in deprived areas it is essential that large family groups live together. The child may go for security to a grandparent or an uncle who serves as a substitute for his parents, or another adult may be in the home while the parents are at work. The child is usually one of a number of children living in the household, who may be brothers, sisters, or cousins. These are the people to whom he belongs.

The characteristics of the family group described above may not be those of the middle-class family. The interrelationships and the child rearing practices may be different and there may be less conversation and less demonstration of love, but this still is the family that means the most to the child and is his only source of security and safety, which are among his greatest needs. The parents may have a very negative attitude concerning the value of education, which many times results in lack of effort on the part of the child and encourages poor attendance at school. But the chief cause of this attitude on the part of the adults is probably the experience that each of them has had in his own schooling. They themselves may have been dropouts, or the children of migrants, who experienced little if any satisfaction in their limited learning experiences. Perhaps they blame their own failures on the failure of the school to prepare them to earn a better living.

Riessman gives this description:

> The home is a crowded, busy, active, noisy place where no one child is focused upon. There are too many children for this, and the parents have too little time. Consequently, the children spend much more time in each other's company and with the relatives.
>
> Individualism and self-concern on the part of the children is much less likely to emerge and is, in fact, discouraged in this more family-centered home. (124:37)

Inherent in this quotation are evidences of a positive value, particularly the lessening of self-concern, which many of us know to be a problem with children of more affluent circumstances. Riessman also points out that there is less opportunity for jealousy and competitiveness and little danger of overprotection, and that the deprived child learns early the meaning of very simple cooperative living and sharing. The conditions of living for a large family in very small quarters demand a form of discipline that requires the child to learn that he must take the consequences for his wrongdoings. This usually means a physical rebuff. However, there is no evidence that the child thinks of this punishment as withdrawal of love. Rather, punishment can be an assurance of it, if the child receives punishment only when he has done wrong and he understands the reason for it immediately.

\ There is need for careful study of the effect of the home and family structure on the deprived child as he develops, particularly on the formation of attitudes and the more permanent characteristics of personality. Gordon reviews the results of research studies that have been carried on and reaches the following conclusions:

\ These environmental studies provide some insight into the home experiences of disadvantaged children, but few represent systematic long-term investigations conducted in naturalistic settings. Too much of this work tends to be speculative and is based on relatively small and unrepresentative samples. The findings, nonetheless, point to the importance of environmental studies. Interpretation of such findings, however, will be greatly limited until simple enumeration and description of environmental factors are replaced by ecological investigations designed to show the relationship between certain features of the environment and certain behavioral characteristics. (292:379)

One study recently completed by Elliot Liebow, however, gives us very good insight into the thinking and feeling of the man who is one of the group on the street corner. In this case these are the poor, uneducated Negroes who have recently arrived in one of the northern cities. It is this thinking and feeling that each man carries to his home with him and shares with his family, for it is the expression of himself and his friends.[4]

Margaret Mead[5] recently pointed out that all children today must learn to confront the unfamiliar. It may be that the parents of deprived children are teaching this to their children in a more fundamental way than the parents in the other class structures. Confronting carries the individual beyond merely withstanding or tolerating to the point of reacting.

One of the sad commentaries, primarily concerning the Negro family, is that of the absent father. (138)(114) This situation reveals one of the important differences between the average white family and the average Negro family that lives in the poor districts. The white family is thought of as headed by the father, who does carry the major responsibility and who makes many of the decisions. It has been stated that about 25 percent or more of the poor Negro families are headed by women and the fathers are absent. It is the father who has been lost as the Negroes have progressed from slavery toward the process of integration. It was the father who was the slave, and who suffered from the name-calling for the sake of his family. It was the father who suffered in the transition from dependence to independence and found too many times that he was no longer needed by anyone. He has been the one seen lounging on the street corners (138:40) and standing in line at the welfare office, and generally pictured as shiftless and unwilling to work. He has had little to encourage him to hold his head up and to fight through for employment, and this has forced open the door for the wife and mother to become the head of the household. Many times she is able to find household work, which in turn makes her more readily accepted. Even in the days of slavery the mother had charge of the children because the father was working long hours and was sometimes away from home. This responsibility for the children has strengthened and given the mother even more right to them as the father, discouraged and hopeless, has separated himself from his family because of the loss of his own personal dignity as a result of his inability to provide economic security. It is not all family circumstance that has brought this about. It frequently occurs that the Negro woman gains a certain social prestige in her closer relationships with white families and, in order to maintain her feeling of superiority, carries on the belittling of the Negro man. He has not yet found the freedom which was to have been his.

The Negro family feels the loss of the father in two ways, and the situation has brought about serious conditions. American society, being built upon the father as head of the family, is set up in such a way that it is through the father that the family benefits. The Negro household headed by the mother finds it hard to understand and take advantage of welfare relief assistance, medical assistance, and opportunities for socialization within the community. The more acute effect is upon the children. Although the Negro family feels that any male living within their larger group serves as a father substitute, the Negro children of today, by comparing themselves with others in their school or with the American family pictured in the press and on television, are becoming aware of their loss and of their difference from other children. Opportunity must be provided for the Negro father to gain status within his own society through a change in the patterns of education. Much can be done by the larger society in offering to the Negro man the opportunity for retraining and for employment with pay, not lower but higher, than that received at the present time by the Negro woman. He must step back into his family and provide for his children the leadership and stability they need. Can the larger society return to a man the dignity and the personal value that it destroyed some two hundred years ago? Any plan for an educational process that is to be developed to meet the challenge of today must be broad enough to reach not only the children but the parents and must be important enough to them to permit this change to be a part of their lives.

In any discussion of the Negro family, mention should be made of the earlier study known as "The Moynihan Report." The conclusion was that conditions for the Negro are becoming worse and that only the effect of national effort can combat or change what Moynihan considered the most serious of all the social problems with which we are faced. In his own defense he continues to urge for the poor urban family full employment, re-education, and subsidization.[6]

As some of the characteristics of the deprived child were described in a previous section, fear was mentioned as one of the basic problems. It is from his parents that the deprived child learns this fear. The purpose might appear to be to protect the child from prejudice and overt acts against the less fortunate, but Robert Coles, who has spent considerable time as an investigator among the poor in various parts of this country, feels that this fear may be due instead to anger and spite. He cites the following statement from one Negro mother who found the words to say what she felt:

> I guess we all don't like white people too much deep inside. You could hardly expect us to, after what's happened all these years. It's in our bones to be afraid of them, and bones have a way of staying around even when everything else is gone. . . . White people are a real danger to us until we learn how to live with them. So if you want your kids to live long, they have to grow up scared of whites; and the way they get scared is through us; and that's why I don't let my kids get fresh about the white man even in their own house.[7]

What is our answer to this?

Uniqueness and Classification: Determents to Education

Are the deprived different? If they are different, with whom are they being compared? Are they basically different human beings or have they been forced to become different? Why must these people be labeled? Is it necessary to classify them in order to learn more about them? Assuming that the deprived are different, must they remain different? Do the labels that we give them deter their education? Whose education is deterred by our efforts to single out, to categorize, and to remove from the general stream of American society those people less fortunate than we? It is most likely our own.

It is important to know that there are those who strongly feel that the problems under discussion should be studied with a scientific, biological approach. It is indeed important, before planning the studies and the programs for improvement in relation to deprived people and the conditions under which they are living, to know and to understand the significance of such basic information.

Dr. William Shockley, a Nobel Prize winner in physics from Stanford University, urged the National Academy of Sciences at its Fall 1966 meeting to "foster research on the effects of heredity, including race, on human behavior." Although Dr. Shockley himself has not carried on research on this type of genetic problem, he offers his opinion that the "marrow" of the slum problems may be their genetic aspects. He feels that we hesitate to search into this area for fear of having to admit our ignorance. He suggested that a summer study group be organized "to seek new approaches to utilize scientific imagination to reduce the environment-heredity uncertainty." It is his feeling that research in the connection of heredity with behavior and intelligence will give information concerning intelligence distributions of minorities, especially of the American Negroes.[8]

One attempt to seek an answer through research in this area was recently reported in a short newspaper item. Dr. Wallace A. Kennedy, Staff Chairman of the Humanities Development Clinic of Florida State University, was quoted as saying that a recent study of 216 culturally deprived mothers and their babies indicated that "emotional and chemical changes in the mother can get through to the child she is carrying, changing its normal pattern of growth." Dr. Kennedy's conclusion was reported to be that the "inability of a culturally deprived person to function in society may be passed from mother to child as a permanent condition. . . ."[9]

It may be that through careful research studies the biological sciences will be able to resolve our basic uncertainty in dealing with the education of all people at all levels. The impact of environment and of heredity on the learner, especially as it relates to the diversity of living conditions and cultural backgrounds, is indeed the basic question being faced by the anthropologist, the sociologist, the psychologist, the behavioral scientist, and the educator.

In comparing the deprived child or the deprived youth with the "typical" American child or youth, the differences are obvious. If we are willing to face the fact of the deprivation of experience, recognizing that in many instances it is the educational system that has created the differences in experience, we can then search for the most expedient ways of erasing them. If the term "deprived" is to be used, it should be used with the understanding that it indicates a need rather than a handicap. We can then take a positive approach and determine the kinds of experiences that each one of the deprived needs, as an individual, to help him arrive at the level of experiencing that is commensurate with his ability and essential to intercommunication and interaction in the world just beyond him.

When both the deprived child and the deprived youth can think of themselves as capable of learning and as respected citizens, and when through a positive education they can set their goals, use their abilities, share the high standards of living, and discover that life can hold rich experiences, the necessary changes in our educational program will have been made. Then we will discover that differences can be positive, for there will be respected differences in personalities, in abilities, and in potentialities. Each person will have the right to his own positive uniqueness and will use that uniqueness in finding not only respect but a place where he may be useful to others and to the larger society to which he belongs. Labels will no longer be necessary. In using labels we have deterred the education of all people. It is only by removing the labels that we can see the situation clearly.

We should listen to the words of the "Friar Tuck" of the Capuchin Order, Father Capistran, to the people of the Spanish Harlem he has served so well: "It hurts me to think that many people considered this to be a bad neighborhood. . . . This is not so. We have good people here."

REFERENCES

[1] Robert Coles, "When I Draw the Lord He'll Be a Real Big Man." Reprinted from CHILDREN OF CRISIS: *A Study of Courage and Fear*, copyright © 1966, 1967, by Robert Coles, with permission of Atlantic-Little, Brown and Company, Publishers.

[2] Alvin F. Poussaint, "A Negro Psychiatrist Explains the Negro Psyche," *The New York Times Magazine* (August 20, 1967), pp. 52–80.

[3] Vernon E. Anderson, *Principles and Practices of Curriculum Improvement*, 2nd ed. (New York: The Ronald Press Company, 1965), pp. 345–348.

[4] Elliot Liebow, *Tally's Corner* (Boston: Little, Brown and Company, 1967).

[5] Margaret Mead, "Rearing Children To Live In a Changing World," *Parents' Magazine and Better Homemaking* (January, 1966), p. 33.

[6] Office of Policy Planning and Research, United States Department of Labor, *The Negro Family: The Case for National Action* (Washington, D.C., March, 1965).

[7] Coles, p. 75.

[8] Harold M. Schmeck, Jr., reporter, "New Study in Race Heredity," *The New York Times*, October 18, 1966.

[9] Associated Press item from Memphis, Tennessee.

Concept and Challenge

The manner in which this nation is going to nurture, conserve, and deploy its most vital resource—its brainpower—is probably the major concern of thinking Americans today, although it may be stated in other terms at other times. We are at a pivotal moment in our history. The decision we make, the action we take, the manner in which we use our people today, will sharply affect the destiny not only of 200 million Americans, but the destiny of millions around the world who look to us for leadership.

We are a changing nation, and the major changes are being wrought, not from without, but from within by the application of men's minds and talents to the processes of living. We have evolved rapidly from an agricultural to an urban society. Seven out of ten Americans now live in urban areas. We have come through the industrial revolution of the eighteenth and nineteenth centuries, and we have launched a technological revolution which . . . profoundly affects the lives of every American.[1]

This quotation very clearly expresses the task of the broad educational process. Brainpower is our most vital resource. This does not mean the brainpower of a few or the brainpower of the upper 50 percent, but rather that of every citizen within the country. We need the sum of the abilities of every person used to the maximum in the most creative way in a continuous program of development, cultivation, expansion, strengthening, and discipline. This demands an educational process that begins at birth and continues throughout life and is far greater than the school, which serves only as its instrument. Thus, this process becomes the responsibility of all social institutions and determines the goals for all, for it is through this vital educational process that Americans will inherit their birthright.

53

Our educational process bears a rethinking, a redefining particularly of its purposes and of the depth and breadth it must assume. The school can do much for this newer interpretation of the process of education once the structure of the process is determined. Our responsibilities are not fulfilled when we float more school bonds, erect larger buildings, pay more teachers, put more teaching machines in the classrooms, open the schools the year round, extend continuing education, extend the elementary schools down for the four-year-old, and extend the size of our graduate schools. This is not the vital educational process.

The very best of living and learning is confronting every experience that life has to offer with one's whole being; it is resolving the problems within each experience with the feeling that one's best abilities have been put to use to the fullest, and concluding each experience with a sense of satisfaction of having done one's best; it is using each experience as a stepping stone toward experiences of greater depth and greater breadth, anticipating with excitement what tomorrow may bring; it is respecting the possibilities of knowing other persons and sharing with them all aspects of daily living; it is marvelling at the wonders of the natural universe and sharing personally or vicariously in man's acquaintance with and use of its laws; it is choosing a vocation commensurate with one's abilities and talents and using it to grow and to extend one's knowledge and personal worth; it is desiring to know about and to enjoy another man's efforts to express his innermost thoughts in words or by whatever avenue of self-expression is his and in turn finding one's own way of expressing feelings and ideas that they might be shared with others; and it is recognizing with humility that the goal of living is guiding and sharing with others along the way. All of this is the broad and vital process of education, and it can be accomplished only as each one of us educates himself and assumes the responsibility for fostering the education of his brother. To help another extend his reach beyond his grasp creates a heaven for both, to borrow from Browning.

Education demands that each individual first of all respect himself, then respect others and have the respect of others. It is only through this mutual respect that a process such as this can even be launched. It involves every individual and holds the highest expectations for each. At the same time it recognizes the differences within what each person has to offer, and accepts these as the component parts of his individuality, uniqueness, and worth rather than as the bases for odious comparison. Thus education becomes a process in which each person is constantly involved, a process that does begin at birth, with the early formation of attitudes, habits, and relationships. It does not end with the closing of the door of the high school or the college, but, by opening the doors of all schools, a person is permitted to see beyond and to understand that his education continues on in a richer and deeper way throughout life. No person is denied his opportunity, nor does he in turn deny it to another.

Can such a process function? Can this country refocus its sights, create anew its educational thinking, and find ways to afford a program that can produce these results? We need only look at the beginnings of this country to recognize that the ideals of democracy to which we have paid homage, if put into operation, will demand the shifting from our unrealized educational ideals to such a vitalized and dynamic process. The situation is urgent. The time is short.

What then is compensatory education? Is compensatory education necessary? If so, what is its role in the newer view — perhaps we should not use the term "newer" view, but rather the *vital* and *broad* view — of education that we propose both as a concept and as a challenge?

In the current literature the term "compensatory" has been used regarding educational programs particularly designed for adults and children within the culturally disadvantaged groups. Benjamin Willis, in a recent report issued from the Chicago Public Schools, first states the fundamental purpose of education and then gives a definition of compensatory education in relation to that purpose:

> The fundamental purpose of education, as developed by the citizens of our country, is to help boys and girls develop their full potential so that they may become increasingly more effective members of our American society and enjoy the personal satisfactions of a full life. . . .
>
> Compensatory education refers to educational programs, practices, techniques, and projects designed to overcome the deficiencies of children from culturally disadvantaged homes to enable them to fulfill the fundamental purpose of education.[2]

Bloom, Davis, and Hess contribute the following clarification concerning the use of the term "compensatory education":

> Compensatory education as we understand it is not the reduction of all education to a least common denominator. It is a type of

education which should help socially disadvantaged students without reducing the quality of education for those who are progressing satisfactorily under existing educational conditions. (11:6)

Having seen the need to revitalize the total educational process, we shall find that compensatory education means helping all of those who have received insufficient challenge in our current educational system toward a meaningful education in the light of our restated goals. However, the chief consideration here is to meet the needs of those not merely deprived by our current educational scheme, but deprived of the basic fundamentals of life that affect them physically, mentally, socially and emotionally. These are the children of one fourth to one third of our nation, and for them there is even greater urgency for providing an immediate compensatory educational program. Their compensatory education may provide the opportunity to see that the values sustained are worthy of the effort for change. Compensatory education should permit us the opportunity to prove that we have gained, through recognizing our deficiencies, the insights neccessary to rise above the overworked terminology and to use what we believe in as the base for planning a functional program. This will mean planning for the child or the youth or the adult whom we have left behind, or whose value as a person we have not recognized yet. "What is a weed? A plant whose virtues have not yet been discovered," said Ralph Waldo Emerson.

In the following discussion of the needed compensatory education for the deprived child, youth, and adult, we shall deal with the school as one of the instruments of the total process and its larger goal, in an attempt to provide an expedient means by which these deprived persons may find as soon as possible their places in the larger, continuing education as contributing citizens.

There are certain aspects of our current educational picture that need a quick review. One concern has been the failure of approximately 300,000 young recruits each year on the simple aptitude tests given in the armed forces. This has been blamed not only on the school program but also on the teachers who fail to give the necessary background of knowledge and who create an atmosphere of boredom, confusion, and noncomprehension. The military services themselves are taking on the task of teaching basic skills that the recruits lack, such as grammar, reading, and arithmetic, as well as the necessary technical skills. The success of the armed forces programs in lowering the percentage of failures has been due to several rather concrete practices, which they recommend that all schools might put to good use: going from the concrete to the abstract, letting each learner work at his own pace, maintaining a low student-teacher ratio, and putting the stress on the essentials.[3]

In a recent newspaper article it was reported by Hechinger[4] that Sargent Shriver is challenging the quality of the present elementary education and is suggesting that the more successful elements of the Head Start Program be used as a basis for revision of the whole elementary program. Shriver also calls for smaller classes and would accomplish this through the use of teacher aides, who would need less professional training than teachers and thus help to resolve the teacher shortage. He feels that the Head Start Program, even with its many weaknesses, has given those who have worked with it an insight into the possibilities of a program that should be afforded all children.

One of the very urgent reasons for improving public education can be found stated in almost every piece of literature concerning compensatory education. It is the sizeable number of pupil failures in the current educational system. Such general estimates as these are given: Approximately a quarter of a million of our youth fail to complete their elementary education, and of those who go on, another million leave school before completing their high school education. Twice as many Negro youths drop out of the high school as white, and almost 50 percent of our laboring group are school dropouts, as are two thirds of the unemployed group. The challenge is to furnish a purpose in any planned compensatory educational program in order to give to each student a reason for accomplishment and for the completion of his formal schooling. This means that the program must be one worthy of completion.

Many are unaware of or uninterested in the statistics that indicate our ability to provide education for our children. For example, enrollment in institutions of elementary, secondary, and higher education has increased 31 percent in the last 10 years. The number of degrees conferred by higher institutions in the same 10 years has risen by 77 percent. Such figures show a widening gap between the youngsters left behind and those who are going further in their schooling. The total spending for all schools in the United States in the past 10 years has grown by 124 percent.[5] One might quickly assume that all children had benefited from this increase, and yet we find that for the year 1964 the cost per pupil in the South was $337, while the average for the remainder of the United States was

$507. The average teacher salary in the same year was $4,973 in the South and $6,105 in the remainder of the country.* According to the 1960 census, in the South 15.1 percent of persons 25 years of age and over had had less than five years of schooling, while the corresponding figure for the rest of the United States was 6.3.[6] Inequities of this sort should be erased in the process of providing equal educational opportunities for all persons equal to their own individual abilities.

Will a national assessment provide further needed evidences of the weaknesses of our educational system beyond our present awareness? Will this mean more statistics, more generalities? Or can it furnish pertinent information on the individual learner so needed? Will the recommendations be geared to helping the individual or will they result in "big business" promotion of better mass production? Considerable thought is being given to such an evaluation,[7] and until answers are available, we must move forward on the present evidence. We are indeed aware of much as we do focus on the needs of the learner today.

In considering the mental health problems of deprived children, we find that certain aspects of the current educational program tend to foster a feeling of inadequacy early in the lives of some children, which blocks further learning. Some of the children may fail because standards are set in a uniform manner, making any success for them unobtainable. Too much competition constantly points out the child who is not doing well. There is a possibility that the child who wins constantly does so at the price of failure for others. The scheme of organization of the classroom and of the school often permits the children within a class to know very soon which ones are repeating a grade and which ones are in the lower groups; their failure then becomes the interest of the public. We know also that where there is lack of enthusiasm and concern on the part of the parents, their children seldom have a reason for finding real pleasure in learning.

Too many times in the average classroom the ill-prepared pupil is earmarked early, and as his weaknesses are pointed out to him he sees himself as one who must always be inadequate. There are those who complain that boys are not given a chance to succeed. Even though we know that some learning differences are developmental, the school standards do not change, and the boy has trouble keeping up with the girls in learning the tool subjects and even in the process of socialization. At the high school level we suddenly find evidences of fear on the part of the school authorities and teachers that the adolescents are apt to cause trouble. Additional rules are set up, there is less freedom as students go from class to class, there are constant checks, and students are removed from the classrooms at the first indication of mischief. The young adolescent soon learns that he is considered irresponsible and a nuisance, and is generally mistrusted. The formality of the average classroom itself prohibits the talking, exchange of ideas, and physical movement so necessary during the growing years, so the students are anxious for the closing bell.

Teacher-pupil ratios must permit the teacher's knowing the individual child. Grouping should be based on developmental differences or similarities rather than upon chronological age. Evaluation of learning should contribute to a positive picture of the progress of the individual's total development, thus aiming to build self-confidence rather than encouraging a negative analysis. There should be close cooperation between the school and the parents. This would include parent education. The school then becomes important to the learner, and status within the school is gained in ratio to the degree of interest he has in being in school and in what he is learning. The curriculum is organized to meet his needs, and standards are set for him according to his capacities. This will demand that the teachers understand the entire educational process and be able to see their own work as well as the children's in the light of the total span rather than just according to single grade expectancies for the average child. A rich environment, constant contact with the world outside, time, encouragement, opportunity for thinking, and ample ideas will provide conditions for good teaching and learning and encourage initiative and creativity. All of these factors seem at first to be mere ideals, but if the larger goal is to be accomplished they must become essentials.

Is it possible for us to see the worth of each deprived child, youth, or adult, regardless of how he has been labeled, and assess with kindness where he *is* in his personal growth, development, and behavioral life patterns? Can we plan for him from day to day exciting learning situations that bring him success, set the standards to meet *his* needs, and help him to stretch a bit each day and to be excited about tomorrow? Will we provide for him an atmosphere of security and respect, plan his curriculum to challenge his abilities, and free him to think creatively and to learn with success?

The School

> . . . *the school has for so many years been thought of as the panacea institution of a troubled society struggling to realize democracy for all its citizens. Not wishing to appear impotent as a social agency, it has attempted to be all things to all people. Lately, however, educators have gained new insights into what the school can and cannot do. They realize that no school system can overcome single-handedly the social, cultural, and economic handicaps under which many children live in their non-school hours.* * (89:58)

This statement by Vontress clearly pictures what the school has been attempting to do alone for too long. Society has put the burden of training for citizenship and of the totality of education on the school. In view of the problems now facing society, the school is a very important social agency, but it must also know the limits of its responsibility. This is essential if the values and the strength of what the school can do are to be made clear. At the same time, the school is not absolved from assuming as much responsibility as possible, for it is the instrument of the essential type of education. The school will have to assume the leadership in cooperative planning with other agencies. It is the school that knows the child, the youth. The school cannot close its doors and forget him for the major part of each day. The school will not only play a very important role in carrying out the goal of the new vital education; with concern for the child in his home and in his community, it will relate itself to all that happens to this child, wherever he is, at all times.

The school represents our fund of knowledge concerning the teaching-learning process and the child at all ages. We have the results of the research and thinking of those in the fields of educational theory, philosophical and psychological learning and teaching theory, child and adolescent psychology, and educational psychology. It is this information, combined with that offered by the scholar of child and human development, that gives us our knowledge concerning the individual. It is important for every person, administrator or teacher, who is concerned with education today to understand these theories and processes and translate them into guidelines for the full educational process for which the school assumes responsibility. The school must give evidence of this re-

---

* Used by permission of Phi Delta Kappa, Inc., Bloomington, Indiana.

source of knowledge in its organization, in its teaching procedures, in the learning expectations that it sets, in its recognition of the individual child and in the experiences it offers him, in its relationship with homes and parents, and in the total educational guidance that it provides.

This fund of knowledge permits the school to take the stand that any good educational program begins with the child where he is, taking into consideration his immediate environment and his own culture, and encourages him to use his heritage actively from day to day, using his own words, expressing his own ideas, and thus making his own contribution to others. This knowledge permits the school to stress that the elements of readiness and maturity often account for slow beginnings in learning, and that at no time should slowness alone be interpreted as low ability or poor intellect on the part of the child. The school, then, is able to recognize the fact that emotional, physiological, social, and academic maturity levels are evidenced in the behavior patterns of each individual child. All schools, including the slum school, have the responsibility to maintain a high level of quality in teaching and in learning as these relate to the children at hand, stressing at all times that the evaluation of quality can be made only on the basis of the personal development and changed behavior patterns of each child concerned. The school is challenged to work closely with those theorists and researchers who make this information possible, and to involve all who understand the child and his learning in the educational process itself, thereby closing for all times the gaps between knowledge and theory and practice.

It is on the basis of this same fund of knowledge that it is possible to evaluate the various programs for compensatory education within the school and the changes that will be taking place in the structure and content of the curriculum in the various types of instruction, in the organization of groups for teaching, in the quality of teachers, and in other essential aspects. All of these changes must be made with the young child, the growing child, the adolescent and the adult in mind, for the growth process up through the years is clear, and at each step along the way we are able to see the characteristics that point out specific needs. Each school that is built upon the knowledge available to it will meet change with change, as each of the children within it will then learn to do.

What will the school endeavor to provide for each child? It will give opportunities for adequate stimulation through rich experiencing, the acquiring of needed skills for building the foundations for learning, the successful completion of the child's own developmental tasks. It will give him opportunities to move ahead at his own rate within a program designed for him, to acquire a sequence of enriching experiences that grow in depth and breadth according to his readiness and maturity, to become proficient in each of the basic tools, and to develop broad concepts based on his current knowledge. The school will have teachers who understand him, and who know his parents, his home, and his community. They will know his needs and will serve as guides in his development, learning, and living. These provisions, with their many ramifications, will lead each child toward the very important goal of learning how to think. The process of thinking implies exploration, adaptation, flexibility, acceptance, and judgment. This should be the all-important objective of any school for any child, and particularly of the school maintaining a compensatory program for the child who has much more to learn as he learns to think.

These services offered by the school prepare the youth for responsible citizenship in his immediate environment now as well as in the future. When the boy or girl has reached the age for assuming responsibility, society in general has failed in giving opportunity to do so. The school's fear of the youth, previously mentioned, is no doubt a product of his restlessness, which is engendered and enforced by idleness, the only "activity" left in the after-school hours. We are only now beginning to realize the positive strength and power of the adolescent group. These young people have the energy and the drive to do, but even the small odd jobs in the community and around the home are fast disappearing. They have little to turn their hands to, and the school as one of the social agencies must face a share in the responsibility for providing some type of activity, commensurate with their interests and abilities, that these youths will feel gives them the opportunity to assume the responsibility for which they are ready. It is being suggested that the schools themselves be open many more hours each day as well as throughout the year in order to answer this need for activity and to channel it toward constructive ends.(114) The school has the knowledge about the adolescent. It must take the step that leads to an understanding of him on the part of his parents and his community so that plans are made for some work and other constructive outlets to extend the teaching of responsibility beyond the school hours. As the school becomes the community's school, the organizations and businesses within the community will be able to work with it on setting up such a program.

Can the school face current criticism? It has been stated that the time is here when we must close the gap between the theory and the practice of education in the schools. We must also close another gap. This one exists more prominently in the minds of the deprived peoples, about whom we are most concerned. These people have given at times the impression of a negative, uninterested attitude towards the school, but when asked about education for their children they show a real concern and interest. This fact challenges the school to assume the responsibility of informing the public, the parents, and the children that the school stands for all that is good and all that they hope for in education. The school can exemplify a vital philosophy of education by recognizing the worth of each individual. In being a part of the community, it can give evidence that it does provide the education so needed and desired by the people in that community. The school must offer a place in its program for each citizen, with the opportunity for his involvement.

The school can face criticism if it is willing to admit that it must change in order to keep up with the progress in our social order. While doing this it has every right to be proud of its past, for it did meet society's need in many respects before the migration from the South and extensive urbanization. The school can, as it puts into operation its more vital education, begin the process of eliminating the discouragement of persons and of their efforts, which is sometimes the effect of the attitudes of those involved within the school. Such attitudes can be replaced with a desire to know, to understand, and to appreciate each individual and his efforts toward improving his own life and his community. The school must find its strength while recognizing its limitations, and keep the avenue of communication open to the public so that its program for all can be made known. The school has the responsibility of the highest value. This responsibility is to know each and every child, understand him, and guide him to the best use of his capabilities by stimulating within him a high level of motivation. All of this should be accomplished within the framework of a positive attitude toward coping with his environment and of the positive self-concept so necessary for this coping.

What are the dimensions of the school providing compensatory education for the deprived? Compensatory education has been described as a "crash" program. There can be no doubt of the need for speedily reaching out to the deprived, making contact, and involving them in a program to meet their urgent needs. In the vertical dimension, every indication points to a program beginning with the young child of age three or four and preparing him through basic experiences in the process of living that will assure him of success later in the educational process. The school at this early level helps him to improve:

—— his verbal ability
—— his understanding of himself and others
—— his perception and understanding of the environment
—— his store of understandings to be applied to future situations
—— his emotional and cultural resources through experiences which are satisfying: joy in music, art, poetry, stories, color, rhythm, materials, pictures, books, and friendships (102:5)

With this as the beginning, each phase of the educational program will guide the individual learner up the necessary steps he must take toward his own self-realization and self-actualization. As society demands of him he will demand of himself, and he will then expect that his education will extend, through the use of the upper limits of his own capabilities, to a satisfactory completion of that phase of program most befitting him, be it the high school, the vocational school, the college, or the graduate school. As the guidance of the individual within the school increases and includes the determining of potentials, the program will in turn be broad enough at each step to permit the fulfilling of the variable needs found within any group. The school will be the instrument that realizes and demonstrates the vital education that has been described, and the product of each part of its program will be a thinking, interested, creative, participating, and responsible citizen who finds his active place in his social group. Above all, he will be free to become a thinking person. James Russell presents a vivid picture of this free person:

We need men who are — as we say in that convenient shorthand which permits us to express a vast congeries of values in a word — free. The free man is aware of himself and of his environment and of the forces shaping that environment. He is aware of his own passions and of how they affect what he perceives. He knows that he perceives the world through the screen of his own personality, that the person he is colors the things he sees. He has considered his own values, the values of others, and the consequences to which these values lead. He is

*free, in sum, not because he is without passions, but because he has
examined his life and mastered it with his mind. He is slave to no
man, to no doctrine, to no ignorance. He is free because his mind
has set him free.*

*To give every American a chance to become this man — this is the
central challenge of education in our time.* (131:47–48)

In the horizontal dimension, the school must be extended to provide
for all groups needing compensatory education. It is significant that
considerable evidence and pressure point toward putting the emphasis
on the needs of the inner-city child and youth, for in the inner city
is the largest concentration of deprived persons. However, it will
behoove us to remember those in the rural areas, those still in the
South and the Southwest, and the most neglected of all, the children and youth of the migrant workers. The context of the program
to be offered must be closely related, in each instance, to the particular needs of each of these groups. One other group that has
received little attention but does play an important role in our
current social situation is made up of those who are illiterate and
those who have had little experience with any part of a formal educational program. The public is now being made aware of the
various groups of people whom our own society has failed or who
have failed themselves. It is gratifying to note also that this concern
includes the American Indian. Compensatory education should be
provided for each individual group to the full extent of its basic
and educational needs, for if any program of compensatory education
within the school is to succeed it must be applied to every individual
regardless of age or circumstance. There is no longer time to wait
for our Head Start children to be educated and form the adult
society of which we dream.

Still within the horizontal dimension, the school with its vital
education now must find a way to include as a part of its responsibility the guidance of the youth and adult as well as the young
child toward the best use of their abilities and toward the most
rewarding opportunities for the growth and use of their potentials.
Any limitations on this type of guidance will continue to place
inadequate persons into society, where they must exist. Lack of
preparation and guidance removes from their hands the tools
needed for successful coping with environment and, hence, successful living and the ability to be independent and free. Higher education must face this challenge.

Can the school also serve the parents? (44:389–394) In both the vertical and horizontal approaches to education, and particularly to compensatory education, the parent is most essential in the successful education of his child. Through the provision of vocational education, retraining, and further education for adults, many of the parents are reached. But of particular concern to the school and to the family is school and parent cooperation, which is possible only when there is joint involvement in the educational process for the child and youth. The schools that have attempted just this have been rewarded by the change from a negative to positive attitude on the part of the parents, and hence by a fresh, new positive attitude on the part of the children toward their own learning. As parents help out in the school, go on trips with the children's class, and take part in workshops offered to help them with their own personal and cultural needs, they begin to see the efforts made by the school for their children, and to have a clearer picture of the purposes of education as well as its values. They come to understand that they must help their children, in forming their attitudes, to give attention to their work, to have a time and place for study. They then share in the pride that is rightly theirs as their children experience success. Not only do parents share with the child in the pride of work well done, but as they become involved in an educational program of their own, they also have pride in what they are accomplishing and have something to share with their children.

Facilities and Implementation

What consideration is being given to the school as an entity? In the literature, concern is expressed for the overcrowded city school — for the obsolescence, the dreariness, the dirt, and the resultant atmosphere of neglect. Just how important is the school building itself? There is confusion in the minds of many as to the value of new schools within the ghetto areas, but some evidence is now being given that a new building with ample space, light, and color does more for stimulating and encouraging the deprived child in the educational process than such a school would do for the child of the middle class or of the affluent group. There is opportunity to build pride, to teach the elements of respect for property, and to give to the people of the area a feeling that they are worthy of the expense of such a structure. The deprived child needs space for movement, needs to belong to the small class, needs to have a rich environment made up of many things that will stimulate the senses, and needs a teacher who has the materials necessary for this stimulation. Will a more vital education be accomplished more quickly if the money is spent for schools for the deprived?

In the trend in school construction it is obvious that architecture is being influenced by the general tendency toward mobility and change. Jonathan King makes the claim that if the architectural transformation now being promoted were to take place in the urban schools, it could serve as a strong force in blocking the migration of the middle and upper classes from the cities. He speaks for operable walls, which provide for the accommodation of large groups or can form smaller rooms. The amount of space required for specific learning tasks can now actually be created by merely moving the walls and rearranging the movable equipment. Allowing for this kind of adaptability is called "humanizing" the school. King clearly states his point of view when he says:

> . . . the school house itself cannot cure all the ills of education. But it can complicate them or simplify them. It can either facilitate or restrict learning. It should at the very least get out of the way of education. The building can teach little, but it can say a good deal to its occupants and its community. (62:136)

If these are the plans for the schools of the future, one wonders when many of our deprived children will have the opportunity to occupy them. One is reminded of Cardinal Cushing's statement that was quoted in a Boston newspaper: "The Ghetto binds the Negro child to the local school, where most often he finds reflected the deprived neighborhood in which he is imprisoned. Overcrowding, obsolescence and isolation take their toll in spite of the most dedicated teachers, while compensatory programs only touch the surface of a long neglected problem. . . . Plans for new schools turn yellow on the drawing board while decay eats away at existing institutions, and a generation of young Americans finds its future very nearly foredoomed . . ."

The American people have one important decision to make in relation to new school buildings and that is where the money can be best spent. The education carried on in the many beautiful buildings across the country is proving to be less than adequate. It is expected and taken for granted. Administrators and teachers seem satisfied with less than the best, the children are neither neglected nor challenged, and the space, color, and design of the building relate little to the learning and teaching within. Those administrators and teachers are to be commended who are able to create within old, outdated buildings an atmosphere of enthusiasm, purposeful activity, and concern for doing their job well. One can soon forget the water stains, cracked plaster, high ceilings, and dirty beige walls where dedication exerts its power. The children learning in such buildings are the more fortunate.

Anyone who has had the experience of moving into a new school building or the privilege of beginning a new program is fully aware of the overexcitement and overenthusiasm that sometimes accompanies the opportunity of looking through catalogs and choosing those items that would make both the school and the classroom an alive and exciting environment for a child. Too often the choices are left to a purchasing agent, who may not be well acquainted with the environment and who is even less acquainted with the children who will be attending. Facilities, equipment, and teaching materials have a way of becoming status symbols for the "good" teacher or the overambitious administrator. Each September, after a teacher has been allotted her yearly amount of money for supplies and has filled his room with exciting pictures, materials, and games, he watches for the glow and excitement in the children's eyes as they enter. Often he is disappointed because he has forgotten that the children have come into a room that is his room and not their room. It is the teacher who has gained the pleasure — the children are forced to accept the situation. No purpose has been set up, nor do these children yet relate the objects they see to what they are learning, for they have not begun to learn. How much more bewildering it must be for a deprived child!

One question should be asked: In the light of the statements that have been made previously concerning the new approach to a more vital education, what are the guidelines that should be followed in the choice of facilities and materials for a school providing compensatory education for the deprived? The concerns of a compensatory program suggest the following as basic ideas:

1. Compensatory education should bring a richness, a depth, and a breadth to everyday learning and living experiences.

2. Compensatory education must translate the broad and vital education into appropriate and enriching experiences that take the individual step-by-step toward its goal.

3. The child's own culture furnishes the framework for the structuring of his life's activities.

4. The deprived child and the deprived youth must answer these questions from a positive point of view: Who am I? What am I uniquely able to do?

5. Deprived children need time to think, to feel, to see, to listen as they work through self-discovery toward a positive self-concept.

6. Deprived children and youth must begin compensatory education simply, slowly, without pressure and with encouragement, and arrive at success.

7. Learning is discovery through stimulation.

8. Education must become a continuous program of development, cultivation, expansion, strengthening, and discipline of all one's capabilities.

9. A vital education becomes the best of living through total confrontation and resolution, excitement, knowledge, marvelling, enjoying, creating, and sharing.

10. Within a rich environment, the child discovers himself in touch with the world, and he needs time, encouragement, and opportunity for thinking and for the development of initiative and creativity.

11. The teacher begins his program with the child where he is, noting his levels of readiness and of maturity, takes into consideration the child's immediate environment and culture, and guides him step by step toward the gaining of broader concepts and deeper understandings, toward richer and more varied experiences in living, and, through participation in interaction with others, toward a life of realization and responsibility.

12. A truly vital education will develop men of creativity, sensitivity, and intellectual curiosity.

These guidelines not only assume but demand that a teacher know well the environment from which his children come to him. He knows the experiences that they have had and those which they lack. He knows what materials are basic to the home life of the children and what materials they have access to in their play. He is aware of the parents' attitudes and of demands that parents put upon the older child. He knows of the opportunities and the lack of opportunity for constructive outside activities for the older child and work for the adolescent.

With his understanding of child development and of the process of learning, the teacher can assess each child's language ability, academic level, and readiness for new experiences. This background of knowledge enables the teacher to structure the necessary experiences needed by the children for whom he is responsible. He himself is enthusiastic about choosing materials to promote these experiences, and takes a keen delight as each child slowly becomes acquainted with his school world through the very carefully chosen, simple, but appropriate materials around him. He may need to start by learning to name the furniture in the room; he may need to begin with observing large pictures for the purpose of slow but sure identification of and with simple objects within them. Perhaps he is ready for the opportunity of feeling as well as seeing and hearing. Equipment and materials are introduced gradually as he indicates his ability first to become aware of them, then to explore and gain new knowledge concerning them, and finally to use them properly in his experiences within the school. The teacher is able to develop anticipation and excitement in the child as he looks forward to what may be new for him tomorrow. His school environment offers him possibilities for extending his learning through materials and equipment only as he is ready for the new experiences that involve them. A large mirror in which the child can watch himself may be far more important to him than an expensive piece of equipment that remains unused.

When the child is ready the teacher recognizes that he can go beyond the simple concrete objects to the use of more pictures, books, and films. In the experiences he plans for listening and talking and responding creatively, he sees the opportunity for providing materials that will stimulate the necessary interests and ideas. He will recognize that it is also through responding in a creative manner to the concrete situations as he begins to draw, to paint, to sing, to dance, that this child has made the experiences that he has offered his own, and thus has found that he has ideas and feelings to express and to share.

If the child is ready to extend his horizons and to discover the world beyond him, every opportunity should be given for him to express his curiosity and his interest through questioning. It is through these explorations that the teacher discovers his ability to deal with newer materials and ideas. It is the child's growing and maturing intellectually, physically, socially, and emotionally that determines the increase in the use of materials and in the variety and complexity of those materials. All that the school does for the child must encourage and promote learning, helping him to move slowly from the simple to the complex, from the concrete to the abstract, and from the personal to the vicarious experience. With the older children the range of materials needed widens because interests become more varied, and differences in maturity and ability also begin to make demands for variety. There must be equipment and materials on hand at all times for the child who takes strides ahead as well as for the child who slowly, through repetition, builds and rebuilds his simple experiences.

As the teacher works with the older child and the adolescent, specific equipment and materials are needed for gaining necessary experiences, for practice in skills, for extended realization of the relationship of ideas, and for an appreciation of the world and the opportunities it offers. Each child, at any age, desires to know about his peers — what they enjoy, what they do, how they live, their hopes, and their attitudes. For it is through identifying with others that he gains further interest and desire for newer, richer, and broader experiences. Materials then become related to areas of knowledge, to fields of study, to people, and to ideas and interests. The child begins to see the possibilities for the use of knowledge as man confronts his environment. He discovers the intricacies of nature, of man himself, and of man's ways of living and working in the world.

It is, then, through the proper choice of facilities, equipment, and materials within the school that the child experiences, learns, relates and interrelates, learns to know himself and others, discovers his strengths and his weaknesses, discovers his abilities and his desires, builds his own unique behavior patterns, discovers his independence of thought and action, and acquires a sense of responsibility.

Within these guidelines the total school environment becomes one of encouragement to explore, anticipate, and share in discovery. This can take place in the classroom, in the art room, in the library, in the science room, in the auditorium, as the school makes the effort to introduce new experiences and new ideas only as the child sees a purpose in each for himself and is ready to use them to the fullest.

The Urban School

As sprawling urban expansion engulfs the nation, escape from the city — for rich and poor alike — becomes increasingly impossible. The choice for both is: to live in deteriorating neighborhoods amidst crime, tensions, and frustrations, with slums, poverty, and infectious ignorance undermining progress and human happiness; or to create healthy,

attractive metropolitan communities, economic opportunities for all
and centers of moral and cultural strength.

The instrument for achieving the latter goal — the humanized city
— is education. The challenge is to design systems and programs of
education for urban schools that will free the mind and spirit of each
individual to live abundantly with the benefits that well-organized
metropolitan life can provide.[8]

This statement was made by Stiles and Chandler in 1962, when
migration from the rural areas to the cities was posing more and
more problems and the direction of change for the near future was
becoming more evident. They expressed a hope for what education
might do at that time, but the speed with which the change has
taken place and the far more serious situation that exists now are
even beyond what was feared a few years ago.

The irony of the situation should make all of us take time to
think about the future. As has been indicated previously, slum
clearance is forcing further mobility of the poor population, taking
their homes but providing little in return, for few can afford to live
in the new complexes taking shape where their homes once stood.
Delinquency is on the increase. There is less and less opportunity
for any type of constructive endeavor on the part of the youth; as
a result crime, with its high cost to the city, mounts. The large
cities are making every effort to increase recreational and cultural
facilities in order to provide for the leisure time of the more
affluent group, yet those who are able to take advantage of them are
retreating to the suburbs and so the city is faced with a increased
transportation problem. The cost of the new cultural and recreational opportunities places them beyond the reach of those who
remain in the city. What hope can be given to these persons who
appear to be facing a future with less and less opportunity for social
interaction or cultural development? Is it possible that education
alone can give to the children and the adults in the inner-city
ghetto a reason for building a positive self-image, a need to raise the
levels of aspiration, or even a reason for wanting to learn? Is the
often-stated goal of helping the children of the ghetto reach the
levels of the middle-class society a realistic one if middle-class society
is no longer available to them as an image in the city where they
live?

At a time when there is considerable discussion concerning integration, the inner city itself is becoming a more segregated area.
The very purpose of educating the children and youth, to enable

them to cooperate in a program of interaction with other groups, is being denied. The urban area presents a picture of concentrated poverty and its attendant conditions. The result is an intensification of the many social, economic, and educational problems.

The survival of the American city will depend upon the solution to many crucial problems. At first they seem diverse, but they can easily be placed under one heading, making the city livable according to modern standards — pure air and pure water, adequate housing at a reasonable cost, efficient transportation, recreational and cultural opportunities for all, attractive surroundings, and safety. To these essentials for drawing people to a living area there must be added the all-important one of good schools.

It is the child and the youth in the urban school that is our deep concern. Recent literature is vividly depicting the crisis in urban education through descriptions of those involved—the child, the teacher, the principal.(73) Jonathan Kozol in his recent book, quotes the apt statement of Eric Erikson: "Some day, maybe, there will exist a well-informed, well-considered, and yet fervent public conviction that the most deadly of all possible sins is the mutilation of a child's spirit."[9] Deprivation of experience, the degradation of ignorance, the destruction of hope, and the apathy of the bureaucracy of control too often describe the ghetto school.

The urban school must accept the challenge for change. This is the school that is recognized as being the most difficult, having the most serious conditions, and needing to make the greatest change. It is the inner-city school that must solve the educational problem, by proving itself an instrument for the improvement of the society surrounding it. It must assume the leadership for meeting immediate social needs as well as long-range ones. Its educational program must be pertinent and dynamic. The school must point the way to immediate assistance for the people concerned. Above all, it must involve everyone within the community in this change and improvement. This can be done only if the school proves that it can provide the best education possible by giving full evidence of its new and vital philosophy, through dedicated administrators and teachers who know the people and are able to work with them, speaking their language, thinking their thoughts, and leading them toward higher goals. The school will then have a curriculum geared to the children within the school and planned by the teachers, who provide the appropriate subject matter, experiences, and teaching materials for these children, daring to follow growth lines rather than grade lines, fully recognizing and accepting learning and language differences, and respecting the children for their own worth. This kind of school will be far more than an innovation. It will represent a changed point of view, built on basic and vital purposes and substantiated by research, which must continue on a long-range basis to serve in the development of this *education for meaning.*

The urban school must become a new school — new in spirit — at the center of a new community. It will be desired and appreciated by educators and parents alike because it is the result of their purposeful interaction. This school will begin with each child where he is, and lead him step by step as he makes his own basic generalizations, forms his own concepts, lives the experiences he should have had and should be having. Any evaluation of the school program will be made in terms of the most important end product, the growth of the child. The city or inner city supporting this school will have little difficulty in holding its people, or of drawing them back from the suburbs. This community school will become for those who are involved in this effort for better community living an example of integration at its best, of social interaction, and of social responsibility, for these will be held as essentials for living within the community.

Compensatory education as it has been discussed can and must be the present educational program of the urban school. For the immediate present it may be a "crash" program, but it need not remain one. With long-term planning it will continue to evolve as change takes place within the schools. The success of this program in the inner city will soon make it evident that the need for improved education extends beyond the urban school. This new urban school can succeed, for it will build upon the worth of the child and the worth of the adult, recognizing their strengths, their potentials, and their talents.

Each school must be available at all times to its community. Its service as a social agency, in addition to its provision of a vital educational program, will be as strong as the involvement of each person in the community in the total program for improvement. The need for this new urban school is urgent. The change must take place while there is still time. It is not too soon to remove the pressures from the teachers and from the children. It is not too soon to show appreciation for those teachers who respect their children and are endeavoring to remove from the educational scene fear, resistance, and poor discipline, and to replace these with self-respect and the desire to learn. Is it too late?

It is not too late. There are schools and teachers who have already accepted the challenge and who are quietly and successfully reaching the deprived child and the deprived youth. One should be able to read about these people and their successes in the educational journals. There should also be more articles on the strengths of the deprived people. It is to be hoped that the research currently under way will stress the positive factors that the schools and the teachers confront and show by what means the negative elements, of which there are many, can be translated into positive goals.

People must recognize that the inner-city schools have failed the children. Fewer of their graduates are admitted to college, business is hiring fewer, and an alarming number are being rejected by the draft. This is especially true in our eastern cities, but the trend is moving westward with the migration. As a people we have seldom dared to look for the reasons for the current situation. We quickly approve the yearly expense of $800 to $1,000 for a first-grade child in the suburbs, but we are appalled at the idea that perhaps the same amount of money should be spent on a deprived child in the inner-city school, when actually that figure would have to be tripled in order to bring the education of the deprived child up to the level of the education offered in the suburbs. A recent newspaper report of a talk, "The Collapse of American Public School Education," given by Hauser of the University of Chicago to the Education Writers Association stated that the child in the inner-city school has access only to a third- or fourth-rate education as compared to the child who is privileged to live in the suburbs. Hauser also claimed that even the white child in the metropolitan area, in contrast to the Negro child and others of the deprived areas, has access only to a second- or third-rate education. These facts must be accepted as basic to action. What role will the community play?

The people of this country are faced with the necessity of making very important demands at this crucial time. First, general apathy and complacency must be replaced with positive action in the interest of quality education. The hard fact that this education is costly must be recognized. Second, the public must demand education, not equal for all, but equal to the potentialities of each child and youth, and make this possible by paying an equal amount for it. Third, the people must be concerned with the important roles of both state and local government leadership, and demand that this leadership assume the full responsibility for equal education for all areas and all peoples. Fourth, there must be a demand that the administrators of the schools represent and support current educational thinking and have a thorough knowledge of children, of the learning process, of school organization and curriculum, and of the community in which each school is located. Only as there is mutual respect among educational leaders and cooperation of all responsible for this education can there be any assurance that expectations can be kept high for all, and that those who teach can be free to carry out the purposes of education. Fifth, opportunity must be given to knowledgeable educators to assume leadership in the social changes that are demanded at the present time. The schools will then be in a position of leadership rather than remaining the mirror of society. Sixth, it is the responsibility of those in government at all levels to demand that the best education and the best schools be located first in the areas of the greatest need, to meet the urgent demand of the present and to provide an example for the future improvement of all schools.

In assuming responsibility for education within a community, its people also assume responsibility for the improvement of the other facets of its society. In order that the action taken may be constructive, well structured, and forward-looking, they must use all of the resources at hand, become knowledgeable concerning the research being carried on by the various social institutions, and respect and work cooperatively with the leaders of those institutions, thus permitting the way for improvements to be opened. The action must go past mere referral to intelligent involvement. Value-promotion must take the place of value-conflict.

> Basically, the problem is perennial: that of technological changes occurring faster than man's ability, or willingness, to deal with the results in a planned and sensible manner.[10]

Thus Cox very succinctly sums up the urban situation, in his introduction to the discussion of possibly involving the urban university as a resource in saving the cities. He points out that in the past the university has bridged the gap in town and gown relationships by preparing students to become professional workers in the areas of education, recreation, and welfare. He contributes a listing of seven categories of programs that colleges and universities might now undertake in participating more actively in the "fight against urban decay":

> (1) *Academic credit can be given for some types of community work. (2) Students and campus organizations can be encouraged to work in volunteer projects in the community. (3) Departmental programs can be developed with the objective of aiding the community in which the institution is located. (4) College summer camps for slum children can be established. (5) Settlements or youth centers can be set up in depressed neighborhoods. (6) Programs not intended to lead to a degree in social work can be developed. (7) Alumni organizations can be encouraged to undertake service projects in their communities.*[11]

J. Marton Klotsche[12] considers it the responsibility of the urban university or college to promote understanding of the present urban condition as a national problem, to see how it may improve conditions within its own area, and to determine how it may fit into the community as an involved institution. He sees no conflict between the educational purposes of the university and its community responsibilities, for here is opportunity to put into practice the concepts that are taught in the classroom, thus demonstrating the university's concern for those beyond its doors. Klotsche's book should serve as an excellent guide in the use of a resource seldom tapped before.

In the interest of considering the role of the urban college and university in the understanding and resolving of some of the urban problems, attention is being drawn also to the Negro colleges and to Negro students in other colleges.

First, reports are now being made concerning the actual involvement of the students from the city colleges and universities, such as Antioch's experiment in the ghetto,[13] the work of Boston college students in the Roxbury project,[14] the plan to build an urban welfare center on the campus of Newark College,[15] and the proposal by M.I.T. to set up urban laboratories and information banks.[16]

Second, concern is being expressed about the future of Negro colleges and about improving the education they provide. David Riesman has written about the poor quality of their offerings.[17] Will they or can they improve before the educational program for their students prior to college entrance is improved? And third, there is concern for the Negro students in integrated schools where it is obvious that they are isolating themselves. Integration at all levels must carry into the activities of the "life" of the institution. Ginsberg does report favorably, however, from his study that middle-class Negro students find color no barrier.[18]

Universities are also having to defend themselves against possible charges of discrimination that can grow out of conclusions from reports of studies or surveys. A recent statement of this nature was made concerning the University of Michigan[19] as a result of the Coleman report in 1966. (158) Every effort is being made by many institutions of higher education to admit qualified students from minority groups.

The Rural School

In discussing the school for the deprived and its position in the social scene, we should not ignore the rural school, which still plays a role in our country. So much emphasis has been put on the problems of the migrants from the rural areas that we tend to forget the millions who remain in the hinterlands and who continue to make the effort to support themselves and educate their children. Because of the pattern of mobility there seems to be less need to differentiate the problems of the rural and urban areas. The emphasis is upon poverty and the characteristics of poverty wherever people are found.

In considering the poor in the rural areas, Isenberg lists the following general characteristics of both children and adults:

> . . . a low level of aspiration, a tendency to set only short-term goals, values which differ somewhat from acceptable norms, and a general unfamiliarity with cultural activities which lead to enriched living. (44:244)

These characteristics are similar to those of the deprived in the city, but it is essential to note that the same types of characteristics can result in different backgrounds and hence themselves vary in meaning in relation to individuals. Resolution of the problems in the situation that fosters these characteristics depends upon the resources available, the peculiar needs that have to be fulfilled, and the basic desire of the people themselves for improvement. The urban situation has somewhat eclipsed the rural, but there is evidence that an effort is now being made to consider the rural area as important and worthy of assistance.

With the new mobility has come a change in the meaning of the word "community." The concept is now more fluid, sometimes designating a large area, other times, an extension of the city itself. It would appear that all people, urban and rural, are now striving toward the type of living that puts stress upon material gains, the importance of the wheel, and city standards of living. Values are changing to reflect these desires. Patterns of behavior, of culture, and of recreation are being set in the cities for those in the rural areas as well as for those in the inner cities and the suburbs, bringing about a greater unity of aspiration.

In the more isolated regions the school is often the one social institution, and must assume the responsibility for endeavoring to meet the needs of the people in the area. Rather than a concentration of problems, there is in the rural area a scattering of small, self-contained communities and a lack of communication with the outside world except through radio or television. Too often the welfare agencies serve only in the city and those who would be of help to the school work solely in the urban areas. The consolidation of schools, which has been going on for some time, has proved helpful to the rural areas, permitting them to hire better teachers, build better facilities, and offer a broader program of curricular and extracurricular activities. These larger schools are reaching out into the countryside, from which they draw the children and youth. In many places the schools have become the community centers where representatives from other agencies find the people who need help. Monies are being made available by the states and by the federal government for needed educational and community programs in rural areas. Through rural community action, legal services have been brought to the people. The Youth Corps has reached out to the adolescents. Opportunities for the young adults to gain employment have been made available through the formation of youth centers. VISTA holds forth a promise as volunteers reach the more isolated areas. Since the importance of farming as a source of income has decreased, efforts are now being made to help the people develop other skills that can be used in their own communities.

Even with the addition of such programs, the rural school carries a heavy burden of responsibility for maintaining a broad area of opportunity and for reaching out to bring the people to it. The school also has provided a service to those of the rural population who are on the move. Further provisions must still be made for the migrant child and the migrant parent for better housing, better schooling, the enforcement of the child labor laws, participation in some form of community endeavor, and assistance from health and welfare agencies. These are added to the concerns of rural education in its larger sense.

Perhaps one of the greatest challenges facing both urban and rural schools at the present time is that of informing the citizenry of actual conditions as they exist in the various types of communities. This information should spell out concrete ways in which all can work together to bring about the necessary improvements.

The School Administrator

If the schools are to accept the challenge of informing the public of its responsibility and of suggesting concrete ways in which this duty may be assumed, there must be a clear indication of the structure of the school organization and evidence of the leadership within. As citizens, we are jealously proud of our form of government and of our schools, but too often we are poorly informed as to the depth of the responsibility that the leadership within must assume. We know too little about the roles played and the variability in these roles across the country. In our concern for local control we approach the larger problems through a scattering of independent efforts. The patterning of organizing for a broad national endeavor appears to have to move from these small individual projects, through a gradual pooling of ideas in local, state, and regional centers, to some form of national organization before guidelines of significance can be developed and the public as a whole can be made aware of what is basically needed. Poor planning and the lack of information resulting from inadequate local leadership have led to wasting time, of which we have little, to lack of recognition of the good work that is being done in scattered areas, and to failure to use many of the resources at hand. A structure of operation is essential, and this structure must be made known to the people.

Compensatory education, to be effective either on the local scene or in a well planned national program, is dependent upon the structure chosen for it. We are now at the point of having to take time to discover the good of what has been done, to see the possibilities for further programing and organization, and to determine some of the bases on which the evaluation of programs and projects may be made. We need to study the evidence of wasted time and effort, to discover the relationship between the projects carried out by schools and the social changes taking place within the communities surrounding these schools, and to set forth more clearly the essential changes that must be made in the broad educational program as well as the nature of the immediate and necessary compensatory education. We must then spell out the type of leadership required for a positive sharing of ideas, a recognition of untapped resources, a clarification of goals, and an organization within which this leadership may function for the purpose of meeting the goals. Cooperation at all levels is essential. The time for trial and error is past. Constructive planning and the delegation of work to responsible and well informed leaders must now form the basis of any new or revised structuring in order to realize the new and vital education so essential for our children and youth.

In any consideration of the newly defined modern school — the school that offers compensatory education, the school that offers the new and vital education not only for the deprived but for all children — it is essential that its administration also be defined. Although the teacher within such a school, regardless of the organization or the details of the program offered, is perhaps the most significant single factor in promoting a good education for the individual child, this teacher's success is dependent upon the support given her by the principal, who represents the administration. This dependence is both a referral and a deferring, representing the essential acts necessary in the carrying out of policy. These same acts are present in the hierarchy of administration, not only from the teacher to the principal, but also from the principal to the superintendent, the superintendent to the board of education, the board of education to the city government and state legislature, the state legislature to the federal government and the federal government to the president. Hence the democratic structure of our schools does have an organization. But the successful operation of this organization is dependent upon the personnel and upon the roles played by each. Through the election and appointment systems the people decide and act, thus determining the quality of persons, the defining of responsibility, the appropriateness of legislation, and the shaping of the policy. Although the role of government will be discussed briefly in Chapter IV, it may be well to state here some of the major problems upon which policy must be made.

The larger problems of this country and the decision-making policy in relation to their solutions should be dealt with through national legislation and judicial pronouncement. Here, as at every other level, those making judgments and policies should have at hand all necessary information concerning changes taking place and the needs created by these changes. To be sure, this must be true at every level in the hierarchy of the administration of education and of each school.

Definition and clarity are essential in the statements and restatements of both decision and policy in order that at each level the responsibility for implementation may be seen, not only in the total country, but down through the states, cities, and rural areas and in local situations. There appear to be at present three major problems that call for action at all levels of administration as it affects education. These are integration, the distribution of the tax dollar, and the reallocation of responsibility. All three are basic to the successful launching and continuous processing of a vital education, first, for the deprived, and secondly, for all children.

As it was stated earlier, the problem of integration has not been resolved far enough for conclusions to be drawn or evaluations made. Definitions of the pertinent terminology, however, are clear. They are, according to Weinberg:

> Segregation. A *socially-patterned separation of people, with or without explicit legal sanction.*
> Desegregation. The *abolition of social practices that bar equal access to opportunity.*
> Integration. The *realization of equal opportunity by deliberate cooperation and without regard to racial or other social barriers.*
> Deprivation. The *socially-patterned withholding of opportunity from selected groups of persons.*
> Clearly segregation and integration are opposites; desegregation is a step (but not the journey) to the latter. Deprivation is relative to privilege, as mighty or puny as the prize might be. Segregation has so often been used to allocate opportunities among the deprived and the privileged. By its very nature, however, integration cannot so be used. Problems of segregation and deprivation are compounded by considerations of race and class. All the deprived, whatever their skin color, are segregated.[20]

Thus, he not only gives us clarified definitions, but relates the problem of deprivation to these terms. Integration in the school is a stated national policy. We are in the process of searching for and trying out various means for achieving equal opportunity. Each attempt that is made brings about its own special problems. Both time and distance from these attempts will be necessary to gain perspective. We need now to keep pace with efforts and results. There are indications, evidenced by successive polls, that the American people are increasingly aware of the necessity for integration within our schools. The mobility from the cities, however, is creating a serious situation. The cities themselves are becoming segregated areas of the deprived, leaving these people with little access for communication and interaction with other groups. There is hope that the improvement of the inner-city school and its surrounding community will encourage the return to the city of those who still recognize the advantages of city living. This will once again create the opportunity for the interplay of social groups and the instituting of a truly integrated education for the children and youth designated by the lack of discrimination.

The second major problem deals with the financial support of education. There is need, as shown by Strom, (143:67) to consider a change in our way of supporting the educational program we desire. At the present time only two to three percent of the American dollar goes to education. The distinct change that has come about is in the actual spending of that money. We have moved from the time when 80 percent of the tax dollar was both collected and left for spending in the local district, to the point where the federal government collects and takes over the spending of nearly 80 percent of the same tax dollar, leaving only about 20 percent to the local district, county, and state. However, according to the national average, over 90 percent of the cost of both elementary and secondary education is still carried by these same local districts, counties, and states.

Another aspect of the financial problem relating to education was mentioned previously with regard to the inner city. Not only is the improvement of the existing educational program essential here, but this is where there is greatest need for compensatory or special programs, which are indeed even more costly. This need is occurring in an area where the tax rate on property value for the support of schools is low in relation to that of other metropolitan areas and the suburbs. The accomplishment of the necessary and urgent improvements in the inner city will have to depend upon outside financial assistance. The inequity of tax income is also obvious in the rural areas, where this situation has also helped to bring about poor schools. Some measure of equalizing the income for the schools from the tax dollar must be realized.

The third problem to be solved pertains perhaps more specifically to the inner city, but also in some measure to the rural areas. There must be some form of redistricting in the state and in the city, and a reallocation of the responsibility for the education of the children of small communities within larger communities. It has been pointed out that the newer and more vital education demands that the administration be carried out by those within the situation, who can relate to it and are knowledgeable concerning it. The intention here is not to destroy or to give up the basic democratic hierarchy, but to take a new and realistic view that does demand the delegation of responsibility for specific situations and, with this responsibility, the power to act. Again, it is the people who must intelligently determine the solutions of all three of these problems with their many ramifications. Their solutions will free qualified teachers and administrators to carry out the type of vital education that we are beginning to see as essential for each American citizen.

The superintendent is highly respected by the board of education, principals, teachers, parents, and public. He gains this respect only as he becomes fully versed in both the assets and the needs of his schools and of the people involved. He is well informed, and he in turn must inform well. He not only knows the strengths and weaknesses of his own schools; he builds his forward-looking programs upon the strengths and in turn strengthens the weaknesses. He must inform and he must act. It is to this superintendent that the principal of each school must refer and defer. The success of each principal as he governs his own school will be determined in considerable part by the support and understanding given to him by this superintendent.

> The role of the principal in the education of the disadvantaged is crucial. Where a depressed-area school is successful in educating children and retaining teachers, it is almost certain that the teachers have the leadership of an understanding, competent principal.[21]

There are those who insist that the principal holds the key administrative role in the schools. And, although it has been said that the teacher is the one important single individual, this is stated because of his or her direct contact with the children. His success is still dependent upon the leadership and support of the person directly above him, as is the principal's.

Attempts have been made to list the characteristics of a good principal. These should be the same for one who directs a school promoting a program of compensatory education for deprived children and youth. (143:59–62) Those qualities should be stressed, however, which seem to be essential above all others for the person who takes on this special role. They are: (1) a commitment to service, (2) selflessness, (3) proven skill in interpersonal relationships, (4) a spirit and practice of empathy, (5) a marked degree of sensitivity, (6) an insightful awareness, (7) a mixture of humility and courage with an absence of fear. Any good school at any level of the educational process will be a better school if its leader possesses these qualities in full measure and if its purpose and philosophy acknowledge that these qualities are as necessary as the academic preparation.

It is the principal who creates the atmosphere so essential to good teaching and to good learning, and who permits each teacher an independence with support to find his or her way of personally reaching each child and creatively teaching that child. With this independence and support, the principal must give a knowledgeable guidance to those on his staff in the planning of the curriculum, and in the organizing of activities. The principal is responsible not only for the establishment of the program, but also for its operation, through which broad basic policies are implemented and goals realized.

The school that initiates and operates a rich, vital, and creative program of compensatory education at any level must have a principal who sees within his role of leadership the responsibility for establishing an appropriately structured learning environment. This single responsibility involves guiding teachers in working within this environment, establishing the proper attitudes on the part of the teachers and the children, and accepting this environment and the expectations built relative to it. The principal must provide constant personal encouragement, to both the teachers and those who are learning, to work toward increasingly higher aspirations and standards, without undue pressure or the creating of frustration. The principal must also give recognition and expressed approbation upon each success, no matter how small, of each person working with him, teacher or child.

Levine clearly states the seriousness of the responsibility assumed by the administrator of a school for the deprived.

> What we ultimately face, then, is a challenge to the competence, integrity, and wisdom of the administrator. To revise thoroughly the educational policies in low-income schools will imply past negligence in not having made these changes sooner. Administrators who react defensively to criticisms of their persons or their schools are not likely to rise to the occasion. The easier and safer alternative is to search out and reiterate reasons, many of them valid, which explain why the

situation is not better than it is. Only the administrator who is secure enough to give more attention to exploring the possibilities for the future than to justify the failures of the past can hope to meet the challenge.[22]

It is to the machinery of the "local control" of the schools that attention is drawn, for it is here that there have been evidences of prejudice and of the very pettiness of politics. The workings of a democratic procedure too often allow for the mismanagement of ideas and of funds, for acts of favoritism, for the juggling of facts, for the lining of pockets. Democracy assumes the honorable discharge of responsibility and selfless concern for the good of all. "Local control" has shown its weakness in the administering of poverty funds, and in the lack of interest and concern for those to whom these funds were to go. The failure of some of the antipoverty programs has been attributed to human failure to put need above the desire for personal recognition and personal gain. As a result, there is under consideration a structure of greater centralization in the management of the schools in smaller communities, setting boundaries by larger community needs — centralization for more efficient, more professional controls in a tighter, safer organization, with those assuming responsibility who see the need for being responsible. The hierarchy will in turn work more efficiently and in a more dedicated manner. This is proposed at a time when there is a beginning of decentraliztion within the larger cities in order to more nearly understand and meet the varied needs of the smaller communities within them.

The Curriculum

Solutions to the problems of children, particularly of minority-group children, involve the creation of social forms that can assist the youngster to achieve self-respect, identity, motivation to achieve, and intellectual purposes consistent with the changing necessities of our social system. In many respects, the awareness of the retarding effects of social deprivation associated with ethnic group and social class membership offers an opportunity to develop procedures for all children who function below their intellectual capability. Much in middle-class affluent America tends to destroy individual identity and tends to alienate young people from any purpose outside the self. Many of these children, subject to contradictory and at the same time confluent social stresses, never become sufficiently motivated for intellectual achievement. At times, in middle-class children, the need for status replaces the need for individual accomplishment, thereby fostering an apathy toward substantive intellectual achievement. . . .

The school can become a socially "therapeutic" instrument through its primary educational function by consciously developing broad-scale curriculum formats that will operate in such a way as to establish and reestablish cultural and educational, and school and community, continuities. This is true for the behavioral as well as the learning areas.[23]

Here we have a challenging statement made by Martin Deutsch. He clearly places the school within its immediate social context and charges the school with the performing of its primary educational function. Deutsch also clearly indicates that the formats for the curriculum must be planned so as to span the cultural and educational, the school and community, and the behavioral and learning areas, not as separate areas to be related, but, through continuity, to be "part and parcel" one of the other. Educational planning can no longer ignore the cultural background and "roots" of the people it is to serve. The school can no longer be considered a separate entity but must be recognized and organized within the context of its community. Neither curricular content nor the consideration of the learning process itself can be isolated from the fact that the end result must be the changes within the behavior of the learner. If the curriculum formats for all schools are planned with this approach, a truly therapeutic education will be available for the treatment of the ills so obvious at the present time. To a greater degree but in the same manner, deprived children and youth will profit from this approach and, as a result of skillful teaching of the curriculum, will be able to disprove the deficits that now serve too often to identify them as "slow."

Revisions within the curriculum in content and content organization are taking place at all levels within the formal educational program. They are evident in the manner or style of reorganization of the personnel contributing to these changes. Many who write on curricular changes include in their discussion the terms "innovation" and "reform," endeavoring to emphasize a newness, or a substitution of something radically different, too often for the sake of being different. Care must be taken that these terms do not hide the true value of changes that are soundly based in knowledge and research. Change based on new knowledge is called for, not change for its own sake. Sound evaluation should run concurrently with the introduction and the use of new ideas and new material, and must be in terms of the overall effectiveness of the total program as it relates to the life, the learning, and the behavior of each child, youth, or adult.

Even though we are giving Sputnik credit for awakening us to our problems, it is now the happenings in the world about us that appear to be forcing us to relate curriculum content and learning itself to the child in his changing world. Population mobility is necessitating a certain type of flexibility within the curriculum, whereby the child who goes from one area to another may be able to step into a new school situation, find his place easily, and continue on with his own learning process. This demands a broad understanding as well as a broad interpretation of experiences that make up the curriculum. This does not, however, prescribe that every school in the United States must be teaching the same thing at the same time at the same level so that the child who moves will find identically the same educational program going on regardless of where he is. This uniformity is neither meant nor implied literally, for if the modifications in the curriculum are to keep pace with broad social changes we must also consider those specific changes within a rural district, a suburb, the city or the inner community.

Social changes have considerable impact upon what we teach children. Technological improvement has altered the type of work available to man. The increasing diminution of our world and universe, with its concurrent increment in our awareness, knowledge, and concern regarding all world citizens and the problems engendered by our closeness, often brings about a fear of our ability and theirs to cope with change, and to plan a way of living together peaceably without loss of identity on the part of anyone. The school carries a tremendous burden as it accepts the responsibility for preparing children and youth to meet these changes and others to come, and for providing for them an interpretation of the past and the present. In the light of new information concerning the process of learning and the development of the learner, we must change our teaching approaches and our expectations. It is essential that we now add to the goal of knowing that of *thinking*. The learner must strive toward many ways of thinking as he determines more creative approaches to the building of attitudes, to the channeling of desires to know more, and to his effort to learn how to learn for the future. The curriculum becomes the means.

Many persons have a concern in the revision of the curriculum of the school today. The situation demands the scholar, the informed administrator, the creative teacher, and interested, cooperative, and informed parents and public. It is essential that all agree upon the importance of curriculum, upon the direction of changes to be made, and upon the time needed to carry out these changes in a constructive manner. Necessary too are good communication, money, and appropriate materials and facilities within the proper setting. Finally, all must recognize that, as change is met and dealt with, there must also be a meeting of the now unknown concurrent changes, for we are living in a world in which progress is open-ended and continuous.

In updating the broad school curriculum it is essential that scholars within the several disciplines contribute, through their research, the current basic concepts that must be taught. In many instances they can also suggest the sequence of these concepts and methods of presentation that will permit the greatest understanding. When this information is linked with the research by the educators in child development and in the teaching-learning process, the question of timing and of pacing can be answered. With this combined effort, it is possible to see a format for the curriculum emerging—an appropriate sequence of knowledge within a discipline and between disciplines, to be taught from the early years, through the elementary and secondary schools, and at the college level. With the present trend toward learning through discovery, involvement, and problem-solving, there is need for new and enriching curricular materials that will both implement the concepts and supplement teaching materials already available. It would appear that this new programming will put the responsibility for learning more and more into the hands of the learner. For it is through this procedure that his own interests are stimulated and his analytical thinking and his own creative approach are realized.

The development of new curricular formats puts a far greater demands upon the teacher. He must be knowledgeable, prepared to interpret the formats, and, most important of all, creative in their use. Although he is provided with a substantial amount of prepared materials and teaching guides that give suggestions for ways of using them, it is still the teacher who has to adapt these materials to the children whom he is teaching. In his consideration of their backgrounds, abilities, and patterns of learning, he must assume the responsibility for the "placement" of each child on the developmental scale of concepts and determine the pacing that will allow for the greatest understanding. The danger in this type of programming is that it will be used as a dictated and required program by an untrained, insensitive teacher as material to be covered within a certain period of time, all with little regard for the children. The steps that have been taken in this curriculum revision are only the beginning ones in a long-range effort. Hopefully the educators concerned will find a way of providing guidance in the use of this new material so that we do not return to a subject-matter-oriented curriculum more exaggerated than that which has helped to create the tremendous problem now facing the schools. It is also hoped that these educators can remove from the American educational scene the stigma associated with not achieving certain arbitrary expectations at stated times and levels, and instead will place high value upon each child's learning how to think and discovering how to learn through acquiring both broad and deep understandings of the sequential concepts and their accompanying skills within the several disciplines in an interrelated structure.

The parents must share in the responsibility for this curriculum and its implementation, for now in the life of the child there can be no separation between the quality of the living process in the school and that in his home and community. There can be no separation in the values he learns in the school and those he learns at home and in his community. The levels of both must be high and challenging.

If this new concept of curriculum can be accepted and put into operation, it will be possible to remove two emphases that have been strong deterrents to educational progress over a period of years. The first is the emphasis placed upon the need for remedial teaching; the other is the focusing upon grade level expectations as the basis for evaluation of progress. Both of these emphases are based upon the assumption that there are fixed standards that each learner must meet regardless of individual differences in background, basic needs, ability, potentiality, interest, personality, or maturity. If the teacher accepts each learner where he is on his own scale of development, maturity, and learning, and he realizes his responsibility in taking this child step by step from that point toward greater personal development and toward new and richer understanding and learning, we will be able to erase from our vocabulary those labels of discouragement such as "remediation," "failure," "slowness," and even the negative interpretation of the term "compensatory education." The terms "remedial" or "compensatory" would need to be used only in recognizing the temporary gap between accomplishment and the full potential of the learner. There would be those who would need an individualized structure within the organization of education to meet their own special needs, helping them to bridge this gap and designate progress in terms of growth rather than grade levels. In essence, then, education would be for every learner a compensatory yet positive one, for the effort would be directed toward helping him to reach toward his potential. The process itself would be on-going, forward, and encouraging to the learner. This same approach to education would be most appropriate at the secondary and college levels and also for any program of continuing education for adults. Differentiation would not be according to the levels of education but according to the needs, abilities, and potential of each individual. The structuring for him would be according to his own pattern of learning within the larger, broader structure. All would then know the true meaning of dignity, respect, opportunity, and realization.

This new approach to the curriculum appears in the suggested revisions of the curriculum specifically planned for the deprived children and youth. The deprived youth, particularly, must learn through a process of discovery, of exploration, and of involvement. In his present state of deprivation his rate of learning is slower, as are his assimilation of ideas and his thinking, but the creative teacher soon discovers his individual growing edge and builds from that point again, step by step, within the structure of good learning. Some form of structure is important for all. The deprived child needs, temporarily, a more detailed structure in his experiencing and learning because of a lack of experiential background from which he may draw in order to see relationships of ideas and build generalizations and concepts to use as tools for further learning. Neither his apparent slowness nor his need for more structure at this time indicate any less ability, although they do indicate that he needs more time. Analytical thinking and creative problem-solving are possible for him as he develops the skills of thinking and a background for thinking.

There is misunderstanding with regard to the use of the term "readiness" with the deprived child as with the average learner. Too many interpret it to mean an actual waiting to present certain materials until the child evidences a need for and an interest in them. The discovering of a child's readiness should be the determining of the point we have stressed several times previously—where he is at the moment in his own process of learning. Actually the deprived child is more ready for more experiences than the child with an adequate or enriched background. But it must be determined where he should start. Nor does readiness mean that there are certain stages in the educational process at which a new area of knowledge should be introduced or the concepts of a certain discipline developed. In the reorganization of a vital and meaningful curriculum the child is ready at all times for some aspect of each discipline. This is the meaning of Bruner's statement: "The foundations of any subject may be taught to anybody at any age in some form." (16:12) If basic understandings and concepts are structured from the simple to the complex and from the concrete to the abstract, each discipline finds its way into the normal, continuous process of learning.

It is now possible, with the information at hand, through the observation of deprived children and youth, to know the areas in which, within a new curriculum, stress must be placed in order to narrow the gap between the lack of experiential background and the potentials they evidence in ability. Deficits do appear in the lack of development of a self-concept, in cognitive development, in the understanding and use of language, in inner motivation, in sensory and intellectual stimulation, in spatial, time, and number concepts, in the basic understanding of their natural and social environments, in the ways of solving social problems, and finally in the areas of appreciation and self-expression. These deficits tend to group themselves according to the various separate areas of learning or the separate disciplines, but we must keep in mind that we need to go a step beyond the separateness to the interrelatedness in order that these children may have facts, knowledge, and understanding to use as a foundation in building both skills and experiences for use in solving problems that must necessarily cross the lines of disciplines.

As we consider this approach among the disciplines, we need to recognize that in this structuring there must also be a crossing of lines as far as levels of instruction are concerned. Individualizing does mean that all that is taught must be taught at all levels at the same time to meet variations in ability and in readiness for each step in the development of a discipline. This raises the question of organization within which the curriculum operates. There are those who feel that if a teacher is to be prepared to do just this he must have time to concentrate on fewer of the learning areas and go into his "specialties," such as social studies, reading, mathematics, more deeply. As a result, an organization for team teaching has been promoted. This same concern brought about a recommendation for ungraded schools. This need was discussed previously in connection with rigid standards of expectation. Grade-level lines have indicated that within a particular grade there shall be both upper and lower limits of the material taught. We now know that these limits cannot be arbitrarily spelled out but are set by the make-up of the learners within any group. Teachers do need help in the structuring of experiences to provide for the wider range of need on the part of the children. But if we are to give each learner a feeling of satisfaction there must be provided some means of recognizing progress so that the child himself has a realization of success and experiences recognition by others of the specific forward steps he has taken. It is not simply the removal of what we have had that will answer the problems. There must be a positive substitution in the light of the new philosophy and the new curriculum that will help the teacher and the learner to meet them.

Another consideration in planning and implementing the curriculum for the deprived child and youth is the understanding and acceptance of the background and culture with which they come to the school. There is a tendency to consider only the deficits and to assume that the child comes with only a vacuum in place of the desired experience and information. This is far from true, for in his home and community he has been coping with his environment, he has been experiencing, he has been communicating, and he has been forming values and loyalties. This is true to a greater extent as he grows older. The problem is not how to erase what he has had, for no one can take this from him. No teacher has the right to further undermine this child by ignoring or refusing to accept his culture or the experiences that he has gained for himself as his only means of identity. There will be times when it is possible to build directly upon this culture. There will be other times when the teacher recognizes that, because of a wide differentiation, the language that he learns at school is for him a second language and school experiences are those of a new world. He should meet him on the level of his own language, his own experience, and his own culture as he begins learning the new. He knows these are the bases for the only means of self-expression he has.

A structure for a generalized form of curriculum for compensatory education is emerging within the literature now available. As the young child is accepted with the tools he brings with him, no matter how meager, we are finding that it is essential that he be given ample time to build and to organize within the area of perception. The ability to perceive accurately is essential to the formation of the simple concepts that are to follow. The school activities then ". . . should be heavily oriented toward the development of language skills, even if an unusually heavy emphasis on language arts — particularly reading — necessitates a corresponding de-emphasis on other activities."[24] This should in no way mean a deleting of other activities, for they form the context for using his language skills. It is through the success that the child experiences in developing communication skills that he can begin to identify himself in the other learning areas. Learning to converse and to read opens many doors for him and if each step taken in the building of these skills is a successful one, the very danger of his being a future reading dropout is diminished. We are also recognizing that the language experiences that begin with the young child continue throughout the educational program as skills are refined and used with increasing ease and speed. There is no longer a cutoff point in learning language skills as one discovers the new approaches in general curriculum revision in the area of linguistics. Language is an exciting area that knows no limits.

As the deprived child grows older, the creative teacher finds that his curricular experiences need to be based on a broadening of his interests to strengthen his inner motivation. Each area of the curriculum expands his horizons as he assimilates knowledge and experiences through problem solving the excitement of building concepts and ideas that lend themselves to creative thinking. Many teachers are finding that the development of accompanying skills in creative expression permits the child to carry his experiences beyond the point of assimilation to one of re-creating his learning in his own terms. These teachers have discovered that many times there is a freshness in a child's use of words, color, movement, and sound that makes one aware of the reservoir of creative ability seldom sufficiently tapped. As the experiences within the curriculum for youth are deepened and broadened there is still no limiting of perceptual and conceptual emphasis. Both purpose and success in each and every experience are essential for the learner at every age; with the adolescent it is vitally important that he not only see the purpose in the immediate but that he look ahead with realistic expectations for the future. The school and the teacher play an important role here. The learner will form expectations in line with those set for him that spur him on and help to reveal to him his own possibilities for the future.

The same principles of learning apply to the deprived child as to the privileged child and should be kept in mind in the planning of any curriculum program:

Children must be interested in what they are to learn.
They must have purpose in learning.
There must be a basis in experience for understanding the new.
What is put to use is best remembered.
Ideas that are interrelated are best remembered and available for future use.
It takes time to learn, and each child learns according to his own timetable. (103:8)

If the educational program can be started in the preschool years, it is here that the bases for the curriculum are formed. Language and the development of concepts are the emphases of the preschool curriculum. Here the deprived child learns to understand himself and others, to perceive and understand his environment, to improve his verbal ability, and to build his store of understanding through varied experiences. All of his learning starts in the simplest forms, such as seeing himself in a mirror and being able to identify his nose, learning the names of the most common objects, such as chairs and tables and the names of his peers, learning to say "thank you," learning to put two words together and then three, and seeing, feeling, tasting, smelling — as he gets to know the small world about him. Teaching is a slow, careful guidance and preparing of the child for the more formal disciplines of reading, spelling, writing, mathematics, social studies, and science. The child prepares himself by listening, playing, observing, talking, responding, taking part, and discovering the excitement of learning.

As this child enters the elementary phase of his educational program the curriculum continues along the same lines, allowing for the depth and breadth of ideas and the learning of further skills as his maturity warrants and his experiences demand. This deprived child slowly learns to talk more, to become more related to the world around him, and to listen to others with a purpose.

Teaching to read has been considered the most important responsibility of the elementary school. It is interesting to note, however, that reading instruction has reached a state of upheaval. There is agreement only that the level of achievement of our deprived children must be improved. This important need is expressed particularly for them, but the answering of it no doubt will have considerable effect upon the teaching of reading for all children. At the moment, wherever reading is being taught in a program for the deprived, the approach, the procedures, the methods, the materials, and even the desired results vary from situation to situation. Sound experimentation and research is going on, but unfortunately there are also changes being made just for the sake of change.

As a result of the work being done in New York City in the field of reading Lloyd proposes eight avenues of attack in meeting the reading needs of the deprived child.

1. New types of tests must be developed to give a clearer picture of the disadvantaged child's capacity to learn to read.

2. It will be necessary in the future to encourage earlier language development and the building of necessary concepts. This will of course mean the extending of public education downward to take care of these young children.

3. The preparation of urban-oriented materials must be accelerated so as to be made available to the programs ready for them. The reading materials must be revised in order to clearly picture through its vocabulary and stories the experiences of every type of city child, including the deprived. This would apply not only to basic readers but also to tapes, recordings, filmstrips, packaged materials and programmed material. The same type of new reading material must also be prepared for the other areas of the curriculum such as social studies and science.

4. The pre-service and in-service preparation of teachers of reading must be improved in order for the teacher to make proper use of the new materials and to understand their purposes. It is recommended that this skillful reading teacher also have a sound background in mental hygiene and child guidance and a thorough understanding and respect for the various cultural and ethnic groups. New York City is using television as a substitute for courses and thus is able to reach more of the teachers at one time. Specialists in reading are also assigned to school buildings where they may assist the teachers. It is also predicted that the involvement of certain college personnel will result in the beginning of language arts resource centers where the teachers may go for professional consultation, demonstration, and assistance with special reading problems.

5. There must be an increase in both the quality and the quantity of special personnel assigned to schools in the disadvantaged area. Speech specialists, library teachers, reading counselors, social workers,

psychologists, and psychiatrists working individually or as a team within a clinic are needed to increase the level of reading success for these deprived children.

6. It is suggested that adequate reading records be kept of the children's progress because of the excessive mobility of their families. In New York City a Reading Record Card is being used on an experimental basis, and is sent to the next teacher when the child moves. The child's progress in reading skills and the listing of the materials he has used are recorded on this card.

7. Research studies in beginning reading will in the near future serve as a basis for change in both method and materials being used.

8. It appears that only by stretching the school day and the school year will we be able to provide the required reading instruction time so necessary, particularly for the deprived child. New York City has established after-school Study Centers in elementary schools, junior high schools, and high schools. These Centers are open for two hours after school during the week and for two hours on Saturday morning, and the teaching is done by members of the regular faculty who are familiar with the needs of the children. (364:471–476)

Again, learning to read is of vital importance to the deprived child. It has proved in many cases to be a status symbol for the child not only at school, but at home. This ability gives him a place at home as a source of information and a help to his parents and brothers and sisters, for he is able to read to them and take care of certain business arrangements. He soon learns that reading opens many doors of information and brings a satisfaction he has not known before.

Some of the experimental approaches to beginning reading for the deprived child include using child-dictated experience charts, teaching the alphabet as an initial step because this would satisfy the parents, determining the effect of intensive initial phonics, and teaching the child to write what he is reading as he reads step by step. Some schools are using the typewriter with young children before they are ready to write. Programmed reading materials are being used in other experiments, but the advantage seems to be in the appropriateness of the material as compared with the traditional reading texts, and this does not appear to outweigh the disadvantages seen when the children are all working on the same material at the same time. This does not permit grouping for individual differences. For the older children, intensive programs of remedial help and practice in study skills are being planned for both in-school and out-of-school times, with the incentive for organizing these programs coming from the children themselves. The strong desire to improve and the effort applied to the work have resulted in tremendous gains for these children.

One interesting approach has been used in New Haven.[25] Because of the inadequacy of the available reading materials, an enterprising teacher took pictures of familiar scenes in the area, and together the teachers and children wrote their own text with their own words. Out of this experiment have grown eight basic "albums of urban studies" dealing with such topics as growing up, the family, and the neighbors. The children were particularly proud of the photographs of themselves and of places they could recognize.

There is also renewed interest in the Montessori Method, which is being adapted to meet certain specific situations. Pitman's Initial Teaching Alphabet is also being recommended as an approach to beginning reading for the deprived child. The security of knowing that the sound of the word will be right when he follows the symbols seems to provide a satisfying beginning step for this child until such time as his sight vocabulary and his ability to transfer have developed.

The introduction of social studies and science moves slowly, for both are built upon basic concepts drawn from experience. The measurement of the teaching of these several subjects cannot be in terms of the traditional content usually prescribed grade by grade. Instead, with each new experience provided come concepts that can gradually be related. Evidences of thought, of recognition of cause and effect, of appreciation for the world that is his, and of the desire to extend his horizons can be seen in this process. These are worthy of the term *progress*. A child is studying science as he looks at a rock under a magnifying glass; he is studying social studies when he learns to converse with his peers. With this attitude one need not be concerned with quantity. Piaget encourages us when he recognizes that as the child learns, the desire to learn more develops.

In learning mathematics the deprived child lacks the understandings and use of symbols, much as he has in reading. Only as he learns to manipulate objects and discovers groups can he begin to form the concept of number. The teacher cannot hurry this process. It is hoped that the research on the cognitive development of the child will not become so concerned with the minute detail that the picture of the movement and progress of the child in relation to his experience is lost. The deprived child who is learning to count sticks or blocks needs a much longer time to manipulate those sticks and blocks and to feel their shapes before he begins to see the differences or similarities or to use words to describe them. But even here we can begin to use the proper terms with the young child who is putting two and one together. Why not a "set" just as well as a "bunch"? We must never be afraid to teach what the child is ready for, or to teach with the idea of stretching his abilities and his experience just far enough beyond him to catch his interest, his eagerness, and his effort. We would do well in teaching to make more use of concrete materials not only at the beginning of learning in a new area, but also at the beginning of each new level of learning in that area as the child reaches it. The "new math" has been used successfully with deprived children. The School Mathematics Study Group (SMSG) has prepared special methods and equipment that will aid the children in compensating for experience and language deficiencies. Again concrete materials play a large role in the developing of concepts.[26]

As changes take place in the curriculum for the deprived child, he must have readily accessible many books on many subjects that might interest him and a wealth of concrete objects to view and to feel. With these and the help of the understanding teacher, this child must have the opportunity to discover himself, who he is, and what he can do. One of the most important areas, which would not appear on a stated curriculum is mental health, for this child, as he becomes acquainted with himself, needs to be helped to improve his self-picture, to gain courage, to be freed from self-pity, and to find a new hope that will grow out of the effort he puts into his learning.

In a summary of the current thinking on curriculum within a program of compensatory education some important considerations appear to form a framework around which further planning and evaluation of efforts can be built. These are listed here and can be applied to each broad area of content. They will have more meaning if applied to a program of interrelated experiences that cut across these learning areas or disciplines.

1. Knowledge and skills.
2. Concepts and generalizations.
3. Individual differentiation of backgrounds, abilities, potentialities, and personalities.
4. Scope and sequence of experiences.
5. Depth and breadth of learning.
6. Readiness and maturity.

7. Levels of expectation and of aspiration.
8. Discovery and creativity.
9. Evaluation and guidance.

A curriculum built around this framework should result in a sound educational program, both compensatory and general. The personal outcomes for each learner should be a high level of motivation, the development of a positive self-concept, and opportunity for self-realization and self-actualization. These would be built upon the foundation of an evolving set of dynamic values that would serve as determinants of behavior.

Curricular Materials

The following statement by Strom sets the tone for this discussion:

> It has . . . been shown that these children have a lengthy interest span for that which is familiar to them. Lamentably, most of the materials in texts . . . do not represent the type of life to which they have been exposed, so their attention span is unfairly considered shorter than that of middle-class children. It is hoped that some of the strengths of children from the culture of poverty may become functional in the school if our aim to encourage and enhance self-esteem is to be realized.[27]

Including a separate section on curricular materials means an arbitrary separation of this topic from its rightful place in several areas, specifically the curriculum, the learning and language needs of the children, and the specific needs of those representing various types of background. This section must, then, present the general trend of thinking in relation to materials as they would serve to enhance learning. In compensatory education in general, the choice of curricular or teaching materials by a school, principal, or teacher is dependent upon the stated philosophy and objectives, the attitudes that are to be built, the needs of the child for living within his specific community, the availability of community resources, and, finally, the availability of the materials themselves. We now have evidence of studies that have been made, experiments that have been carried on with various type of materials, and the efforts of many to produce appropriate materials. It would appear, however, that we are still searching for the answer to what is appropriate, how it can be stated, and who shall determine it. Little evaluation can be made of current and future curricular materials until the the curriculum

is developed that will best serve the deprived child. It will further
depend upon greater understanding of how the deprived child learns
and a more careful determination of what is involved in teaching
him.

The curriculum is currently under consideration as a result of
some of the important changes that must be made to further the new
philosophy, to meet the needs of the deprived children, and to make
the curriculum a realistic one in terms of their everyday problems as
well as preparing them to meet future problems. There are certain
trends in the consideration of the materials that should be used
within this curriculum. The first has been toward preparing materials
that would give the deprived child further opportunity to learn
through the development of his senses. Thus there have been
emphases upon providing for the development of visual and auditory
perception and discrimination and for increased experience in becoming more intimately acquainted with everyday objects. With
this trend comes the warning that these materials must not limit the
child to experiences needed only within his very narrow environment. He must also be introduced to materials that will extend the
use of his senses and his ideas beyond the immediate and thus extend
his world of seeing, hearing, feeling, and knowing.

Another trend has been toward promoting the publication of reading
materials with a multicultural approach. This has been encouraged because of the criticism of many books that contain only pictures and text representing the middle class. Many times the clothing, toys, games, activities, and surroundings that form the context
of these stories are beyond the knowledge of the children of the
inner-city slum school.

School boards, superintendents, principals, and teachers have also
exerted pressure for the preparation of multicultural materials in
order to foster an attitude of integration, which all feel is their duty.
It is being urged that these materials be used in all schools as well
as in schools for the deprived child. Any child, then, regardless of
his background or culture, can find at least some representation of
the life he knows, which allows him to identify with the characters
about whom he is reading. But once again there is the possibility
that these materials, which may be predominately representative of
certain minority groups, may limit the child's vicarious experience
to the environment he already knows. In some cases, he would read
only about games that can be played on city sidewalks. It is felt
that he should also read of the pleasures that are available to others

in other types of communities, and that eventually will be available to him. This would give him a better understanding of what is going on in the larger community and help him to recognize his aspirations of working for a life that extends beyond his present. These warnings are extremely sound, for they do recognize the need for taking the child where he is and clarifying his understanding of his present experiences, but at the same time recognizing that only as this child's self-knowledge and experience are stretched beyond where he is can he set goals and aspirations for the future. Learning for each person is motivated as his objectives are not only met but reset for an extension of his interests, effort, and personal success. This does not mean that the early reading books should be multicultural in nature and set within the deprived child's own immediate environment, and then carry him forward to a better picture of the middle-class white community. It does mean that he should be carried beyond the immediate to a realization that there exist better surroundings, greater opportunities, and further cultural experiences for each of the representative groups including the Caucasian. It is truly hoped that the upper limit will be more than the static middle class. If we are to erase the lines between poverty, lower class, and middle class, let us continue and erase the lines beyond. Can we accept the fact that we are living in a pluralistic society?

Still another trend that seems to have resulted from a scrutiny of our curricular materials is the discovery of misinformation and discrimination in many of the books accepted and used widely in American schools. The correcting of historical material and the more honest presentation of current material may prove to be one of the valuable outcomes of the present educational upheaval — as important, in fact, as meeting the need for materials that are far more closely related to our understanding of the child, of the child as a learner, and of the learner as a citizen.

In the present era of change, the teacher who aims to keep pace with new educational thinking must be forced to fight a losing battle if she is bound to the use of traditional teaching tools, techniques, and texts. It is true that it has taken time for the newer materials to be appreciated and purchased for use in classrooms, and that as a result it has been only recently that publishers have been willing to risk producing the more appropriate materials. Even now, in the newer readers, textbooks, and supplementary materials, it appears that an effort has been made to "straddle the fence" so that they might be used within a new curriculum and within a deprived area, and also be used by the teacher who is still traditional in his thinking and in his teaching and who has developed little concern for the changes taking place around him. Perhaps this is a step that has to be taken in making progress. (143:105)

The term "curricular materials" today includes not only books, but the variety of audio-visual aids that now appear to be part of the normal equipment in each school. The same thinking applies to these materials as to the others in relation to the deprived.

Crow, Murray, and Smythe (31:262) make recommendations for strong action that should be taken in order to push the preparation of the certain types of materials that would be helpful in a school for the deprived. The first would be a compilation of texts, practice books, photographs, films, and slides that are oriented to the urban child and that reflect the life and the cultural contributions made by minority groups within the urban area. This material should cut across all curricular areas. Secondly, they recommend that some of the books in the classrooms should be in the languages that the children speak at home, such as Spanish or Italian or French, and that suggestions should be made for their use. In many cases English is a second language for these children, and an effort should be made to encourage them to continue using the language spoken in the home while they learn English in school. Third, it is suggested that pilot studies be made to determine the best use of audio aids, visual aids, closed-circuit television, television, and tapes and recordings. Fourth, it is also recommended that pilot studies be carried on to explore the variety of ways in which material already at hand may be used. This would include the various types of community facilities available to the school. Fifth, as more and more programmed instruction material appears on the market an effort should be made to use it in the most effective way possible. Sixth, the very good suggestion is given that within each deprived area there be one school that tests out the various types of materials and proves their value before they are adopted in other schools in the area.

Since programmed teaching materials are more abundant and more easily available to the schools in the disadvantaged areas at the present time, it seems advisable to mention some of the ideas and research in that field.

Riessman (124:121–22) includes teaching machines in his discussion of programmed learning. He even recommends the use of both at the preschool level. His reason for promoting this approach is that programming can be related to the culture and to the thinking of the deprived, and, of course, the teaching machine is a vehicle for such material. Riessman feels that in using programmed material each child can have an individual program so that he may proceed at his own rate and avoid both the shame and the possible anxiety about what he is doing that can result from being compared with other children. Another advantage is that if the child moves from one school to another he can take his program with him. In addition, (1) the teachers who are having difficulty adapting to working with underprivileged children find the use of programmed material a safeguard, (2) programming breaks up the information that is given into very small sequential steps, which are presented to the child frame by frame, or if a programmed book is used, page by page, and (3) the step-by-step approach fits in well with the prescribed inductive, structured style of learning demanded by the deprived child. Since these children are physically oriented, it may be that the mechanical aspect of the machine itself has enough appeal to give them the impetus to carry on through the program, testing themselves, receiving a proper reward for being right, and being freed from competition against other children in the class.

Gotkin,[28] in presenting some of the implications of research in programmed learning, suggests that the difficulty is in the testing of the program once it is made. The programmer is too closely involved with his product, and the teacher who tests the material is too often oriented towards the teaching of groups rather than individuals. Gotkin warns that techniques have not yet been satisfactorily worked out for the evaluation of programmed instructional material.

Riessman (124:115) presents an excellent example of the need for having materials available at all levels in which the children are reading. He states that certain junior high school teachers claim that they have to spend considerable time during the year teaching the deprived how to read before they can start work on the content in the course they are supposedly giving, such as social studies. Is there any reason why not only the reading text but the subject matter material in social studies, in science, or in other areas cannot also be available to the children on their level of understanding and ability in reading? We will make very few strides in teaching these children until we refrain from speaking of them as slow and are able to judge progress on an individual basis rather than according to the expected grade levels set for the privileged child.

In a recent report on some of the new curricular materials being made available, a teacher stated that the children identified with the material in one of the social studies texts so well that some who had scarcely talked before began to verbalize their emotions, for they recognized themselves in the characters of the material. In a new history text particularly suited for Negro children, the so-called "integrated" illustrations were so vivid that one child in Chicago's John Marshall Upper Grade Center remarked, "I guess we've finally arrived."[29]

After considerable evaluation, the following list of materials was recommended in 1965–1966 for use with deprived children:

1. The Holt, Rinehart and Winston urban social studies series begins with material exemplifying real life experiences of a group of seven-year-old children who live in an integrated New York housing development. In this group of five are two Anglo-Saxons; the others are Negro and Puerto Rican.

2. Webster, McGraw-Hill's 1965 Skyline reading series for the elementary grades, portrays urban realities for children of different ethnic backgrounds. This set uses Spanish names and depicts in pictures and content children living in apartment buildings, playing in the street, and sharing a bedroom with brothers and sisters, and endeavors to show that the urban child is not an isolated child.

3. Macmillan's Bank Street reading series contains stories about real people rather than make-believe or the stories of talking animals found in the average textbook for these ages. This was one of the first series of "integrated" textbooks, and the eight books in it are widely used at the present time.

4. Benziger Brothers' recently released eighth-grade history of the United States, entitled *Land of the Free*, was adopted by several of the large cities shortly after publication. This has been judged, after some controversy and revision, a well balanced book. Its competitor is a revised edition of Houghton Mifflin's *This is America's Story*.

Following this listing, it was suggested that some of the new so-called "integrated" textbooks have not been warmly received because of fear that their use would stir up further racial antagonism and, in one case, because the pictures of one of the minority groups showed them as professional people rather than unskilled workers. There is still little thought given to the reaction of the children to omissions of the minority groups from the texts, but it has been found that the Negro children, for instance, do not want to read some of the material because it is not about the people they know.

Another handicap to the increased use of the integrated texts, which give fair coverage to the minority groups, has been the placing on the market of supplementary reading material geared to information about these groups alone. This type of material keeps the minority groups separated just as much as the all white middle-class materials do.[30]

It is encouraging to note the gradual increase in new materials, with greater stress on stories, pictures, and films used in a complementary manner, giving the child the sense of recognition of and identification with the characters, the scenes, and the situations. These stories are based on experiences that are shared by city children — children of varied ethnic groups as well as of varied social groups. The vocabulary and patterning of ideas are recognizable by the children too, and thus aid them in reinforcing and furthering their own oral expression.

There is a new stress appearing in the literature on the children's level and on the adults'. The importance of each of the ethnic groups is seen in stories, permitting the development of pride in background and identity, stressing that they are reading and what they are reading about. We can now know, for example, what the Negroes are reading and also what they are writing. In this way the importance of language, words, ideas, and creative expression is being related to the importance of sharing these with all people while experiencing pride in the accomplishments of one's own group.

Some public libraries are now offering a valuable service to the public and to the schools. They compile lists of books for children and for adults of all groups. They are endeavoring to choose books that might not only entertain, but inspire and encourage further reading and further learning. For the public, these lists provide an excellent opportunity to become informed about the various ethnic groups and to understand more fully the contributions these groups have made.

Films have been used to extend the knowledge of children in school situations. It has been found that they not only supplement other teaching materials, but often provide the visual images that are so needed to strengthen the sometimes weak and meager concepts that the teacher is endeavoring to teach. Again, such attempts are as valuable for the children within the middle-class, affluent schools as they are for the deprived.

In addition to series of readers and history books for the upper levels, new books on the social studies are appearing to be used as readers, thus serving two purposes, one to continue with the teaching of reading skills, and the other to further the understanding of the deprived children concerning their own broader backgrounds. An example of these is the series entitled *Citizens All* recently announced by Houghton Mifflin Company. As publication of such books continues and extends to the other learning areas, we may find that they serve as an incentive for schools to reorganize and renew their curricula and promote the need for integration.

At the adult level effort is now being made to prepare materials for use in programs for the under-educated adult. One is the Mott Basic Language Skills Program recently prepared, tested, and issued by the Allied Education Council. This program is planned in such a way as to take each individual where he is and proceed in a sequential manner with materials that are interesting to adults towards the development of reading skills to aid him to meet and solve the situations he finds in every day life. The content material used gives him information he needs for meeting these situations, by presenting such topics as housing, health, social security, safety, job application, and money.

As curriculum revision continues and new materials are prepared to implement it, there is every need for the people taking part to maintain a type of intelligent maturity and stability and to watch closely in order to evaluate carefully the possibility of a mushrooming of "big business" in the mass production of ready-made curricula and a form of gadgetry that which has little meaning.

Learning Problems

Any discussion that treats the learning and the language of deprived children and youth as separate items removes them from their proper context. In considering the deprived child and his education, any aspect of our understanding of him or any part of the planning of a compensatory program of education for him must be constantly seen in the light of this child as a whole and his need for a total educational process. It is important that this child have the opportunity to be constructively involved in his social world as a whole person, and it is hoped that the program planned for him will be based upon the promotion of the interrelatedness of his physical, emotional, social, and mental development. Until such time as we know this child well and he has the opportunity to adjust to the vital education under consideration for him, can we do less than accept the fact that he is capable of a high level of intellectual development within the context of a high level of total development?

Thus far we have discussed the characteristics of the deprived child and the nature of his environment, and have proposed a form of education that should be vital to him in meeting his needs and in preparing him not only to cope with life as he finds it but to live creatively according to the best of his abilities and potential. In the discussion of the school and the program it has been urged that the child be accepted as he is and where he is in his developmental and learning process, hence removing from him the stumbling blocks for intellectual development that our present educational system has placed in his way and in the way of every child. Warnings have been given against labeling this child as slow or dull or as merely a physical learner. It has been pointed out that one of his important needs is the development and maintaining of a positive self-concept, which is most difficult in the light of discrimination, lack of acceptance, discouragement, and failure, all too familiar to him. The effect upon his attention span, his ability to remain aware of the things around him, his ability to respond to various stimuli or even to shift from one type of stimulation to another, his ability to control his behavioral reactions, and the ability to evidence a sensitivity or to discriminate easily through the senses is evident. We are still in the very early stages of experimentation and analysis of the influences playing upon the child and the degree or depth of their effects, whether temporary or permanent. We must withhold judgment on estimating the deprived child's basic ability and labeling the seriousness of the deficits that seem to characterize him at this time.

At this point we must add another factor to the study of the interrelationship of environment, intellect, and language—opportunity. Only as we study the effects of the opportunity granted to this child to live within a stimulating environment, allowing him to be free to live as the kind of person he is basically can we be sure of the possibility he holds for mental development, for the use of language, for the development of personality, and for the revealing of creative thinking that may be his. It is most important that all of us who are interested in this deprived child watch closely the results of sound research and the programs planned to facilitate the shift from deprivation toward self-actualization. We need to formulate theories, but we must go beyond theory to further knowledge, sound evidence, and the results of carefully planned experiences. It can only be through an enriching of the child's total environment, including an enrichment of the very stimulation that will spur him on toward maximum growth and development that we know of the possibilities of his intelligence. Mental stimulation in a condition of physical, emotional, and social deprivation can neither survive nor give evidence of these future possibilities. We are fully aware of the natural ordering of development that appears when it can occur within a free and positive context. We must not forget that in this ordering the satisfactory completion of the first steps is necessary to those that follow. The success of each step, including the first, is dependent upon the learner's perception of himself.

As we relate the study of learning to success in an educational program, there is every indication that research in learning needs to be reorganized. The concept of a new and vital education could provide the best basis, for it is evident that not only has current education failed the children, but its sheer lack of relationship to what we know about children and about the teaching and learning process has made it unsound as a basis for research. Further meaningful research, to have any value for the formulation of new programs so needed, must be built upon acceptable theory and evidence from appropriate research.

Before reviewing some of the pertinent study material on learning, it should be pointed out here that the concept of individualization must be related to the learning process itself. Such was meant when the terms *structure of learning* and *learning patterns* were used. A teacher does need to know, in becoming acquainted with a child, what that particular child's pattern appears to be. Although there is considerable stress at the present time on learning through discovery and creative thinking, there will always be learners who are literal in their approach and are willing to accept whatever they hear or whatever they read, and have little impetus to go beyond. There are also those who must use a process of trial and error. Not all learners are capable of using the creative approach. Those who cannot should not be labeled as less able intellectually. The problem-solving approach to learning appears to be the most practical and the most meaningful. It does mean, however, that both the learner and the teacher must recognize the possibilities within this method for the process of thinking, for variation in ideas, and for originality. This approach is an excellent one for the deprived child, but it does demand that he have a reservoir of experiences and a fund of knowledge that can serve him in his exploration and thinking. If this approach is used in its simplest form with the deprived child at the beginning, he can have the pleasure of seeing and knowing the value of assimilating further knowledge as he is able to use it.

No child will gain from experience, no matter how carefully planned or how complex, unless that new experience is built upon his own past experience and contains meaning for him. All experience should begin with a purpose, should relate to the past, and should hold possibilities for direct meaning and related meanings to be used as determinants of his own thinking and action and as a base for further experiencing.

It is not possible to discuss learning or experience without clearly realizing that it is through some form of language that we know whether or not learning has taken place, whether experience has been meaningful, and whether the experience is being used. Language is an active, component part of an individual's behavior and his most common means of expressing himself, his avenue of communication.

Some excellent research on the learning and language of the deprived child is being carried on at the Institute for Developmental Studies in the School of Education of New York University. In reporting on the effects of environmental deprivation on basic psychological processes, Cynthia Deutsch hypothesizes that the development of both language and perceptual ability is influenced by social experience, that there is reason to believe that stimulus deprivation in varying amounts will result in functional deficit. She recognizes that social background has considerable effect on language structure and use and that these, in turn, strongly affect performance in school, particularly in the areas of the language arts. In addition to perception and language, she adds as a third process affected, that of attention. She predicts that we would gain some very pertinent information from what she calls stimulus analysis of the classroom, which relates closely to the efficiency of the learning process of the child. In relation to these points, she recommends that there be further study of the effect upon the learning of the deprived child caused by the communication problems between the several social classes. Her paper concludes with this statement:

> Early language training and early cross-class experience may come to be important factors in positively influencing later scholastic performance . . . . As we define links between environmental conditions and

perceptual and linguistic processes, we arrive at an even more critical understanding of the relationship of social process or environmental factors to basic learning and learning skills in children.[31]

In still another paper, Cynthia Deutsch states that "it is not the learning ability per se of the slum child which is deficient, but only his background of experiences."[32] And in a report of research concerning auditory discrimination and learning, she says:

> Auditory discrimination is clearly a function mediated by the nervous system; yet it can be profoundly influenced by the conditions of life of the individual, and it, in turn, can affect his relationship to his environment and the people in it . . . the nervous system of the developing embryo is very susceptible to influences from the mother's nutritional state, and this in turn is strongly influenced by the socio-economic status of the mother. Thus, not only does man's environment influence him, but it may be that it plays a role in molding his very reactive processes to it. This holds out great promise for the potential effects of programs such as our preschool enrichment which are designed to vitiate the deleterious effects of deprived environments. Such programs might really effect lasting changes. (240: 294–295)

John, in a study of the linguistic and cognitive behavior of certain Negro children in which three levels of language behavior — labeling, relating, and categorizing—were analyzed, concludes that the lower-class child has less opportunity for developing precise and abstract language, and for learning to categorize and to integrate within his language structure for the type of learning which is necessary. By showing clearly the close relationship between the use of language and conceptual tasks, she shows that the educational methods used for children in any class may be improved. At best we know little about this and there is still confusion about the best way to help these children. (331:813–822)

Hess and Shipman, from the University of Chicago, recently wrote: ". . . in this paper we will argue that the structure of the social system and the structure of the family shape communication and language and that language shapes thought and cognitive styles of problem-solving. (319:870) Their research subjects were 163 Negro mothers and their four-year-old children. These mothers were chosen from four different social-status levels ranging from the college-educated professional group to the unskilled; in the latter cases the father was often absent and the families were supported by welfare.

The testing situation involved a session in which both the mother and child were present and the mother was taught three simple tasks, then asked to teach these same tasks to her child. These sessions were observed, analyzed, and studied in relation to possible social-status differences as they related to language usage. Both the mothers and the children were asked to give responses to a standardized sorting task and the responses are recorded in tables in the article. To quote again from Hess and Shipman:

> . . . the mothers of the four status groups differed relatively little, on the average, in the affective elements of their interaction with their children. The gross differences appeared in the verbal and cognitive environments that they presented . . . the objective of our study is to discover how teaching styles of the mothers induce and shape learning styles and information-processing strategies in the children. The picture that is beginning to emerge is that the meaning of deprivation is a deprivation of meaning—a cognitive environment in which behavior is controlled by status rules rather than by attention to the individual characteristics of a specific situation. . . . (319:884–885)

These and many other studies clearly show that one cannot study the cognitive development of a child without taking language development into full consideration.

Language Difficulties

In considering the importance of learning and language in a formal teaching situation, Martin Deutsch states:

> I would like to point out here that social-class determination of linguistic styles and habits is an effective deterrent to communication and understanding between child and teacher. To illustrate, the child is unaccustomed to both attending to, and being the object of, what are for him long, orderly, focused verbal sequences. Yet this is the primary scholastic teaching and discipline method. Further, because the disadvantaged child is less familiar with the syntactical regularities and normative frequencies of the language, he has difficulty in ordering its sequences and in both deriving meaning from, and putting into, context. This is all the more disadvantageous for the lower-class child because he has a short attention span for the verbal material to which he is exposed in school. Consequently, he is likely to miss a great deal, even when he is trying to listen. For such a child it is extremely important to feel some mastery in handling at least receptive language. . . .

This discussion keeps returning to the need for helping the educator to develop a comprehensive consciousness of the psychological, as well as the learning, difficulties of the disadvantaged child; the real potential for change; the specifics involved in training children, for example, to ask questions, or to become aware of syntactical regularities, or to use auto-instructional materials; and the imperative need to maintain as high as possible the level of stimulation and relevancy in the classroom. Here the research and insights of the behavioral sciences should be able to contribute significantly, provided the educational albatross takes a few "risks" to accommodate social change. (5:56)*

In the serious study of the deprived child, we are beginning to recognize the real impact of much that we have known concerning learning and language but have taken for granted. The average young child picks up the language of his family, and then that of the school, and has, without too much concern on our part, been able to communicate, to demand, to increase his vocabulary, to speak and write in a manner that is acceptable to his society, and, for some, to reach the level of language where he may use it as a tool for the ordering and reordering of his thoughts leading to the expression of creative thinking.

We have also taken for granted that it is through vocal sounds that we are able to convey thoughts to other human beings, that the spoken word is a distinguishing factor of the human being, that a native language relates one in a deeply emotional sense to his native culture, and that progress made by a community in sharing, in believing, and in setting up a pattern of living is through a pattern of language. In other words, language is one's culture, and one's culture is identified by one's language. One of our deep concerns about the deprived child is his apparent lack of language as we know it, and the effect of that which he does acquire on his intellectual development and his social adaptability. We are aware of the decrease in both the quantity and the quality of language in almost direct ratio to the decrease in the level of cultural advantage as we move from the middle class to the lower class. We must think of language development as we do of the other areas of development, and recognize that it proceeds depending upon opportunity, need, incentive, competition, and challenge. In the area

* From Beck, John M., and Richard Saxe, eds., TEACHING THE CULTURALLY DISADVANTAGED PUPIL, 1965. Courtesy of Charles C Thomas, Publisher, Springfield, Illinois.

of language the culture may demand of this child nothing more than sheer imitation of sound and single-word responses. It may provide a life so barren that there is little need to identify the things about him verbally and, through fear, he may be discouraged from responding even to what he hears about him.

In normal language development we do know that for the child the next step following the stage of sheer imitation of sound must be vocalizing his demands, together with labeling things within his surroundings. Once past identifying and labeling objects because they look as they do or feel as they do, the child's language continues to develop through an interchange of communication, and he begins to structure his thoughts. Only as he has opportunity for further intellectual and emotional development and a higher level of social adaptability for the exchange of ideas will he proceed to the higher language levels. The deprived child arrives at his place on this scale according to the degree of opportunity.

The deprived child does have a language. Again, one helps him to improve by beginning where he *is*, never assuming that he has nothing to offer. Language becomes a problem for the deprived child when he first enters a schoolroom. His success here and the possibility of his progress in learning will depend very much upon the acceptance of *his* language and *his* level of intellectual ability by the teacher. This gives us reason for emphasizing the need for preschool situations for the young child, where the simplicity of his language, abilities, reactions, and behavior make it easier for the teacher to work with him and to see from day to day evidence of the progress he is making.

There must be no intent on the part of any teacher at any level of instruction to destroy the expressive language of the child's own culture. It is interesting to note that in a recent news item the National Council of Teachers of English suggests that children in the primary grades use the dialects of their own homes and that the teaching of more formal standard English begin in the intermediate grades or at about age nine. The Council also stresses the need for practice in oral language at all levels, suggesting the use of imaginative literature for reading, which permits expressiveness, identification, and personal interpretation. It may be that as more use is made of the linguistic approach at the elementary school level, teachers will have a clearer understanding of language and will be better able to help these deprived children to make the transfer from the dialect to acceptable expressive language. We often enjoy hearing the dialects of the Irish and the Scots; perhaps we might add a bit of color to our own language by preserving some of the dialects of our own people.

In some of the adult education programs and in numerous colleges in the South, English is being taught as a second language. A New York City school official calls this second language for these people a "new pair of shoes." He suggests that they wear these shiny new shoes when they go for job interviews, but that they have every right to wear their old comfortable shoes when they get home at night. At the secondary level, some 40 school systems are using a procedure that was developed by a Detroit teacher, Mrs. Ruth Golden, consisting of tapes for group instruction that include phrases that the students misuse but need to hear and speak correctly when applying for positions. The students mimic the phrase, which they hear spoken correctly, then hear themselves on other tapes. It has been found that their speaking improves rapidly.

It is predicted that in the near future bilingual programs will be offered in our elementary schools. The first of these are now in the Southwest, where they are needed for both English-speaking and Spanish-speaking children. This was the purpose in the introduction of the bilingual American education bill by Senator Yarborough. In our educational planning we have been slow to recognize that we have more than three million citizens who speak Spanish and more than one million who speak French, and a total of nearly 11 percent who have a mother tongue other than English. These figures were reported in a study by Fishman of Yeshiva University.

Although considerable research has been done and even more is in progress concerning language development, there is need for further study concerning the relationship of language development to intellectual development and learning success within the school environment, and also of language ability, not only to general ability, but to reordered and creative thinking.

Testing

Considerable emphasis is being placed upon the need for research as the basis for decision making in providing an education commensurate with the needs of the deprived. This is, however, an area in which there are many questions to be answered. It may be found that it is far easier to change the format of the curriculum, the organization of the classroom, and the responsibilities of both the administrator and the teacher than it is to change the basic thinking on the evaluation of learning and school progress. Being able to produce an IQ figure or to state a grade level of attainment in a particular subject matter area has been a safeguard for many an administrator and teacher when called upon to explain either the failure of a child or some form of unacceptable behavior in a formal classroom situation. These figures have too often explained away the need for looking into the reasons for both.

As we begin to understand the deprived child, youth, and adult, we realize that present tests or means of measurement of accomplishment in formal learning cannot be applied to them. Not only are the content and the wording in these devices geared to the middle-class education, but it has been found that the sheer element of timing is a deterrent when the tests are used with subjects of meager background and lack of experience in test taking. The test results, too, are stated in terms of measured ability and grade placement for those learners who can be assumed to have a background of adequate experience and a readiness for responding in appropriate manner to middle-class requirements.

Among those who are working in the field of research relating to a determining of change in the educational process for the deprived there are two points of view. First, there are those who urge an immediate revision in the already available testing material so that it will relate more closely to meager backgrounds and experiences; second, there are those who question the need for having to pressure the deprived with standardized tests and endeavor to rate them by present norms. Some would go so far as to remove from the scene, for the time being, all use of standardized tests and depend upon hypotheses, theories, and the results of carefully controlled observations as bases for evaluation of the success of the newer approaches in curriculum and teaching within a compensatory program. Martin Deutsch, however, presents what might be considered a "middle of the road" consideration, especially while the deprived must be helped within the setting of the present educational program:

> My tendency would be certainly to reduce the standardized tests, particularly those that are standardized on middle-class children. At the same time, there is a problem here. These tests are discriminatory, but in a sense they measure the kinds of capabilities that are going to be required if the children are to function successfully in high school and if some of them are to go on to college.
>
> I do feel that intelligence tests on a group basis with these children should be dropped, except as a research tool. However, achievement

tests do yield a base line of what's wrong and how far behind national norm expectations the group, or the individual child, happens to be. Knowing that, you know where you stand as a system, and you know something about the practical difficulties a particular child is going to have at later stages. So one has to be very cautious. I would not want to eliminate the tests, as inadequate as they are.[33]

All persons working in the field of education, and particularly those concerned with the provision of a vital education for the deprived, fully recognize the need for some way of evaluating progress. There is a challenge here, for the points that have been stressed for emphasis within this vital education do indicate a type of measurement that would be helpful. Emphasis has been placed upon each child's reaching toward his potential, on each child's knowing where he stands in relation to expectations set for him, and on the need for teachers to know where the child should be placed on a scale of knowledge, information, or concept building being used. The teacher also needs help in setting expectations within the reach of each child. At the present time there are no tests that accomplish these points. Other terminology also enters here, for we are reading that tests should be "culture-free" or "culture-fair." In the light of our present thinking the term "culture-free" is hardly applicable.

Experimentation is in progress for developing tests that will more clearly meet the needs of our new thinking in relation to the deprived. It is hoped that the positive results of this experimentation will also influence the testing of the privileged child, thereby giving all teachers a fairer insight into their children. The best standardized tests still give us a very inadequate picture of the mental abilities of children considering our current knowledge of the learning process. For the present it would be best if all teachers refrained from using the results of these tests as single measures of ability or accomplishment, but considered them only an indication of performance at a particular time. A sensitive and knowledgeable teacher who knows each child well, including his background and previous experiences, is able to analyze and predict for the child more accurately than the current measures available in standardized form.

The Society for the Psychological Study of Social Issues has made available a report, *Guidelines for Testing Minority Group Children*, which should be used by any persons concerned with the evaluation of the abilities of the deprived. These guidelines will serve to protect both the tester and the tested and yet permit the intelligent use of existing tests. Introductory and concluding statements from this report more sharply accent the difficulties in the use of standardized tests as implied in this discussion:

> (1) they may not provide reliable differentiation in the range of the minority group's scores, (2) their predictive validity for minority groups may be quite different from that for the standardization and validation groups and (3) the validity of their interpretation is strongly dependent upon an adequate understanding of the social and cultural background of the group in question. . . . In testing the minority group child it is sometimes appropriate to compare his performance with that of advantaged children to determine the magnitude of the deprivation to be overcome. At other times it is appropriate to compare his test performance with that of other disadvantaged children to determine his relative deprivation in comparison with others who have also been denied good homes, good neighborhoods, good diets, good schools and good teachers. In most instances it is especially appropriate to compare the child's test performance with his previous test performance. . . . Many comparisons depend upon tests, but they also depend upon our intelligence . . . to undertake proper remedial and compensatory action as a result. The misuse of tests with minority group children, or in any situation, is a serious breach of professional ethics. Their proper use is a sign of professional and personal maturity. (268:130, 144)

One of the recent developments in the field of testing has been the effort to find some way to measure creativity. (90:603–605) Commendations should be given to those making this effort and to those experimenting with measuring potentiality and the many variables of intelligence. However, in the reporting of tentative evidence from research, very generalized statements are being made indicating, for example, an intelligence quotient of a single given figure to be used for certain minority groups. This may be the result of the administering of a specific test, but it would be far better to report fewer of the results at this point if there cannot be some recognition of individual differences on tests for these minority groups. This should be part of our culture-fair treatment of testing in general, for there are those in teaching and out of it who intentionally take such "discriminatory" information out of context. We must be fair in documenting all statements to the effect that the results are insufficient in depth, only indicative, or far from complete. This same warning should be given to those in the behavioral sciences as they make generalized statements concerning the effects of deprivation as they attempt to isolate, group, and measure them.

Much of the value of forward-looking research is destroyed at the beginning by the publicizing of preliminary findings and the making of generalizations on insufficient evidence. The school systems of New York City and some other cities have discontinued the use of group ability tests and are leaving the evaluation of the children to the teachers within the schools until there are more accurate and fairer measures.

Progress has been made in the preparation of assessment materials for preschool and primary school children. These materials are being designed and used in such experimental enrichment programs as the one being carried on at the Institute for Developmental Studies at New York University. Continuing research reports from this and other centers are worthy of study by those who are dedicated to the task of endeavoring to learn more about the specific patterning of the abilities and the relation of certain environmental factors to these patterns in the deprived child. In the educational literature announcements are being made of developmental measures of readiness, visual perception, concept building, and learning potential. One of these (Kindergarten Education of Learning Potential, KELP, designed by John Wilson and Mildred Robeck, McGraw-Hill Book Company) serves as a method of teaching leading to measuring development of "real learning ability" on three levels. Again, it should be repeated that it is essential to learn of the use and validity of such efforts in research reports in order to determine their appropriateness for the deprived child.

All who are interested in the future of the deprived and in the development of a vital education for them must watch closely for the more complete results of good research within the next few years. There is no doubt that the greatest gains will be made first by those who are working within the areas of perception and performance, where the endeavor is limited to small aspects that can be easily seen, controlled, pondered, and evaluated. With the results of these kept in their proper proportion, progress can be made in our insight into these children, their behavior, their development, and their academic progress.

Guidance

In considering deprivation and compensatory education any use of the term *guidance* immediately relates to the role of the teacher. No one can dispute the fact that the teacher is the single major influence within the educational situation, compensatory or not. To go a step further, it is through the interaction between the teacher and the learner, who in this case is deprived, that this child's success or failure within this program will be determined. In the many projects and programs that have been set up to facilitate education for the deprived, the primary concern has been to create a situation in which warmth, sympathetic understanding, and mutual respect make up the tone of the interaction between the adult who leads and the child who follows. It will be noted in the following section, in the discussion of the teacher for the deprived, that the qualifications set up as most important in the choice and continuous employment of a teacher within a compensatory program are those that might also serve as the most important characteristics for a person responsible solely for guidance. The question must be raised: Can the classroom teacher, in assuming the task of teaching deprived children or youth, also carry the burden for the guidance of these children and their parents? Can this teacher carry out his important and responsible role as teacher without assuming the role of guidance for each child and his parents? In recommendations concerning the size of the classes in a school offering compensatory education, it is noted that the number of pupils should be kept small so that there is considerable time for the relationship between the teacher and the child to be on a one-to-one basis for this guidance.

There is a wide variety of opinion being expressed at the present time concerning the need and provision for guidance in both the elementary and secondary schools devoted to the education of the deprived. For example, recently a first-grade and a fifth-grade teacher were asked to discuss briefly their findings regarding the classroom needs of the deprived children within their own groups. Both teachers responded by saying that they did not know which of their children were considered deprived and that they had no information concerning the backgrounds of the children. In this particular school system it was deemed important that the teacher not have "inside" information concerning his pupils so that he would treat all alike and have the time to spend on preparation for his teaching of the total group; all of the children would then receive identically the same teaching and use the same materials and books, thus avoiding any type of discrimination or favoritism. Whatever information there was on children who might be considered deprived in these two situations was kept by the principal of the school, and this proved to be scant. When children arrived from other areas and brought no information with them, little effort was made to gather any that might help in understanding them. Needless to say, the deprived children within these two groups were considered by the two teachers to be slow, of low mental ability, and unable to listen or to learn. They were marked for repeating, and hence allowed to sit and wait to take the work over again another year. This is not an extreme situation. Nor is it necessarily thought of generally as a poor teaching situation, for it is important that the teacher work with those who are alert and receptive and those who test adequately or better than average so that by the end of the year they can meet the grade expectations and help to identify this teacher as successful in the eyes of the administration!

Between these two apparently extreme situations — the one-to-one relationship and the no-information one — much of the discussion within the literature appears to be centered on the importance and training of special personnel to handle the guidance work. Guidance is taken out of the context of teaching and out of the hands of the teacher as far as any process of initiation is concerned. Guidance becomes a business, a job to do, more than a role to be played. We cannot argue with the reasons given at the present time for the need of guidance personnel, for it can be frankly stated that many of the teachers do lack the orientation and training ordinarily expected of those who undertake to work with a special group of children. Those who propose the appointment of guidance persons recommend that they have special training in sociology, in health education, in mental health, in social service work, and in understanding the cognitive process. It is felt that these are the people who can work with the deprived child or youth and his parents and have a real understanding of this deprived child. This course apparently leaves the responsibility of teaching to the teacher.

Will the appointment and use of persons trained in such a manner provide for adequately meeting the needs of each deprived child or youth, and hence improve his self-image and ensure academic success within the school environment? Why is it not possible for this same special preparation to be a part of the training of every teacher who is given the responsibility of working with even one child, whether he be deprived or gifted?

What is the role of a guidance counselor within a school designed for the deprived? (143) Certain experimental projects have included the assignment of social workers and guidance counselors for both lower grades and upper or junior high levels. Their responsibilities

122 · *Deprivation and Compensatory Education*

have been generally designated as working with the children, their parents, and the teachers for the purpose of assisting with certain behavior problems. In some schools special classrooms have been set aside where those children who find it impossible to adjust to a normal classroom environment may work with the counselor until they understand the need for a different form of behavior. Effort is also made to use these special areas for prevention of more serious behavior through careful awareness on the part of the teacher and close cooperation with the counselor. Some of these groups are identified as special classes, remaining as such; in other instances children spend only short periods of time in discussion and in special help, or use these areas as work centers, with the hope that they can return quickly to their own classes. These groups are kept small to provide for as much individual attention as possible.

In working with parents, the counselor attempts to bridge the gap between the school and the home through the planning of both small and large meetings, thus bringing the parents to the school. Also, in visiting homes or inviting parents for individual conferences so that they may more fully understand what the school is attempting to do for their children, the counselors endeavor to help them increase their aspiration levels for their children and, in turn, for themselves. In the initiating of discussion groups where parents may gain information and ask questions concerning child growth, and child health and safety, counselors can suggest ways of assisting the child at home toward a better school adjustment, and can also assist the parents in meeting community problems.

Counselors have worked with young adolescents and their parents by attempting to build an atmosphere of mutual respect and understanding, giving educational and vocational information, and helping them to plan toward the future and to set their sights more in accord with their apparent abilities and potentialities. In this case, particularly, the counselor may have the opportunity to refer these people to other agencies that can give appropriate assistance. Guidance here may lead to developing opportunities for further vocational training or evening work centers, thus saving those who may proceed on to college as well as those who may wish to drop out before having reached the limit of use of ability.

Other responsibilities that seem to be a part of the role of these counselors are testing, the planning of extracurricular cultural activities, orientation programs for those new to the community, planning for parent assistance within the school, and providing child care so that parents may attend meetings, workshops, and discussion groups. They also assist teachers in the enrichment of their programs through the use of community resources, by working with small groups in the classroom, and by teaching the entire class while the teacher himself works with a few of the children or becomes acquainted with individual children and their parents.

Thus we see the range of experimentation in the use of a counseling or guidance service, the important variation coming within the degree of service given. It is felt that in some instances the counselor can enhance the position of the teacher, strengthen his knowledge, and share in service to the children and their parents in promoting the program. When the counselor assumes special duties not coordinated with the teaching, there is the possibility that this work contributes less in the way of assistance to the classroom teacher, and the service to the child and his parents is reduced in value. If a counselor is used within the school, the success of that person's work depends upon the degree of cooperation with the classroom teacher and the knowledge of the child within the classroom. At present the problem of cost is a serious one and those attempting to use counselors find that the ratio of counselors to children is too large for the accomplishment of the purposes set. It is hoped that in meeting the financial problem schools will not increase the size of classes, for an ideal professional guidance approach has not yet been discovered that can or should supplant the value of guidance given by a well prepared and well qualified teacher for a class of deprived children where the numbers are kept small. Is there not some way in which the counseling performed by the classroom teacher can be enhanced by the provision for assistance within the classroom, thus centering the effort where it belongs, where all aspects of the situation as they affect the child are united, where the child himself is learning?

There are two lines of thought at the present time concerning approaches to counseling. The first deals with developmental counseling, which places its purpose on the broad basis of helping an individual to function close to the level of his potential. The following comments by Peters express this viewpoint:

> The focus of developmental counselling is the strengths of the individual—educational, vocational, and social-personal—as opposed to the weaknesses. . . . Developmental counselling purposely interjects stimuli in the pupil's stream of behavior to cause him to think of his development. . . . Developmental counselling is concerned

with examining possibilities for using one's potential. . . . Developmental counselling is further concerned with the analysis of one's choices or possible choices. . . . Learning about opportunities to implement choices with a consideration of deterrents is a key function of developmental counselling. . . . Re-enforcement is the sine qua non factor in developmental counselling. . . . Developmental counselling is part of the process of assisting one to gain an authentic identity through the many and varied life's stages. Developmental counselling is bringing to fruition one's potentialities. This is a recurring process as one's growing potentialities bring on new opportunities for higher-level achievement.[34]

The second trend is a consideration of:

. . . guidance as a means of developing a better understanding of the role of the school in the affective or social learning process . . . centered on a better understanding of teacher behaviors, pupil behaviors and their consequent interactions. The unique objective is to present possible teacher behaviors that are designed to influence pupil behaviors. While the methods presented apply to every classroom, they are especially relevant for teachers of culturally disadvantaged pupils.

The reasoning behind the decision to depart from the more traditional guidance program approach is a commitment to the belief that the real need is not for more exhortation or organizational patterning, but for the examination of teacher-pupil and pupil-pupil interactions. . . .

The ability to make discriminations is probably the most important characteristic of human intelligence. Behavior that shows fine discrimination in response is what is observed in most higher order learning situations. In the context of social learning, discriminaton takes the form of alterng the response and expectancy of response as the situation alters. This social learning is also a product of education. In fact, a case might be made for its central importance in a democracy. Pupils from socially deprived areas have the right to expect that they too will be taught the social discriminations necessary for achievement in our society. (5:89,107) *

In this statement Foley sets forth the current thinking in research on teacher behavior and pupil behavior. It should prove interesting to all persons vitally concerned with the deprived and their education to follow these two lines of thinking and the research pertaining to

* From Beck, John M., and Richard Saxe, eds., TEACHING THE CULTURALLY DISADVANTAGED PUPIL, 1965. Courtesy of Charles C Thomas, Publisher, Springfield, Illinois.

them, for guidance is a very important aspect of the total education of the deprived child, youth, and adult.

The Teacher

Who should teach the deprived child and deprived youth? We have come to one of the most crucial questions, and it may prove to be one of the most difficult to answer, as Riessman's discussion indicates (124:81–97). We tend to come forward quickly and say that this teacher should love to teach, but too often we fail to ask what he would love to teach. We also say this teacher should love children, but again we fail to ask what children he would love.

In the light of the previous discussion concerning the deprived, their characteristics, their needs, and the concept of a vital compensatory program for them, there is presented here a list of 16 statements describing the teacher who should be placed with these children. There could be considerable discussion about each statement and perhaps some disagreement, but if we are to accept the challenge of teaching these children we must take a long step forward and state that the teacher must be a person who:

1. Recognizes and accepts life as it is, knowing that the past cannot be changed and that the solution of the problems of the present forms the basis of the judgment for the future.

2. Is at home with all people, and has the gift to identify with each.

3. Through an understanding knowledge, can cut across class lines and through cultural levels, and share emotional experiences such as those related to beauty, pleasure, self-doubt, self-pity, discrimination, and heartache.

4. Possesses and knows the value of preserving self-respect, self-control, and self-realization with equal amounts of humility and awe.

5. Has a respect for the place of questioning and the need for change if there is to be progress, and has a personal zeal to be a part of that change.

6. Shows to each child a cheerfulness and an enthusiasm, justice, and sympathy where needed, and, as a basis of all of these, sincerity.

7. Recognizes that each child is the unique individual with the unique pattern of living and learning already established, and that his value as a person is found in that uniqueness.

8. Is not fearful of being a whole person, recognizing that the

process of education involves not only assimilation of knowledge but also the gaining and using of it through personal discovery and the processes of exploration, evaluation, judgment, and creativity.

9. Thinks of the process of education as a process of learning to live with one's self and with others, and wishes to make a positive contribution to that process.

10. Sees the curriculum as a body of worthwhile experiences, related to the past, timely and exciting for the present, and essential for dynamic adjustment to the future.

11. Through a rich background of experience in teaching, knows the need for persistence and consistency of leadership and guidance — all based upon an intimate understanding and a "walking with" each person who is taught.

12. Is aware that one of the most important aspects of teaching is not only the sharing of but the imparting through example of one's own values, attitudes, and concerns, while appreciating, understanding, and accepting those of the child.

13. Believes that teaching is a creative process based upon sound knowledge and past experience, and that within this creative process the teacher has the privilege of choosing the approach, the method, the special technique, or perhaps just the right word that will open the door for the child to a positive attitude toward learning, to be followed by satisfaction in learning.

14. Holds to the belief that progress in learning on the part of each child must be measured from the point where he is in all aspects of development and training to the farthest point he himself can reach through enriching experience, stimulation, the building of knowledge, and the use of that knowledge for the interpretation of still further experience bounded by his own set of values and abilities.

15. Recognizes the importance of sound professional preparation in teaching and of the continuation of this preparation while teaching as especially essential in working with the unique child.

16. Prepares for, desires, and requests the privilege of teaching in the school for the deprived because it is an honor to work with these children, to help them discover the persons they are meant to be, and because this teaching has for its reward the sense of success and hope, leaving no room for fear, frustration, or failure.

Once again it can be said that what have been described as best among the qualities of a good teacher for the deprived child should also describe the best teacher for *all* children. If the teacher described above can be identified and prepared for the deprived child, we may be able to work out the way to prepare and identify the good teacher for every child. The present situation may force us to do just this.

The person with these characteristics is the one who has played the role of the all-important teacher in the discussions thus far. This is the teacher who:

1. Provides a richness, a depth, and a breadth to everyday learning and living experiences for the child within the compensatory program.
2. Permits him to be a child before he is a man.
3. Respects and values each child or youth for himself.
4. Imbues the child and his parents with a thirst for knowledge and an excitement in learning.
5. Removes the discriminatory label from the deprived child and replaces it with self-respect.
6. Challenges the learner where he is and leads him step-by-step in successful progression toward higher, self-determined aspiration levels.

What of those teachers who have become satisfied with the educational program that is no longer acceptable and have no desire to work with the children and youth of poverty and deprivation? Not all of the deprived are within the inner city, in the isolated rural areas, or members of the migrant force. There are deprived children in every community and in every school, who exist and learn from day to day with no particular purpose and no awakened desire or aspiration for the future. (11:4) Are not the teachers within these situations who are unawakened to the needs and possibilities within the children whom they teach deprived teachers? There is every hope that we can save the deprived child and the deprived youth through a change in attitude and the implanting of hope. Can we not save the deprived teachers? It is perhaps here that we need to re-emphasize one of the responsibilities within the role of leadership on the part of educators and school administrators. The challenge for them at this time is to recognize and respect the human worth of each teacher and, through a step-by-step process, free that teacher in much the same way as one would free the child or the youth, to become himself or herself, to experience the recognition of challenge, to set realistic goals, and to know the reward of success in helping a deprived child or a deprived youth who is in his own class waiting to share many of these same experiences.[35]

A slum school teacher speaks:

> I can teach the children reading. I can give them the academic tools for social success. I can foster and reinforce their confidence and aspirations, but ghetto children still have a very long way to go. They are capable of it, they are strong enough to complete the journey. They only need someone to help them master the necessary tools.
> That's my job. I'm the tool-giver—the teacher.[36]

The Teaching

There are those who will immediately say that all of this very positive discussion concerning the need for compensatory education, the organizing of a school and a program for it, the deprived children and their needs, and the teacher who affords the inspiration, is too idealistic to be realistic. Let us remember that there can be no value to idealism without its being realized through a process of facing facts as they are, knowing the reasons for the facts, accepting the challenge of the situation, and resolving the situation by striving toward goals set. We do know that the higher the goals, the greater the accomplishment.

What is involved in the teaching of the deprived? We can become aware of the seriousness of the current problem of poverty and deprivation, accept it for what it is, recognize that our present educational system has not met the needs of the deprived nor of any child in the light of current change. We can then assume the negative attitude that we have done the best we can, that there must always be the poor, that the possibilities for education are there if anyone wants to take advantage of them, and, with an air of resignation as teachers, administrators, or citizens, reject the challenges that have been thrown out to all of us, continuing on in what we falsely term the *status quo*—falsely because we know that unless there is progress we can be sure there is regression.

We can also accept the situation as it is, however, and learn all that we can about it, hoping to discover the reasons behind the failures. As teachers we can come to know each child as a human being and accept him as he is now. His only way of fighting against hopelessness may be by striking out, destruction, or withdrawal. He can show no interest in the everyday activities of a middle-class group of peers. As teachers taking part in a new and vital approach to education, we can understand his behavior and give him time and the simple experiences that will gradually help him to become aware of the type of behavior that will bring him the reward of communication and satisfying interaction with others. As teachers we know he cannot learn the prescribed curriculum of the old school, but we are free to help him through a variety of experiences in which awareness leads to learning. Learning eventually leads to a series of concepts about the world around him and the people in it, thus giving him a basis for moving upward in the various disciplines but always with a goal in mind. We are aware of the lack of cooperation on the part of this child's parent and we know the seriousness of the home situation with its lack of communication and interest in the child. As teachers we accept the challenge of reaching the parent and, with time and understanding, we can bring this parent into the larger learning experience for himself and for his child, thus helping both to set goals and to realize the purposes of what is being provided for them.

The teaching of the deprived requires re-interpretation of the teaching-learning process. Concern for subject matter, coverage, and testing must be changed to an exciting sharing of the possibilities of interaction of persons and ideas, the power of thinking, the establishing of one's own values as a contributing member of a social group, and the freedom acquired through the use of all one's capabilities in a creative manner. Change is an expected, inherent part of this process. As administrators and educators we must provide the educational programs of worth and meaning in which this process of teaching and learning can be realized. As citizens we must demand the building of a new and vital education, placing it first within reach of those who need it most. Thus teaching the deprived becomes a deeply rewarding experience of heavy responsibility and equally satisfying, personally and professionally. This *is* idealistic, but it can become reality.[37]

U.S. Commissioner of Education Harold Howe II states the challenge:

> The difficult tasks of this world are always the ones most worth doing. Thousands of teachers are now choosing the difficult task of teaching in our slum schools and are finding personal and professional satisfaction . . . many others . . . [of] warmth, understanding, and professional ability are needed. . . .

Henry Van Dyke . . . once said, "There is a loftier ambition than merely to stand high in the world. It is to stoop down and lift mankind a little higher." This is the lofty ambition which can make teaching a profession rather than merely a job.[38]

Teacher Preparation

To teach disadvantaged children effectively is to display the highest professional competence. Few jobs are more demanding, but few are more rewarding. To help a child achieve the human promise born in him but submerged through no fault of his own is a noble task.

The essential precondition for teaching disadvantaged children is a deep understanding of the causes of their behavior. The teacher must therefore possess both the general background needed for teaching anywhere and a knowledge and understanding of the circumstances of life for the disadvantaged.[39]

Thus a positive note is struck by the Educational Policies Commission.

> Rookie Teachers Get Tough Posts —
> City Puts Hundreds in Slum Schools —
> Some Quit.
> Wanted: Inner-city Teachers!

Thus the negative note is sounded in a newspaper and an educational journal.

If teaching is to be a profession and to be recognized as such, there needs to be a basic plan of preparation that can be agreed upon and accepted as essential to developing ability for good teaching. In addition, there must be standards for admittance to the training programs, and every effort made to reach the high caliber of student who can, in turn, raise the level of the quality of teaching in our country. For too long it has been the pattern for those students to enter into the field of teacher education who do not have the qualifications to be accepted in the outstanding colleges and universities. Why is it not as important to be a teacher as it is to be a doctor or a lawyer? Shall we place the blame for our current educational dilemma on the teacher education programs, on the caliber of students going into teaching, or on the conditions under which teachers must work, or shall we say that all is due to the rapid social changes taking place?

Let us look at the basic areas of knowledge that a teacher needs before being adequately prepared to teach. As in all professions, this person needs an understanding of the historical development of his discipline. Education with its institutions should be seen in the light of social development through the centuries, and in the light of the part it has played in the development of ideas. This should include a knowledge of the importance of education in the development of our own country so that the student will have an insight into the foundation that has been laid for the organization of our present educational program, and be able to identify its strengths and weaknesses in order to work toward change for the future.

A second area of knowledge concerns the development of the curriculum within the institution of the school. The changes that have taken place in the content of subject matter areas are indicative of the needs of our society at various points in our history. The student should be well aware of the importance of public education but at the same time recognize the lag between educational theory and its acceptance and practice in the school program.

Along with the study of any curriculum the student needs to have a clear picture of the development of teaching methods and of various procedures, techniques, and teaching materials that have been used to promote what has been considered the best learning for any particular time. Still another area closely related to this is the knowledge of the learner or the child. In studying the changes in the attitudes about the child and his place in the home and in society, one sees the influence of research in our increasing knowledge of human development. Thus it is important to see the changes that have taken place within school organization, school curriculum, teaching methods, and learning expectations in the light of the historical development of educational theory, educational practice, and the growing understanding of human growth and development.

In addition to these broad areas of information, the student preparing to teach needs a thorough understanding of what we call the teaching-learning process. Incorporated in this is a study of the research on learning as it relates to levels of development. This student should also be aware of the change in the analysis and evaluation of the teaching-learning process; it was much easier formerly to judge a teacher on the basis of the preparation of the lesson, its organization, his presentation, and the learner's ability to repeat it. Now the process of teaching cannot be separated from the process of learning, for we have found that it is a constant interchange of inquiry, discovery, involvement, and evaluation on the part of both the teacher and the learner.

The intern aspect of teaching is a very vital part of the program of preparation. During the time that the student is making an intensive study of child development he should have the opportunity to observe children of all ages in various types of school situations, for it is here that he sees the outward evidence of development that is the behavioral response of the child to different forms of stimulation. During this time the student has the first opportunity to identify in a less active way with the age level that he may be best suited for teaching or, in the reverse, recognize those levels where he would be the least successful. During the study of concept development, methods, and techniques within each curricular area, the student should be in a classroom for intern assistance preliminary to teaching. Then, under the direction of a master teacher, he should have the opportunity to see the best practices in operation — the best for the children within that particular group — as he begins his own active participation.

It is most essential to a student of high caliber that his preparation for teaching not be isolated from serious study in the several disciplines. Today's teacher needs a fund of knowledge in the social sciences, the biological and physical sciences, English, foreign languages, mathematics, and the areas of mental and physical health, music, and art. From this base of preparation and practice, he is then freed to become the creative person and teacher in the classroom with the average child, the slow child, and the bright child we find in our schools across the country.

If we are to promote this type of preparation on a high professional level, how shall this same student receive the additional training necessary for working with deprived children? In order to answer this question, we must assume that following an excellent background of intern experience in teaching under the guidance of master teachers, this person gains good experience as a professional teacher in what one might call a typical school in this country. It is expected that this now experienced teacher has received recognition for his work and has shown the characteristics listed previously. This teacher, who now has the desire to be placed in the disadvantaged area, recognizes the need for further training and looks upon the opportunity of working with the deprived child as a professional "specialty." This would mean that if his previous preparation had been at an undergraduate level within a program of broad liberal arts education, he then faces the training for his specialty in a graduate program particularly planned for the training he will need.

If his preparation was at the graduate level and based upon a liberal arts education previously completed, the program of training for teaching in the deprived area will mean further graduate work. Let us look at the recommendations for this further preparation made by Riessman and Haubrich, who are pioneers in facing the challenge of education for the deprived.

Riessman suggests a Five Point Plan that includes the extending of the teacher's general respect for children to *respect for the disadvantaged children and their families.* This respect for them must be built on a knowledge of the cultures represented and their values, and of the ways in which these people are living and coping with their environments. This knowledge cannot be gained through reading or through listening. This teacher must learn through direct contact with the community, through observation, and through participation in community activities, so that he comes to know the people who are living there. Only then is he ready for the second point of this plan, which is *further intern teaching* — this time with the disadvantaged in their own schools. Again, this teacher should work under master teachers who are skillful in the *special techniques and the special understanding of ways of working with these children.* Through this experience the teacher begins to understand the behavior of deprived children in the light of the environment and experiences with which he is already acquainted. While carrying out this intern teaching he learns the importance of basing the teaching upon those qualities previously mentioned, such as consistency and structure, directness and honesty, and the building of values for the child's behavior to enhance his learning. In order to begin to teach these children he must reach them through "achieving contact" or, as some have spoken of it, by "breaking through to the child."

The fourth point, that of learning the teaching techniques that are appropriate for these children, has little value unless the teacher has met with success on the three previous points. It may be here that the teacher discovers whether he is "meant" for teaching in this specialty or whether he should return to the typical school and the typical child. If he has met success thus far and his interest runs high, this further training must consist of *learning of the teaching techniques* that have proved successful. These are the means by which he teaches the child once he has reached him. Riessman suggests becoming acquainted with materials that are prepared for the teaching of the disadvantaged, the importance of role playing, the ways in which a teacher can accept and work with the language the child brings to school with him, and the ways in which the teacher may help these children to face their own problems.

The final point in this proposed plan for advanced teacher preparation is the development of "effective teaching styles." It is here that this teacher "tries on" the various roles of teaching to determine the styles, not only which seem to work best with the children, but to discover those which he as a person can most sincerely play. These styles, not prefabricated but created by him as a person, become the means by which he proves himself most successful in reaching and teaching the deprived child. (79:95–108)

Haubrich lists the skills that he feels are essential for success in teaching the disadvantaged, regardless of grade level.

The ability to understand and utilize developmental and remedial reading procedures.

The ability to organize and routinize specific classroom procedures.

The ability to reconstruct syllabi, textbooks, and reading materials in terms of the background of students.

The ability to work effectively with small groups within the classroom and to know when to use such procedures.

The ability to adjust new entrants to the classroom situation quickly.

The ability to construct and use concrete materials for classroom work.

The ability to handle aggression and violence.

The ability to use individual and group procedures in gaining classroom discipline.

The ability to know when a child should be referred and to whom.

A knowledge of the language patterns in an area and the ability to correct such patterns.

A knowledge of neighborhood and family to see what effect this has on classroom work and procedures.

The ability to translate the "academic" knowledge of children from depressed areas into specfic procedures for classroom use. (305:502–503)

There are two areas of information that thus far have not been included in the recommendations for the special training for this teacher, but they are indicated in the development of some of the abilities just mentioned. Much of the work that the teacher does with disadvantaged children is in the area of evaluating the child and his progress and of guiding him toward the solution of many of his problems, some of which are school problems and some home problems. This teacher should have an excellent knowledge of ways of evaluating that have been effective and should keep up to date in the research, planning, and production of new measures that may be of help to him. He also needs to know the basic techniques of counseling. It may be true that he might have the opportunity to refer a child with a specific problem to trained counselors, but in the majority of cases, he must rely upon himself and his knowledge to make a judgment for guiding this child in any action he must take. He is the one who knows the child.

It will be interesting to watch the progress of the many programs in teacher preparation that are now under way, all different in organization and intent, but each serving the same purpose ultimately. It is hoped that in the efforts to improve the programs, the purpose for a background of preparation in history, philosophy, curriculum, techniques, procedures, and styles of teaching will be geared to this deprived child as a human being whose greatest need is help in forming his own positive self-concept before he can gain any advantage from any educational program. We do know that the child's self-concept evolves from his own unique biological structure, is affected by the quality and extent of experiences he accumulates, is conditioned by his relationships with his parents or adults in his life, and is affected by his own perception of his successes or failures from day to day. It is the teacher's first responsibility and first commitment to help this child in the formation of his own image. Crow, Murray, and Smythe state:

> A child's self-concept is learned. His perceptions of his environment are filtered through his ideas about himself, and they affect the way he relates to his subsequent experiences. Self-concept influences the way the child perceives his abilities, his status, and his roles. Influenced by physical endowment, value beliefs, and aspirations, the self-concept also involves the way one perceives himself as well as how he perceives his social self — the perceptions he believes others have of him.
>
> The individual's self-concept serves as a guide to future behavior and aims toward an idealized self-image. It provides him with a reference. . . . (31:25)

Present teacher education must change. The demands made upon a teacher today are no longer oriented in the teaching of a specific body of information from a textbook. Instead, they are based on an understanding of our world and of the prevailing economic, social, political, and human problems. It is the teacher who must translate the current events, the explosion of knowledge, and the redefining of values into a language and into a form of behavior that will make possible an understanding of these on the part of the child. It takes courage to be a teacher in these days, and it takes courage to train a teacher. There is no room for fear or self-doubt or self-deprecation. The challenges facing teacher education are those of recruitment, of establishing and maintaining high standards of scholarship, and of finding ways to give recognition to those who have mastered the teaching-learning process and are fearlessly carrying out the vital education so necessary for all children. These challenges also include recognizing those who have the qualities essential for working with the deprived child and with his parents within his community, discovering the wealth of potential in the teachers presently within our schools who, given the support and the necessary further training, will aspire to work in an atmosphere where education holds human dignity, human worth, and human values as important, and finally, making the process of teaching exciting and the entrance into the profession of teaching a privilege.

A new teacher education should promise for the student greater contact with children in school and out of school, and the opportunity for the exchange of ideas with social and behavioral scientists, psychologists, educators, researchers, and those in social agencies. It should mean for the student an involvement with all who represent the school — the opportunity to share in conferencing, in planning, in evaluating, and in teaching. Courses in learning to teach should be challenging and open-ended, giving the students time to explore, to discover, to think, to create. The student must determine that his attitudes, his behavior, and his thinking are those he would have each child respect, accept, and exhibit. Teacher education must be a continuous process, for there is no limit to the understanding of human beings or to the discovery of ways of communicating with and guiding even one child toward a better life. The explosion of knowledge and understanding is exciting. It should mean richer experiences, not only for the teachers but ones they can share — this is teaching. If teaching can become a commitment to the equality and excellence of living, all else will follow.

REFERENCES

[1] Hobart Taylor, Jr., "Higher Education and Equal Opportunity," *Educational Record*, 45 (Fall, 1964), p. 385. Courtesy American Council on Education.

[2] Benjamin C. Willis, *Compensatory Education in the Chicago Public Schools: Study Report Number Four* (Chicago: Chicago Public Schools, August, 1964), p. 1. Fundamental purpose restated from *Elementary Education in the Chicago Public Schools* (Chicago: Board of Education, City of Chicago, 1959), p. 9.

[3] "Three R's in the Army," *Time* (September 16, 1966), pp. 61–62.

[4] Fred M. Hechinger, "Shriver: Overhaul Education," *Boston Herald* (November 27, 1966).

[5] *The New York Times* (September 4, 1966), p. E9.

[6] *The New York Times* (December 12, 1965).

[7] Alex M. Mood, "National Assessment," *American Education,* 3 (April, 1967), p. 11.

[8] Lindley J. Stiles and B. J. Chandler, "Urban Schools for the Future," *School and Society* (November 17, 1962), p. 395.

[9] Jonathan Kozol, *Death at an Early Age* (Boston: Houghton Mifflin Company, 1967).

[10] Eric Cox, "The University and the Decaying American City," *Educational Record,* 45 (Fall, 1964), p. 395. Courtesy American Council on Education.

[11] Cox, p. 396.

[12] J. Marton Klotsche, *The Urban University and the Future of Our Cities* (New York: Harper & Row, Publishers, 1966).

[13] *The New York Times* (June 18, 1967), p. E9.

[14] *The Boston Herald* (July 23, 1967), p. A11.

[15] *The New York Times* (August 4, 1967), p. 1.

[16] *The New York Times* (September 10, 1967), p. 79.

[17] *The New York Times* (May 2, 1967), p. 51.

[18] *The New York Times* (September 10, 1967), p. 121.

[19] Raphael G. Kazmann, "Negroes at Michigan," *Science,* 157 (August 4, 1967), p. 490.

[20] Meyer Weinberg, *Research on School Desegregation: Review and Prospect* (Chicago: Integrated Education Associates, 1965), p. 1.

[21] Educational Policies Commission, *American Education and the Search for Equal Opportunity* (Washington: National Education Association, 1965), p. 14.

[22] Daniel U. Levine, *Raising Standards in the Inner City Schools* (Washington: Council for Basic Education, December, 1966), p. 31. (Occcasional Papers: Number Eleven.)

[23] Martin Deutsch, *Social Intervention and the Malleability of the Child* (Ithaca, New York: Cornell University. Fourth Annual School of Education Lecture, May 6, 1965. Revised November, 1965), p. 5.

[24] Levine, *op. cit.,* p. 9.

[25] *The New York Times* (November 28, 1965), p. E7.

[26] Mary Folsom, " 'New Math'—Too Verbal for the Disadvantaged?" *The Instructor* (March, 1967), p. 26.

[27] Robert Strom, *The Tragic Migration* (Washington: National Education Association, 1964), p. 17.

[28] Lassar G. Gotkin, "Some Implications of Programed Instruction Research for Urban Teacher Education" (New York: Institute for Developmental Studies, School of Education, New York University, 1964), p. 4, mimeographed.

[29] "Integrating the Texts," *Newsweek* (March 7, 1966), pp. 93–94.

[30] Gotkin, *op. cit.*, pp. 93–94.

[31] Cynthia Deutsch, "Effects of Environmental Deprivation on Basic Psychological Processes: Some Hypotheses" (New York: Institute for Developmental Studies, School of Education, New York University, February, 1965), p. 12, mimeographed.

[32] Cynthia Deutsch, "Learning in the Disadvantaged" (New York: Institute for Developmental Studies, School of Education, New York University, 1965), p. 21, mimeographed.

[33] Martin Deutsch, "Some Elements in Compensatory Education" (New York: Institute for Developmental Studies, School of Education, New York University, 1964), pp. 17–18, mimeographed.

[34] Herman J. Peters, "Developmental Counseling," *The Clearing House*, 41 (October, 1966), pp. 111–112, 117.

[35] Levine, *op. cit.*, pp. 26–28.

[36] Susan B. Jordan, "Teaching in the Inner-City School: What It's Really Like," *Grade Teacher* (September, 1967), p. 86.

[37] Levine, *op. cit.*, pp. 8–12.

[38] Harold Howe II, "Where teachers are needed the most . . . ," *Grade Teacher* (May-June, 1967), p. 102.

[39] Educational Policies Commission, *op. cit.*, pp. 18–19.

IV

The Role of Government

The famous Massachusetts School Law of 1647 was designed to thwart "that old deluder, Satan," by making sure "that learning may not be buried in the grave of our fathers." Even more famous is the provision of the Northwest Ordinance of 1787 that reads: "Religion, morality, and knowledge being necessary to good government and the happiness of mankind, schools and the means of education shall forever be encouraged." These are, of course, eloquent arguments for free public schools. Let me remind you, moreover, that they are, with special particularity, arguments directed to the plight of the deprived child — the child who, potentially at least, might suffer deprivation because he lived on the edge of an expanding frontier at a distance from the centers of civilization.[1]

Thus Bestor reminds us that the education of each child has been the concern of citizens and educators throughout our history. It is the location of the areas of deprivation that has changed. Now it is not the distant frontier where deprivation of opportunity exists. Deprivation follows the movement of our people. As this mobility brings them to the cities, it is here that we endeavor to remedy the lack.

Throughout our history the federal government has had an important role in education. It has continuously been concerned with organizing the means by which the American people can know what is transpiring in the field of education, with studying the various problems and needs as they have arisen, and with giving assistance in efforts toward maintaining standards and developing new programs.

Since much has been written about this role of government in our history, there will be presented here only some of the trends that have guided our thinking and brought us to the present consideration. With the speed of change taking place around us, we must keep in mind that what is immediate today will soon be a past development. Our greatest responsibility is to continue to move with this change, attempting to understand the many factors that bring it about.

There are those who claim that a new revolution in education began with the appearance of Sputnik I. It cannot be denied that that event struck a note of concern and discontent, not only with education, but more deeply, with our own self-satisfaction in this country. The role of the government in this concern has been evidenced in the recent passage of legislation relating to National Defense Education, Civil Rights, Economic Opportunity, Elementary and Secondary Education, Education Professions Development, Higher Education, and their many ramifications. Underlying all such legislation is the expressed need for improving the quality of education for all and for providing equal opportunity for the deprived in all phases of American life including education. All have shown concern for education, but when we comment on the role of the federal government we must remember that that role is determined basically by the American people.

We are faced with two current problems that affect education and that are basic to our thinking and to the direction that some of the trends have taken. The first is the continually shifting pattern of mobility of the people in this country, and not only of those who are deprived. With this movement and the ease of communication and transportation, we are becoming citizens not just of a state, but of the nation — the United States. More and more we are requesting that some of the laws that held before for a state now be regularized and apply to the nation.

The second problem is that of attitude. We have become proud of this country because of the great strides we have made in our development and standard of living over a comparatively short period of time. But we find that this pride engenders another attitude, a false concern for being on the "right side of the tracks." As a consequence, those on the right side have looked down on those on the wrong side. This in turn has inhibited the fulfillment of one of the basic principles within our democracy of assisting, sharing, and giving. The term "welfare," for example, now creates an emotional reaction against those who must receive it. This same negative attitude holds between the suburbs and the inner city. Just how readily will those who now have be willing to share with those who have not?

Vice-President Hubert Humphrey, in many of his speeches, quotes from the words of his friend, Ben Youngdahl, who has emphasized his belief in the dignity of man. Three of the quotations are given here:

> In 1949 Ben Youngdahl wrote: "A recipient of public assistance is still a citizen and a person with all the rights and dignity given to all people in our democracy."
>
> In 1952 he said: "Regardless of what programs we espouse or administer, the end result in our minds is always the person, supreme, divine."
>
> In 1963 he sounded a note of impatience. He said: "It's about time to shake loose from the time-worn assumption that people who are compelled to receive public assistance are necessarily immoral or weak."

Only time will tell how deeply rooted this attitude is, but it is hoped that through the attempts being made to inform the citizens of this country of the actual conditions under which many of our people do exist, they will recognize that the moral and material health of our nation is only as good as that of our poor.

In 1960 the government continued its financial assistance to education, but began to give directions as to how the money should be spent. Thus the government began to single out the areas within the total educational program that needed more help than others. At that time there were evidences of the first tentative guidelines to ensure that the money would be spent toward the goals of education that we hold of value in our democracy.

In his State of the Union Address in 1965, President Johnson stated that "Every child must have the best education our nation can provide," thus giving emphasis to the concern for education held at the national level. It was at this time that we began to hear of a possible issue with regard to national standards for education. This was one of the topics to be thoroughly discussed at the White House Conference on Education held in Washington in July, 1965. As noted previously, this Conference was an indication of still another trend. The participants included not only people associated with schools, universities, and various educational associations, but also a generous representation from major foundations, industry, the government, the public, and the press. Here the major problems of education became the major problems of the citizens. The purpose of the Conference was not to solve the problems, but to define them and to stress the need for leadership in their solution. Thus the national thinking transferred from the "New Frontier," with emphasis upon intellectual achievement and academic excellence, to the "Great Society," with its emphasis on improvement of education and equal opportunity for that education for every person within an environment conducive to it. We move, then, from "the educated man," to "educated men."

The anti-poverty program, operating on both the local and national fronts, grew out of the Economic Opportunity Act as the result of the recognition of the need to improve living conditions and salvage the youth of the country. The management of this program demanded a new agency, the Office of Economic Opportunity. The evaluation of this organization and its administration of funds is still under careful consideration. The question becomes one of the method of procedure for the development of our own human resources without its becoming entangled in the politics of the day and the ever present inter-governmental relationships.

Every effort is being made by word and graphic representation to inform the citizens of the responsibility of the government, through the people, to bring into balance the education in this country. One attempt has been made by showing the variation in per capita income, in the cost per pupil in public education, in the rate and location of illiteracy, and in the general increase in expenditure for public school education. The southern states still lag, and hence present the greatest need for financial assistance. This condition is serious, for the other states are also putting forth considerable effort toward improvement at the same time, and the gap continues in spite of great effort and expense.[2]

Congress requested the United States Commissioner of Education (Section 402 of the Civil Rights Act of 1964) to study the education being provided for the deprived children and the progress being made on desegregation. After two years of study, the report, *Equality of Educational Opportunity, 1966,*(158) known as the Coleman Report, shows that in general American education continues to be segregated and that the segregated schools are still inferior. About one out of every five school-age children continues to go to an inferior school. The report also shows that the quality of the school plant has considerably more impact on deprived children and their achievement than it has upon the average child. Teachers are still more important to all children than the facilities; it is found that the children from minority groups still have the least capable teachers. There is also a widening gap between the achievement of the deprived child as he continues through school and that of other children. This report recommended that one of the better ways to help the deprived would be to intermingle them with other children — children not only of other races but of other social and economic levels — indicating that this does not appear to harm the education of the other children.

The role of the federal government in education continues to grow. The time has come to question this growth, to check the competency of management, to evaluate the results, and to determine the source, availability, and amount of further funds needed.

In evaluating the broad federal assistance program, we cannot ignore its negative impact. In the attempt to educate the deprived child, thousands of new jobs have opened up in teaching and guidance, leaving vacancies in the classrooms, where the best trained teachers should be. The Peace Corps, Job Corps, and Head Start Program, in addition to the draft, have caused considerable drain on our teacher supply. And the Office of Education recently estimated that another one million teachers have been lured from the public schools by higher salaries elsewhere. The role of the government thus is felt in both a negative and a positive way. We still must improve the education for the deprived child and raise the quality of our total educational system. We still must ask: How can this be done best?

In looking to the future, Harold Howe II, United States Commissioner of Education, makes this statement:

> . . . I'd say we should place two items at the top of our agenda for American education:
>
> First, eliminate the disparities in the quality of education to be found in every region, state, and locality; second, tailor our educational institutions and practices to fit students, rather than expecting students to conform to the mold our schools and colleges find convenient or traditional or both.[3]

The United States Office of Education has a staff paper that is being studied, entitled "Equal Educational Opportunity Act of 1967." Although, as it is reported, it may not reach the legislative stage, this particular paper does give an indication of the forward thinking of this Office, which can be encouraging to all of us. Two possible points of major emphasis are (1) the need for construction of school facilities in the most pressing areas, such as the inner city and rural districts, for the purpose of providing better educational programs and helping to achieve integrated education, and (2) that grants be given to assist the public schools in the process of desegregation. These would be given to local educational agencies and school districts to assist integrating and to give recognition for excellence in efforts toward it, for assistance in the development of exceptional programs that will attract peoples from all groups, for providing for better salaries for outstanding teachers, excellent equipment, individualized instruction, and reduced pupil-teacher ratios. In addition, grants would be available to continue training programs for school personnel and for the carrying out of techniques, both of which would facilitate integration and attempt to correct de facto segregation in designated communities. Some of the techniques recommended in this paper are rezoning, the pairing, grouping, or clustering of children by grade levels in two or more residential areas, the reorganization of the use of existing schools, and the careful selection of locations for new schools. Others are increased busing to prevent overcrowding, open enrollment, voluntary enrollment and free transfers, possible suburban and inner-city pupil exchanges, and improvement of standards, curriculum materials, and remedial programs.[4]

The consideration of this educational commitment, however, precludes a consideration of the commitments of the federal government in the broad social and economic fields of American life as evidenced in the new programs such as those for health, economic development, resource development, and manpower training. The questions being raised appear to center on the feasibility of governmental management of such a vast array of programs dealing with some $15 billion, a figure which is expected to rise. The seeming chaos at the federal level is caused by the confusion of the administration and funding of these programs by the vast number of departments, agencies, bureaus, and regional offices. At the same time chaos at the state and local levels is evidenced in inadequate administration. Communication is weak, supervision is not desired, and cooperation and delegation of responsibility are feared. There must be a balance of responsibility between these three managerial forces, but it will be successful only as it is carried out by responsible personnel, knowledgeable and qualified for the task. Is this possible? Such persons are not used now where needed.

There is being added to the monumental problem just stated,

newly exposed reasoning that lies behind some of the programs, especially those for the needy. Robert Sherill[5] makes clear that the first surplus food program was enacted to . . . "support and stabilize farm prices, not support and stabilize needy people." Again, the surplus food did not supply minimum daily food requirements — no thought was given to this. The food stamp program hardly faced reality, for management could not accept the dire poverty and lack of the needed cash in some of our own states. We still see only what we want to see — and yet we hold the life lines for those we refuse to see.

This same basic fault may have caused the decline of the civil rights movement and its push for equality of manhood. A token is not enough.[6] And how much of the truth about ghetto conditions has become first-hand knowledge of those who hold the reins of the assistance needed — at any level of administration?

Can a structure be set up by the federal government that will permit the use of available knowledge, the cooperation and communication that is essential in working with the states, the use of the talent and proven ability of those who man the programs toward successful accomplishment without waste of manpower or funds, and the delegation of responsibility in its best sense? If this is possible in other major areas of concern, it is possible in education.

It is clear that any future success in the commitment that has been made to education on the part of the federal government will depend upon the cooperative efforts of those responsible for education at all levels, with the support of the citizens of our nation. The federal government is now involved in the education of each American child from age three through higher education, and it must not fail in carrying out satisfactorily the goals set.

Responsibility of the Public

Public sentiment is everything. With public sentiment nothing can fail. Without it nothing can succeed. [Abraham Lincoln]

It has been continually pointed out that the public is basically responsible for education in our country. It would seem that this idea is so well accepted that we have come to take the education provided too much for granted. We have apparently assumed that as we made strides in the social and economic fields in this country, education would surely follow. We have a right to be proud of the fact that we have assumed responsibility for the educating of children from Colonial days, when the community and hence the taxpayer took over the education of the children. It was first put into law in Massachusetts in 1642 that education would be compulsory for every child and that taxes would support education in order that each child would learn to read and would have some kind of training for work within his community. It was in 1872 that we assumed responsibility for public secondary education, which came about through the Kalamazoo Decision. The financing of the schools has always been of highest importance. It has been assumed that the public would raise the necessary money and that those within the community who are given the responsibility for instituting the school would be responsible for hiring the teachers, buying the teaching materials, supervising the program, and encouraging others in the community to take an active part. These people became the school board as we know it today. It is still assumed that the school board carries forward these responsibilities, allocating and delegating to others trained for the work.

With the addition of other agencies in our communities, with the increase in knowledge to be organized and taught, with the complexities of everyday living affecting the purposes of education, the school board and the people have assumed increasing responsibilities involving decisions both greater in depth and wider in diversity. The public is committed to the individual and to society. Our understanding of both has grown and changed considerably during our short history, but it is still the worth of one individual and the best society possible for him that are the essential elements of consideration. The process of interaction has changed from simple living to one of a complexity difficult to comprehend, but basically this individual must contribute to his society and society must meet his needs, so that living brings about challenge and satisfaction.

The public today is faced with problems it finds hard to meet. Criticism against our current educational program is rampant at times, poverty and deprivation of education have suddenly forced themselves upon our attention, and the diversity of action, reaction, and the meager attempts at solving these problems have momentarily bewildered us as a nation. The nation must attack the educational problem in its enormity in identically the same manner as the first colony met the problem of organizing the first school. By this is meant, all of our human and financial resources must be put to the task of resolving the situation as we find it in order to meet the needs of each child as soon as possible. Every citizen must become involved. It is time that we recognized that when we say "every person" we include the deprived as well as the affluent and we can know real cooperation only when each recognizes that he has a voice in determining what education will be in every area. Knowledge and responsible personal involvement are the cures of apathy, one of our most dangerous social and educational ills at the present time. This is a time of opportunity, but we cannot take advantage of it without leadership. The leaders must come from each level — from the government, from the college and the schools, from the public. With concerted effort the knowledge that is needed by each person to assume his responsibility for what lies ahead must be made available. This leadership must plan the opportunities for the involvement of all. It will not come about unless there is planning, organizing, and a structure for fulfilling the purposes set.

It cannot be said strongly enough. The government is people, be it federal, state, or local. The leadership is the people, for this is the talent, the depth of knowledge, the organizational ability, and the experience. The "local control" is the people, be it of city government, the welfare agency, the health and sanitation programs, or education.

Knowledge of conditions in our country is a privilege of its citizens, a right. If the people demand this knowledge there will be less of a "hue and cry" that we are seeing and hearing too much, and less opportunity for those "at the top" to close their eyes to the seriousness of the needs of their constituents, whoever they are, wherever they are.

Do the American citizens know the following evidence that was brought out in the senate subcommittee hearings on the "federal role in urban problems"? Does the public know that no one can hold a government job or enter a program such as the Job Corps if he has a police record? Yet we have permitted an atmosphere in the inner city in which a youth feels he has not "made it" until, by stealing or committing a murder, he obtains a police record in order to preserve his integrity. Does the public realize that this is what it takes to break into our society, so-called middle class? The deprived youth today is following the only path he knows to fight the "system" that the American public has created. In these hearings one senator "pointed out regretfully the enormous gap between what the government conceives the problem to be and the facts of life for the underprivileged."[7] And the government is the people.

Is the public aware of the accusation that the welfare program "suppresses initiative, breaks up families, abounds with abuses and inexorably grows"?[8] What does the general public know about the welfare legislation being considered? All such concerns as these affect our understanding of the needs of deprived children and youth and hence their education. There are public groups working hard to alleviate conditions as they find them, but once again communication breaks down, for little is heard of these efforts.

How much does the public know concerning the development of a child or the way he learns? What does the public know of the vast amount of new knowledge that has recently become available to us? What does the public know of the condition of our school facilities? And how many of the people are aware of the present cost of the education that too many deem inadequate? Some people are aware of the taxes they pay and concerned only that this figure not be increased. How many people know what percentage of each tax dollar goes toward the education of our children? The majority of citizens talk of investment, but how many are aware of the investment that the public has in education? Many of these people are willing to accept federal money for education, but how many would vote for redistricting in order to equalize both the income and the educational opportunities more easily? How many of those living in the suburbs would vote today to take an active part in the renewal of the city from which they have moved? How many recognize that unless the city areas are improved and revitalized to make satisfactory living there possible, business in general will suffer and each citizen will feel the effect? Just how concerned will our citizens be to learn that the expenditure per pupil in our elementary and secondary schools during 1966 amounted to $564, that the average cost of maintaining one person in prison for that year was $2,690, and that the average cost of keeping a mother and three children on relief was $1,800?[9] Just how concerned is the American public about the need for the improvement of educational opportunities for the deprived of our nation — and for all our children?

Responsibility of Public Education

Since the school is the agency which meets far more children and parents than any other, it should take the initiative in promoting interagency contact and coordination. Responsibility for community im-

provement rests on all agencies and citizens, but the school has a special responsibility and a special opportunity to discharge it. It can make of itself the focus of a community-wide effort at self-improvement.[10]

An attack at the roots of equality of opportunity means education. Prejudice, which is a lack of objectivity, is learned; objectivity, too, can be learned. Therefore, insofar as inequality of opportunity is based on prejudice, it can be fought by education.

A disadvantaged life means a dearth of skills and understandings, a dearth which has a real existence apart from prejudice. The acquisition of these abilities is also a matter of education.

For millions of Americans, the American promise has been largely or wholly unfulfilled. Millions of others have lived their lives blinded by prejudices and by their actions or their attitudes have prolonged a situation of gross inhumanity. The fundamental solution in both cases lies in the greater development of the abilities of all Americans. The public school therefore has before it two jobs of unique and surpassing importance, two jobs which, given the resources, it alone can perform — to make of the United States one nation, and to make it a nation of equal opportunity.[11]

The challenge to the schools cannot be put more strongly than in these two statements. Conditions within our own "world" in this country and in the larger world have changed radically. Situations on the larger horizon have made us aware that we have not prepared ourselves either to meet immediate problems or to face the future.

The first responsibility of the school is to face present criticisms in a positive manner. But these must be faced at the same time by the people through the government, nationally and locally. The school administrators must recognize now the apparent waste of human resources and the inequality of offerings that exist among our many schools throughout the land.

Changes in attitude, atmosphere, and opportunity will mark the new era in education for our country. A positive attitude toward the worth of each individual, the creating of a warm, positive atmosphere conducive to learning, and the opportunity for learning in the exercise of thinking will create an excellence of intellect, which in turn should unlock the door for excellence in living. This is the challenge to the public school.

As the public school cooperates with the federal government it can demand from the public that the leaders who administer the programs be knowledgeable and qualified for their assignments. The school can contribute in the evaluation of the federal programs, and can aid in the interpretation of research. All of this will guarantee a better use of the money that becomes available. At this time money is necessary, but money alone will not solve the problems.

What can the public schools do immediately? Through in-service training the present teachers can be given the necessary knowledge and guidance to understanding the deprived — psychologically, sociologically, and anthropologically. They can then understand the individual deprived child and his environment, accept him at his level of development, value his cultural background, and lead him forward with a positive attitude toward understanding himself and learning, recognizing that we cannot know the limit of his intelligence until he has had ample opportunity to develop it. The curriculum can become a series of valuable, exciting, and challenging experiences for the children through which they may gain basic knowledge and develop concepts to be used in further learning. The schools can remove from their testing program those measures that do not accurately determine the potential ability of the children and that serve only to compare them with children of more favorable background. Confidence in the classroom teacher to evaluate the growth of the child from day to day will provide far more reliable estimates. The schools can lower the numbers of children per teacher to give each teacher time to understand and help each individual, not lowering standards, but raising standards and heightening aspirations by permitting more time. Families can be brought into the schools and into the community; the community can be brought to the school, thus opening up the door of opportunity for employment for some, for greater understanding of each other, and for a sharing of common problems, leading to the involvement of all for the betterment of that community. Schools cannot afford to take a step backward at this point. There are funds and there are opportunities waiting for those in the role of leadership to initiate these worthwhile programs for the tapping of these unknown human resources.

One important responsibility that the public schools must face is that of national assessment. The original purpose of this was given at the 1965 White House Conference by former Education Commissioner Francis Keppel when he stated that "the nation's taxpayers and their representatives in Congress have every right to know whether their investment in education is paying off." The funding of such a national assessment was to be made by the Carnegie Corporation, backed by the Ford Foundation and the government. Such action is based on an Act of Congress of March 2, 1867, which has not been complied with to any extent:

> The U.S. Office of Education is formed "for the purpose of collect- ing such statistics and facts as shall show the condition and progress of education in the several States . . . and of diffusing such information."

Fear is expressed by those representing "local control." This appears to be fear of further federal control, of pressures from possible regional, state and local comparisons, and of a possible cut in funding.[12] Why should an assessment be thought of in this manner, unless the fear of disclosure goes much deeper? Could not a disclosure prove greater need of funds?

A second major responsibility of the public schools is found in the report by the U.S. Commission on Civil Rights, "Racial Isolation in the Public Schools." The unanimous conclusion was that Negro children do not progress as rapidly in predominantly Negro schools as they would in a school of a balance of Negro and white children. Of the eight recommendations made, it would appear that the first, a demand that a mandate for government action at all levels be made to establish "equal educational opportunity of high quality," needs clarification.[13] Is it the quality of education provided in the predominantly Negro school that is poor, or is better education provided when half of the children are white? Do the Negro children respond better when there are white children present? How do Negro children respond to a program of high quality? Those who would improve our public schools need answers to such questions as these before requesting such a mandate.

A third responsibility is that of equalizing costs of education, not through consideration of unexplained increases in the suburbs, but through equalizing costs per pupil regardless of the school location and after the level of equality of the several programs has been balanced. National amounts of costs per pupil still vary, even after efforts have been made to narrow such ranges. Public education represents that education desired by the people. Only the public, through its representation, can improve and equalize its quality for all.

Responsibility of Private Education

When one thinks only in terms of the role of the government and the responsibility of the public and public education to provide equal opportunity for the best education possible for all, he ignores one very important factor in the history of American education: the independent school. This school has not escaped the criticism faced by all of education. The same variation in quality of education exists within the independent schools as within the public schools. That school also, which wishes to be known as one possessing outstanding quality in its educational program, must constantly exert considerable thought and energy to the maintaining of such a program. Not bound by some of the formal requirements, legal or assumed, each school stands alone in providing the kind of education it believes in. The National Association of Independent Schools gives support and recognition to good independent schools, and indeed has served as an incentive for those schools needing to make improvements in order to be accepted in its membership.

The independent school has the opportunity for serving American education in proving the value of advances in curriculum and in teaching. An independent school can be an ideal school by maintaining a small pupil-teacher ratio, by providing stimulation for sound learning within an enriched environment and, by giving evidence of the full meaning of creative teaching and creative learning. Its goal can be intellectual and academic excellence and can be reached as the school demonstrates the value of intellectual challenge and the meaning of guiding children to the highest level of their potential.

The independent school also has the opportunity to conduct research that can be of value to all schools. In the education of the deprived, it may take part in the projects within the cooperative research program sponsored and supported by the United States Office of Education, working closely with nearby colleges and universities. The standards that independent schools have set for academic excellence in their testing programs and their statement of *Definitions of Requirements* have proved to be incentives to forward looking public schools in evaluating their test results and in determining levels of accomplishment in their curricula.

Our democracy has always recognized the need for granting the opportunity for independent enterprise, and American education has profited from the contributions of this enterprise on the educational front. The challenge to the independent school today is to assume the responsibility of leadership in proving the best means by which excellence in education for all can be achieved in sharing in all the endeavors, projects, and programs that make possible this excellence for all those worthy of it regardless of circumstance. The greatest responsibility within this challenge is to be involved in the efforts being made. The independent school, to take its rightful place in the upgrading of all education, must serve as a resource for the public school at each level — not only through communication, but also through a close working together to improve and increase educational opportunities for a wider range of students capable of challenging programs of high calibre. Harold Howe II, U.S. Commissioner of Education, summed up this responsibility in speaking at an independent school meeting:

> *Engage in the concerns of education; reach out to serve more broadly in the community and at the State and national levels. Engage in the problems of our disadvantaged youth, even if it means a change in your admissions policy and a few irate parents. Use your independence to improve the quality of your academic offerings; in time these improvements will show up in our national academic standards.*
>
> *There is nothing wrong with getting entangled in a few alliances that hold such promise.*[14]

The present involvement in summer programs, in the search for talent, in the opening of some doors to the selected deprived, and in the training of teachers must increase in strength and influence if the independent school is to take its rightful place in educational change today and tomorrow.

Legislation

In considering the impact of recent legislation on American education, it is necessary to bring to the fore the Supreme Court's Decision of 1954, which made it most clear that any form of racial discrimination in public education is unconstitutional and that all previous rulings and recommendations at the federal, state, and local level that require or even permit discrimination are also unconstitutional. The decision ended:

> We conclude that in the field of public education the doctrine of "separate but equal" has no place. Separate educational facilities are inherently unequal.

These words can be found in almost every discussion on the subject of integration. Educators and citizens are not only faced with the need to improve our total educational program; this improvement must be planned for, carried out, and evaluated within the framework of the *integrated* school — nursery, elementary, secondary, and institutions of higher education. The South must approach integration by changing its state and local regulations. While the North had set up no such regulations permitting segregation, segregation in the schools is on the increase there as a consequence of the movement of the more affluent from the city to the suburbs and the poor from the rural areas and outlying reaches to the inner city, creating a situation that has brought about the degrading of the neighborhood school. There are indications that this trend in mobility will reach into the South as its schools give up separateness.

The impact of this problem is felt within the schools by both teachers and administrators as they attempt to work out procedures that will eventually lead to integration. Perhaps the strongest force will be the maintaining of the best schools of a school system in the inner city or ghetto areas. This would mean the construction of new buildings, excellent facilities in all schools, and staffing all with the best teachers. With redistricting in mind, these schools built on the fringes may make all who value education willing to intermingle there. This will take time, but as each good school is opened for those who deserve it most, one step will have been taken in the right direction. This good school, by embodying and putting into practice worthwhile learning and community betterment seasoned with the positive attitudes of hope and encouragement, will produce the results expected from a vital education. Public attitudes are changing. The changes in education must keep pace if we are to take advantage of the positive results from many of the efforts being made. All recent legislation points toward the accomplishment of integration, and we must not weary in our efforts nor be affected by the setbacks, for the success of all other goals will be determined by the success in the meeting of this one. Integration has become an issue. By nature it is not only financial and legal, but also a moral, social, and finally an individual issue to be resolved by each person through his own attitudes and efforts. It is basically an issue of the conscience of each American. A positive attitude must become the cornerstone and the building block for the establishing and maintaining of good schools.

An interesting question has been raised concerning an educational

act of some 20 years' standing that appears to have served its useful-
ness and, in the face of the new integration, to be a hindrance.
This is the Fair Educational Practice Act, which stipulates that no
educational institution shall inquire concerning an applicant's race,
creed, or color. Now we are making an effort to recruit Negroes,
Puerto Ricans, American Indians, and students from disadvantaged
areas for our educational institutions in cases where there is promise
of their being successful. Eugene Wilson, Dean of Admissions at
Amherst College, gives four reasons why this Act is faulty and
outdated:

1) Its provisions defeat the very purpose of the act.
*We now know that the academical potential of students from cul-
turally disadvantaged areas (Negroes especially) cannot be measured
accurately . . . . and have a tremendous power for intellectual growth
when transplanted into a cultural environment such as a college . . . .*
2) The FEPA protects the unfair discriminators. . . .
3) The FEPA has been difficult to enforce. . . .
4) The FEPA is undemocratic.

He suggests legislation to counter this to permit, for one of several
goals, free discussion, and to allow the student to feel that the information will not be used against him.[15] This could prove to be
one of the steps in the right direction.

The Civil Rights Bill provides support through financing and assistance to those school systems that are willing to face the problems
of desegregation. In turn it provides the right to withdraw federal
support from the communities or the schools where discrimination
continues to be practiced. "No person in the United States shall,
on the ground of race, color, or national origin, be excluded from
participation in, be denied the benefit of, or be subject to discrimination under any program or activity receiving Federal financial
assistance."[16] This bill cuts across and influences the support provided by various programs.

In any discussion of the need for legislation for integration, for the
improvement of living conditions for the poverty stricken people, and
for the realization of equality of educational opportunity according
to human potential, which demands the overall improvement of
education, certain facts need to serve as bases in stressing the urgency
in this legislation.

Coleman, in his 1966 report, *Equality of Educational Opportunity*

(158), stresses through substantial evidence the fact that environmental factors of deprivation in the life of the young deprived child
so deeply affect him that they counteract the influences the school
would have on his achievement and carry through to remain the
same detrimental attributes of his adult life. Such statements point
to a focus for legislation, the overcoming of the early environmental
influences that negate the future of the deprived child.

Legislation involving funds for the alleviating of the early negative
influences in the life of our deprived and minority child must also
consider the funding for the improvement of educational practice to
meet the needs of this child as he is able to profit from it. Questions
arise as to the proper allocation as well as the extent of need of this
funding. Facts must be made known to help in the answering of
these questions. At the present time some schools are spending four
and five times more per pupil than other schools. It is estimated by
William F. Johntz of the University of California that the spending
of $100 at the elementary level does more good for the deprived
child than $1,200 at the secondary level. It is also important to note
that the average cost of education for a child in this country is about
58¢ per hour. This is pointed out by Sam M. Lambert, Executive
Secretary of the NEA, as he stresses the urgency for spending twice
this amount to meet the current needs.[17] The need for legislation is
clearly seen in such facts as these, and the purpose underlying legislation already enacted to counteract the financial inequalities is being
realized as data is collected. As reports on this information are made
available the needs will become more specific.

The Anti-Poverty Program, which has stemmed from the Economic
Opportunity Act of 1964, at which time the Office of Economic
Opportunity was organized, also provides for direct assistance in
achieving the new, vital educational program so needed for the
deprived. Poverty has proven to be the enemy of education. We
have seen how it stands in the way of the learning of children of all
ages. It is equally essential that we see education as the enemy of
poverty, for it must be through education that the deprived successfully work their way toward better conditions. The various programs
sponsored by the Office of Economic Opportunity have educational
significance. It would appear that much of the effort is centered
upon the adolescent, such as salvaging the dropout and giving assistance in preparing for and finding jobs, an opportunity provided
through membership in the Job Corps.

The chief purpose here is to find the youth at a time that is critical to him, a time when he may become alienated from his school. Attention has also been given to the other critical time in the life of the deprived child — as he begins his schooling — and hence we have had the organizing of the Head Start Program. The initial purpose here was to prepare a program for those children of poor families who lacked many of the early experiences so necessary for the successful start of formal education, for it had been readily shown that the child who begins his education with a deficit too often becomes the dropout later. As work is carried on with both the Head Start child and the potential dropout, a special effort must be made by the school in the changing of the program to meet the needs of these children, adjusting the program to fit them individually. We have learned through sad experience that they cannot fit into the pattern arbitrarily set by a school. The gap in the ages between the deprived preschool child and the adolescent who needs the Job Corps, the Youth Corps, or assistance to stay in high school is taken care of by the introduction of the Elementary and Secondary Education Act of 1965.

Title I of this Act relates specifically to the deprived. It places the major emphasis on the meeting of their special needs. Here again we see recognition of the direct relationship between poverty and educational deprivation. It is here that the federal government has made available the largest sum of money, with the stipulation that this funding is to be spent through local determination of need. Criticism against local management of the funds has been evident since the implementation of this Act. Poor leadership, the unwise spending of money, and inadequate planning of programs appear to have prevented the changes so necessary. Questions also have been raised concerning the allotment of funds on the basis of the number of children from low-income families, for charges have been made against certain groups for misrepresenting the number of children within the prescribed category. The allotment to the state of half of the average cost for education per child within that state would seem to be a fair amount of assistance. However, those states that receive the most could be the ones that can afford the most. Educational programs for the disadvantaged, however, should under these provisions be benefited as they are from Titles II, III, and IV, which permit special funds for libraries and textbooks, for the establishment of centers and services for the schools, and for very needed educational research. A recent amendment to Title I makes the distribution of more adequate grants to poorer sections; the following categories of needy children have been added: delinquent, neglected, and foster children and children of Indians and migratory workers. Under Title II funds have been increased for administration and staffing of programs for state and local agencies. New amendments for Title III permit schools to apply for planning or operational grants when including an innovative program. Projects for the training of teachers and educational research personnel can be funded and in 1968 school districts can request money toward preschool programs and for replacing inadequate facilities. All three Titles include children in Department of Defense schools and Department of Interior Schools for Indians.

In each case where the management of these apportionments is questioned, many feel that the money is going to support the organization rather than the schools and the individual deprived child. It is hoped that through a careful evaluation of the work carried on at the beginning stages of this Act there will be strong evidence of proper use of the money in steps taken to realize good education for the deprived in the form of additional classes for young children, possibly extending public schools down to make available an early education for children of three and four. It is hoped that the programs at the kindergarten and primary levels can be revised to accept these children at their own levels and, through carefully individualized program planning, help them to continue on a road of successful learning to avoid the gap that has been so obvious; that with money for research and grants for teachers they may carry out pertinent innovations; that the teaching methods will be more closely geared to the evident needs of the learners and the curriculum will be fitted to them; that teachers will be given freedom to develop their own methods of approach and will have at hand materials they need for stimulating teaching as they adjust to the learning styles of these children; and that the school and community agencies will have found ways of working more closely together to assist all deprived people.

Another source of assistance for the education of the deprived child comes through the 1964 Revision of the National Defense Education Act, which Congress has broadened to include the teaching of the deprived. It is under Title III of this Act that funds are allocated especially for instructional equipment and materials and for the provision for services at the state level for supervision and consultation, although here only half of the cost is provided by the Act. Also, under Title III, training of teachers is possible through workshops sponsored by the state and through the formation of institutes by the colleges, giving opportunity for these teachers to gain assistance in implementing the curriculum for the deprived. In addition, Title V provides funding for guidance of these children at the elementary as well as the secondary level. It emphasizes that these guidance services be used particularly in the urban areas so that the individual differences of the children may be recognized and used as the basis for determining their needs and making the necessary provisions that the school can offer.

It is important to note that particular attention has been paid, in the setting up of the purposes of these various Acts, to the older youth and to the adult, thus helping those who are past the need for the compensatory school programs but have specific needs in relation to building work skills and finding jobs. Emphasis is also placed on the importance of the family and the finding of work for the employable so that the family may remain as a unit. Plans for adult basic education and for programs and projects geared to a specific community are further aspects under the Community Action Programs. All interested citizens should keep informed of the progress made by these various Acts and the programs they include. Evaluation is inevitable, and essential, and the time appears to be here when this evaluation must be begun.

In reviewing briefly those Acts that pertain particularly to the deprived, it must be mentioned that the many new programs that have been enacted in support of education recently offer assistance for our total educational program from the preschool through graduate school, and provide in some manner for a type of support to institutions of higher education, in addition to that from the International Education Act and the Higher Education Act of 1965. Attention is given at this level to improving libraries, increasing instructional materials and equipment, strengthening the programs of the humanities and the arts, health education, vocational education, teacher education, community services, aiding developing institutions, and assisting toward construction of academic facilities and housing facilities. This affords further impact upon the deprived. If encouragement is given to the able among the deprived, institutions for higher education will be better able to serve them through grants and scholarships in better equipped facilities and improved programs. A new emphasis should also be felt upon the training of personnel who will be better qualified to work with those who are deprived. The present trend in recognizing the importance not only of science, the humanities, and the arts, but also of the special areas of health education, vocational education, and community services should make possible a much broader education and training for those who are going into teaching as well as those who are specializing in these individual branches. It will also be interesting to watch the developing of programs under the International Education Act, which now relates rather specifically to our own country but has possibilities of far-reaching importance if the problems of poverty and deprivation are considered on a broader basis.

A United States Office of Education grant has been announced, made under a section of the Higher Education Act of 1965, that is enabling the colleges of the Ivy League and the Seven Sisters group — Barnard, Brown, Bryn Mawr, Columbia, Cornell, Dartmouth, Harvard, Mount Holyoke, Pennsylvania, Princeton, Radcliffe, Smith, Vassar, Wellesley, and Yale — to extend their search for talented youths who are in need of financial help in obtaining a college education. The grant has been made to Yale as the coordinating agent. This assists in expanding the efforts that have been going on in the Cooperative Program for Education Opportunity (CPEO) since 1963. In addition to helping Negro and white students, the new effort includes Puerto Rican, Mexican-American, American Indian, Oriental, and other minority groups as well as students from the rural areas, especially in the South.[18] The Office of Education also granted for the year 1967–68 $12.5 million for graduate fellowships under Title V-C program for those who were prospective elementary and secondary school teachers. The number of programs at colleges and universities is increasing, and the grant may extend for two years of study for an advanced degree other than a doctorate.

By the fall of 1967 a step forward by the Office of Education was fully realized — the decentralization of the office, with nine regional offices in full operation. These are located in Atlanta, Dallas, Chicago, Denver, Charlottesville, San Francisco, Kansas City, New York, and Boston. Each is headed by a region assistant commissioner in charge of program responsibilities, with a staff to conduct further activities. Each assistant commissioner will be accessible to the problems and programs in his area and has been delegated final authority on a wide range of responsibilities by Commissioner Harold Howe II, within the limits of the Office of Education policy and budget allocations. This is intended to bring about the desired

" . . . closer partnership between Federal, State, local, and private school agencies for the benefit of American education."[19]

Our country has already suffered from the decision to cut back on funds for housing, the anti-poverty programs, and urban development. This, no doubt, will have some effect upon the speed with which education can be improved. School and community improvement should go forward together. We cannot afford a slow-down in integration. But it is encouraging to note the emphasis on the provision for work skills, work experience, and employment assistance for parents in order to make them independent of the public assistance on which they have been dependent and the passage of the Child Nutrition Act, which includes breakfast and lunch for the needy children who have not been included before. These smaller gains are in the right direction, but they can do little alone unless there is progress in urban development and housing at the same time that integration is promoted and is becoming a reality. We must agree with President Johnson when he declares that the federal government should become the leader in encouraging integration, thus giving support for more consistent cooperative endeavor.

New organizations are forming for the betterment of education. The accomplishments of these groups should prove interesting to all of us in the future. An example is the formation by The Compact for Education of the Education Commission of the States. The participation of governors or their representatives from all states in providing for the state's assistance and sharing in information needed for the resolving of educational problems should have considerable influence in expediting the new educational programs and coordinating the many efforts. If such a group can work at the higher level of research and interpret it for their own states, they may well provide the incentive for implement and applying new materials and information in creative ways not envisioned before. The National Early Childhood Research Council, organized recently, has one of the greatest challenges before it. It is hoped that this group of educators and representatives of agencies concerned with the young child can realize quickly their goal of finding and freeing creative people interested in the development and education of young children and, through further funding, make it possible for these persons to spend time in study and research to meet the very pressing problems facing the education of all young children today as well as the young deprived. Such a group as this can do much in planning for the migrant children and for the inner-city children by developing ways for the improvement of the self-image, the language, and the curricular materials so essential to the learning styles of the young.

With the passing of the Education Professions Development Act during the summer of 1967,[20] the federal government through the Congress enters into another area of the education of this country, the professional preparation of teachers, which will raise problems while attempting to solve the shortage of teachers and to satisfy the need for teacher assistance. After July, 1968, schools can apply for federal grants to recruit new personnel for teaching, provide them with short pre-service training and then continue with in-service training while they are on the job. Will we once again place such inexperienced recruits in schools for the deprived, where extra understanding and additional training are called for? Or will they be placed under experienced teachers in the suburbs until such time as they are proven to be teachers worthy of working with the child with special needs? Schools may also apply for funds to recruit and train teacher aides. Will this action be controlled so that the professionally trained teacher will be placed in a more secure position with greater recognition, or will it tend to "water down" a profession that must fight for a fair and honorable place with other professions? What does the fate of the teacher corps bode for this same question? Will such action extend to the other professions as they begin to come slowly under the aegis of our federal government through the introduction of programs aimed at being of assistance to the people?

The positive features of the Education Professions Development Act permit the continuing of the present teacher fellowship program, provide for grants to universities to improve their programs for training college teachers, education specialists, and administrators, and establish a 15-man National Advisory Council to serve as the coordinators between the several governmental agencies and educational leaders, determining needs and unifying efforts.[21] Again, it will be interesting to watch the effects of this Act on the needed improvement of the educational scene.

Education has become big business. It is a national issue. Each new act of legislation for change is indeed an indictment against some failure that has come to light. This legislation will be valuable only as it points specifically to the improvements needed. Otherwise, it cannot combat that which it legislates against. As this country invests in education, what interest is it asking for? What are the bases for deciding whether or not this national investment is sound?

Representative Projects

In the midst of the challenges and charges cast at the many projects underway that have been designed to improve social, economic, and educational conditions, and more specifically to assist deprived children and youth within the poverty areas, we are reminded of President Johnson's interpretation in his 1967 State of the Union Address, when he said that the trial-and-error method has been used and there have been "lots of both." There is, however, a sobering and thoughtful note in all of this confusion, for we can see evidence of an element of stability emerging in the new purposes and renewed goals for our total educational program. It is easy to look at the ledger and see only the vast amounts of money being spent, to listen to the many accusations made against those responsible for mismanagement, and, through hindsight, to see evidences of poor planning and execution in some of the programs. There is one aspect of all of this endeavor that can be neither put on the ledger nor stated in terms of either negative or positive observable results. There is no way to measure the ultimate effect of returning to one person his dignity, of giving to one youth a purpose for furthering his education, or of awakening in a small child the realization of his worth as a unique human being. With this in mind some of the larger projects will be considered here in terms of their several aspects and apparent value. This can only be a consideration, for the first few unsteady steps in a new venture do not always indicate the strides that can be taken in the future. In particular, these programs will be discussed in terms of purposes set up, thus showing the basic thinking that can be of help to future programs, regardless of some of the difficulties encountered in the early trials. Evaluation is made where warranted in terms of these purposes. Problems of organization, management and execution can be corrected. (Information on these projects was gathered from available representative government publications.)

Project Head Start. This ambitious program began in the summer of 1965 as one of the Community Action Programs organized under the auspices of the Office of Economic Opportunity. This program was nationwide, and served as part of the War on Poverty. Its plan was for four- and five-year-olds to meet in eight-week sessions in order to overcome the deficiencies imposed on them by poverty and enter schools with a better chance of success. A director for the national program and two national educational consultants were chosen, and about 560,000 children were served.

The first summer, the needs of the children that seemed most important were improvement in health care, nutrition, living conditions, language development and intellectual development, wholesome self-images, and self-respect. In some areas it was difficult to reach the families with children eligible for the program, and it proved more successful when there were joint efforts by the school people with social workers, family welfare agencies, and the clergy. In some areas it was necessary to do door-to-door visiting in order to gain the support of the parents. It would appear that they resented being labeled "poor" or "deprived," or "disadvantaged." The relationships with the parents were best where they were called in to work along with others in the program either as classroom aides, to help prepare and serve lunches, or to join the children on trips. It was from experiences of this sort that they could take the easy step over to group meetings for parents, which proved to be a worthwhile part of the program.[22]

Teachers were chosen from all levels and many of them made an excellent adaptation to working with preschoolers. It became evident that as the program continues great care should be taken in the selection of teachers, and it is hoped that those will be chosen who exhibit warmth, understanding, concern, and interest in the children, as against concern about subject matter and the behavior of the children and inability to accept the children as they are. It appears essential that the orientation sessions be longer than the concentrated six-day programs that were used the first summer. There is need also for in-service training during the time of the teaching and assistance from those who are experts in child development or in family counseling. It was felt also that the administrators of the programs should attend the pre-service and in-service orientation programs along with the teachers, and that both groups should have closer contact with community workers who could be of help in resolving some of the problems that they faced.[23] The benefits from the first summer indeed outweighed the problems. Perhaps the greatest concern was the future of these children as they entered into the public elementary schools. There was a feeling that much of the gain would be lost and that the Head Start Program would not reach full efficiency until there was comparable improvement in the programs in our regular schools.

The recruiting of the children for these summer groups and the organization of what are known as Child Development Centers is now done by the local schools together with the child welfare organizations or the community planning groups. While this recruiting is going on the Head Start Orientation Program is being planned and organized for those who will be teaching. For the summer of 1966 very specific guidelines were set up for the selection of the institutions providing these programs: (1) The institution must have had prior to January 1st a program in early childhood education or child development under the auspices of one of the departments of the college or university, such as education, child development, home economics, or psychology. (2) There should be available a full-time member of the institution's faculty in childhood education or child development who will serve as an educational program coordinator or director for the project. An institution having only elementary or secondary education without the preschool program is not acceptable. (3) There must be the staff that meets the institution's qualifications for faculty employment and who have the skills to implement the related aspects of the curriculum including parent, community and staff relations. This basic staff is essential for each group of 25 trainees. There must also be adequate qualified personnel in the areas of medicine, dentistry, nutrition, social work, sociology, and psychology. The final requirement is the availability of facilities for the observation and work sessions in premises set up appropriately for programs for young children, preferably with the children present.

Excellent guide sheets have been prepared for the orientation programs and general core curriculum has been set up for the entire operation. This is divided into curricular plans, one for the professionals and nonprofessionals who are new to the Head Start Program, and the other for those professionals and nonprofessionals who have participated previously. The training session still consists of a minimum of 40 hours of concentrated classroom time, with associated outside observation and reading. The core curriculum is based on a series of topics that are worked out in considerable detail for the guidance of those operating the program. The 11 topics are:

  I. The Child Development Centers
 II & III. The medical features of the Center program
 IV. Relationship with social service programs
 V. The sociology of the disadvantaged
 VI. A continuation of Topic V (This includes a study of the subculture of immigrant ethnic groups, including

the Puerto Rican, migrant labor, the Mexican-American, and the "old American" poor in Appalachia.)

VII & VIII.   The educational program

IX.   Coping with problem situations

X.   Using volunteers

XI.   Parent involvement

The participants in the program are given considerable supplementary material that relates to the classes and lectures designed for them. Each person receives a series of booklets, each of which goes into considerable explanation of the topic with ample illustrations and examples.

Evaluation of the program has been going on since the end of the first summer's program, and assessments have been made by specialists in child development, psychology, education, pediatrics and health. Their statements have been gathered at the headquarters of the Office of Economic Opportunity. Many of these specialists have been asked since to give advice to those planning new local programs. It would appear that in spite of a variation in quality of the programs, the strengths thus far have outweighed the weaknesses. However, it will be a number of years before any success can be adequately judged, for we must wait to follow these children through their school years to determine the possible values gained from the few short weeks during a summer. Some feel that the program is moving too rapidly, that the efforts should be concentrated in smaller areas until such time as adequate planning can be made, and that definite steps must be taken to better prepare those working in the program. It is doubtful that a person can be well prepared to work with the complicated problems presented by even one deprived child in a course lasting one week.

Many of the recommendations already made for the qualifications and preparation of a teacher, for the organization and implementation of a curriculum, and for the actual process of teaching itself apply very specifically to those who would work in a Head Start Program if that program is to be worthy of being a first step and a foundation for further experiences. For example, there cannot be a set curriculum within the preschool for all four-year-olds. The teachers are different persons, the children differ, their backgrounds vary, and the curriculum must be flexible and adjusted to the needs of each particular child within each group. Much will depend even upon the way an individual teacher interprets that curriculum, for no two teachers will use it in the same manner. We must apply all that we know about child development and about the child's learning as well as being acquainted with his background and circumstances. This is just as important for the four-year-old as it is for the six-year-old, and there is hope that this may even be applied to three-year-olds in the future. We must remember that learning begins when life begins and ends only when life ends.

There are those who feel certain that the Head Start Program is well past the trial period. They base their thinking on some of the statements made in the evaluation by those considered authorities. For example, the Department of Child Psychiatry at Johns Hopkins University found that following the first summer program the children gained approximately 31 to 40 points over children who had not attended the Head Start Program on the Peabody Picture Vocabulary Test. The Mental Health Society of Staten Island, New York, declared that on an Intellectual Ability Test they were able to measure a gain of some 14 months. From the University of Texas comes the statement that the first-grade teachers found that those children who had attended a Head Start Program came to the first grade more proficient in learning, appeared to be more curious intellectually, and were better adjusted to the classroom. In California, Montessori Schools found the children had gained from a possible four to 12 months in their performance on an intelligence test. It was here that the Mexican-American children, who evidently had started with lower scores, appeared to make the greatest gains. From Cleveland the report came that the children who had attended the Head Start Program were found in their kindergarten experience to have gained in their concept formations relating to color, to form-space, to grouping, and ordering. Little difference if any appeared in those areas of time-sequence and time-duration.[24] We cannot as yet accept such results as reliable, for they are too often based on small numbers and gained in less than the best of testing situations. They can be considered possible indications of improvements.

A most substantial study of Head Start has been made by Max Wolff, senior research sociologist at the Center for Urban Education in New York, sponsored by the Ferkauf Graduate School of Education at Yeshiva University and supported by funds from the Office of Economic Opportunity. Reports of this study state that the educational advantages of the program tend to disappear as the child goes on through the grades. The Head Start child does less well later when the teacher is ineffective, and the desire for further learning created by the program also diminishes with further schooling.

The chief contribution of this study is that it gives evidence that the child who is initially stimulated in a good preschool situation will continue to be stimulated to desire learning, to learn, and to test satisfactorily in direct proportion to the quality of the stimulation of a good learning situation, a challenging curriculum, and good teaching. The report claims that damage is done to the child, once awakened, if he continues under the reverse of these conditions.[25]

It would appear that one of the very important lessons to be learned in a training program for teachers and workers with the deprived would be to keep pace with the literature which is constantly appearing, with the many recommendations and suggestions made, and with the listing of materials, books, guides, and curricular materials, viewing these in the light of our very basic knowledge concerning ways of working with children and the ways in which children work. These teachers must know full well that these ideas may stimulate their own ideas but they themselves, as they become acquainted with *their* children, must be creative in their choice of the experiences and materials for which their children are ready. In the light of the deluge of material which flows constantly to all persons whose names appear on any teaching roster, it would be well for any American child if every teacher were helped through this warning to find the confidence in himself to know that he must be the judge of the children's needs — physical, social, emotional, and intellectual — that it is his interpretation of the individual child which must determine the creative approach which he himself must choose and use.

Project Head Start has involved the largest number of individuals, and is no doubt the best known of the major programs offered in the War on Poverty. The summer programs are to continue, but one of the promising features has been the establishment of the full-year Child Development Project. Another is the health follow-up process.

An excellent example of a Child Development Program is that initiated by the Hartford, Connecticut, Board of Education, which is planned for four-year-old children with a summer session followed by another beginning in September and ending in June. Since it is part of the local school system, a Child Development Center draws from those areas nearby. Applications are made by parents and a part of the parents' responsibility is to attend weekly conferences or group meetings. They are informed of the health regulations, the supervision, and the plans of the program, including such items as field trips, and the flexible schedule, all of which are described in a Policy and Information Booklet prepared specifically for them. In the material prepared for the program itself, and for use by the teachers, care is taken to present the important basic ideas and emphases intended to guarantee satisfactory experiences for these children. In the introduction of this material the following two points begin the discussion:

> I. *The core of a pre-school program is the trained teacher — this includes her knowledge and training, her skill, her planning (based upon her diagnosis, prescription and evaluation), her sensitivity (to the children, the group, and the situation) and her skilled interaction with the children and their parents.*
>
> II. *There are as many different kinds of children in a classroom as there are children in attendance. The range of behavior and values is as wide in the "poor" parts of town as it is in any other section; children are bright, dull, confident, frightened, friendly, withdrawn, curious, talkative, silent — and combinations of these. To try to put them into one or a few categories would be inaccurate.*
>
> *There are, of course, many exceptions requiring tremendous teacher insight into the diagnosis of each child.*[26]

Following the introduction, excellent statements are presented concerning the curriculum, the plan of action and the areas of special concentration. These are spelled out in terms of sound theory and concepts that should serve to guide the teacher in planning the type of program that has been described as vital, forward-looking, and essential for the deprived child of today. The following definitions are given, which indicate clearly the major goals of this program:

> 1. *Education — "preparation for dynamic living — present and future." Education of young children, including that of the culturally deprived, is not an attempt to superimpose middle-class values upon these children, but an effort to extend and broaden their own values and experiences toward optimum functioning of the individual child in all areas of his life. Therefore, this curriculum is built upon real life experiences of the children involved within the framework of current (and hopefully valid) theory.*
>
> 2. *Curriculum — those experiences, not only within the school situation, but concerned with the child's whole life. This definition calls upon the school to attempt to "bridge the gap" between home and school. It further implies that the school and the teacher must be concerned with, have knowledge of and respect for the role of the parent, the parent-teacher relationship, and the family's cultural and value patterns.*[27]

In the follow-up process we once again find those in the health field taking a lead and setting a good example. The Health Department, with its excellent organization, is oriented to the many goals held by education, particularly those for the deprived. One of the strengths in the Head Start Project is its emphasis upon the health of the child. All concerned will agree that it is the healthy child who can take advantage of an educational situation and gain the most from the learning experiences involved. The health follow-up begins with the complete medical evaluation of the child when he enters the Child Development Center. This includes the obtaining of the medical history, an assessment of the child's development, and a physical examination. Screening tests are made for vision, hearing, speech, and tuberculin reaction. In addition laboratory tests are run on urine for albumen and sugar and on blood for anemia. There also is a dental inspection, a completion of necessary immunizations, a psychological evaluation, a discussion with parents, and a consideration of the teacher's appraisal made through observation of the child.

As a part of the follow-up program, suggestions have been made that a person trained in public health nutrition be available for assistance in the planning of the school menus and that a public health nurse be available during the program to work closely within the educational program and cooperate with any of the agencies which might be used. In some situations a form was used to record the results of the medical evaluation of the child while in the Head Start Program, and this was later forwarded to the school in which the child enrolled in the fall. Wherever specific defects were discovered among the Head Start children the follow-up included seeing that the children received the services from the agencies indicated. Some of the needs noted were further dental care, assistance from the Crippled Children Services, correction of vision difficulties, and repeated physical examinations. This is carried on as the child progresses in school if further assistance is needed.

The best program in Head Start is the one that is individualized. This indicates that the learning experiences in and out of school must be considered and evaluated individually. If we believe in taking children as they are, they must move into the more formal schools as individuals, and the teachers' follow-through at the primary level must be on the individual basis. Just as health problems cannot be solved in one short summer but will need watching as the child moves forward, the educational problems also move forward with him. This demands of the primary teachers not only that they recognize the individual differences of the children, but that the children not lose their individuality. It has been said by some that the quality of an educational program can be achieved by individualizing for each child the school experiences he meets and by treating the child as an individual in all aspects. Project Head Start has discovered the value of individualizing and extended this to the parents. As the child moves into the elementary school, can the primary teacher still see the unique human personality in each child, continue to work with the parents in recognizing the worth of that unique personality, show to the parents that all of the teachers care about that one child, thus uniting the efforts of both the home and the school in the concern for him? This concern will create the incentive for understanding and the understanding for assistance. This opens the door to helping the child. If the Head Start teacher can do it, so can the primary teacher, and the teacher of the middle years, preadolescence, and adolescence. Head Start can continue all the way through, but its success does depend primarily upon the teacher.

The Head Start Program was one of the first of the large efforts in the War on Poverty to assist by providing for young children the early experiences, missing in their meager background, so necessary for success at the primary school level. Enough distance has been allowed since its inception to initiate Head Start Evaluation and Research Centers. Ten such centers are based at the following higher education institutions but operating under the Institute for Educational Development by the Office of Economic Opportunity: Temple University, University of Kansas, Bank Street College of Education, University of Hawaii, Syracuse University, University of Chicago, Michigan State University, University of Texas, Boston University, and Teachers College, Columbia University.

This is a decentralization similar to that of the Office of Education, again permitting assessment at much closer range, and studies by research scientists in early childhood development, amid the actual conditions and needs of the different regional areas, and the bearing of these studies on Head Start.[28]

Such statements as that of Jule Sugarman, Associate Director of Head Start — "Head Start can be a false start unless there is adequate follow-through in the early grades" — have been loudly echoed by all those knowledgeable about this program. This opinion has apparently led to the discussion of a Head Start follow-up with recommendation for funds and for a small pupil-teacher ratio (one to 15) with ample assistance in classrooms and a continuing of health services. In order to take action of this nature it would be necessary to determine the administration and the training of personnel.

This fact led to a decision to provide the funding through the Office of Economic Opportunity but assign the administration to the Office of Education. The program, Project Follow Through, began with 30 school district pilot projects in the early grades in poverty area schools in the fall of 1967. These are at the kindergarten and first-grade level for children entering school for the first time.

If this experiment is successful, recommendations can be made for its extension. Some feel that it should be extended through grade three. Will these children not need it throughout their elementary schooling? Will we discover that all children would profit from a program that stresses individualized instruction, small classes, extended parent participation, sufficient medical, dental, and guidance services, and an enriched program? Will this prove to be the initiation of the new and vital education for all? Will the public pay for this for all children? Will not the uncovering of talents, abilities, and creative capacities warrant the expense? If 3,000 children are reached during 1967–1968 and 190,000 during 1968–1969, and the program can be operated satisfactorily by the "local control," evidence will be available to answer some of these questions.

In the announcement of the formal launching of this new Project on July 2, 1967, U.S. Commissioner of Education Harold Howe II and Sargent Shriver, Director of OEO are quoted as saying:

> The program will utilize instructional specialists and new techniques, teacher aides, psychologists, social workers, doctors, dentists, and many others to meet the physical, mental, social, and instructional needs of the children.
>
> Each classroom will be organized to involve the fullest possible social and racial integration. The classrooms will be equipped to provide a variety of educational experiences through individualized instruction and group activity directed to developing each child's self-esteem, his respect for other children and adults, and his own role as an individual in a group.[29]

Whether it will be for Head Start or Follow-Through,

> The structure is there for direction. However, the sensitivity, creativity, and abstraction of content from the children remains the responsibility of the professional in immediate contact with the children — the "Unsung Hero" — the trained teacher.[30]

Peace Corps. The Peace Corps, as an organization that has grown out of government planning and spending, did not originally include in its intent the education of deprived children as such. Many of those who join, however, find themselves involved with the children in the communities where they are sent, and many report that the way to reach the people is through their children.

The training program for the Peace Corps is a rigorous one lasting from 10 to 12 weeks, six hours per day, six days per week. The components of this training might well be used in training teachers to work with the deprived in this country. After beginning with technical studies necessary for the job overseas and for adapting to the host country, the trainee makes a careful study of the language and the historical, political, economic, social, and cultural aspects of that country. His studies also include the analysis of our own democratic institutions, our history and our current political, social and economic problems, as well as contemporary international relations and America's role in the world scene. This is followed by physical and mental health training, including first aid and preventive measures, and physical training and recreation to provide physical conditioning and practice in games of both America and the host country. The final component deals with the role of the volunteer in social and economic development with an understanding of the organization and aims of the Peace Corps. (202:577) These several approaches, if geared to the urban areas and their special problems, would indeed prepare a person for working in deprived situations in this country.

When the Peace Corps began in 1961 there were few who held out hope for its success. It appeared to be an experiment quite foreign to our thinking at that time. The screening of volunteers was criticized, as were the motives of the young people themselves. Parents and others were concerned about various aspects of the program. Even the title of the group came under discussion because of its connotation relating to certain world conditions at that time. But the young people were enthusiastic and the first group of 60 young men prepared to go to Colombia for their first community development program.

Teaching soon emerged as one of the activities most needed in the countries served. It was informal teaching, for the volunteers found themselves in rural areas and in small villages, among adults and children all of whom were hungry for knowledge, for skills, and for a change in their way of life. Within the first five years it was estimated that the volunteers had had personal contact with over one million people, many of whom desired to learn but had no teachers. Some 70 volunteers operated an educational TV program involving about 7,000 teachers which reached over 400 thousand primary school children each day.

This organization appealed to Americans with definite vocational skills, to professional people such as architects and dentists and medical technologists, and to teachers. It was reported recently that in six African nations more than half of the high school teachers with college degrees are volunteers of the Peace Corps, and one third of Nigeria's students are taught by these volunteers. As of April, 1966, 52 percent of the volunteers were engaged in some form of education, half of these for the first time.[31]

In view of the need for teachers the Peace Corps has been working with the National Education Association for some time in an attempt to increase the number of professional teachers for these projects. The response has not been good and efforts are still being made to interest teachers in giving two years to a professional opportunity that would pay far more in experience and value to the individual than a high-salaried position here. It is true that the Peace Corps takes teachers needed for our own city slum areas, and it is necessary to think toward the future to see the value of the experience gained from two years abroad, with the contributions to this country that might result upon return, as against preparing specifically to teach our own deprived. This is an individual matter thus far. Many of our schools grant leaves of absence to experienced teachers who wish to spend two years with the Peace Corps. New York, Philadelphia, Chicago, Kansas City, Los Angeles, and Denver are making this provision.

A person with a college or university degree with a liberal arts background is eligible to teach in the Peace Corps following participation in its training program, which includes both courses in education and practice teaching. Education majors with no teaching experience can be used in elementary and secondary schools and in the teacher-training institutes in the newer nations. Those who have master's or doctor's degrees with teaching experience at the college level qualify to teach in the university programs, and experienced and certified teachers have the opportunity abroad to staff new schools, to train teachers, and to take part in pilot education programs.

One of the exciting aspects of the Peace Corps is the status one receives upon returning to this country. Those who have had teaching experience abroad are being offered the opportunity to teach in the underprivileged schools while they qualify for teacher certification. Both cities and colleges are offering teaching opportunities and scholarships to permit Peace Corps returnees to continue with their education in the preparation for teaching. This appears to be one excellent source of teaching personnel for our urban schools and as one reviews the teaching qualities required by the Peace Corps and some of the experiences that these people have had, one can see that they are similar to the qualities and experience specifically designated as essential in working with our own deprived. It is stated in the Peace Corps literature that the teachers must have patience, maturity, dedication, initiative, imagination and ingenuity. They must be able to improvise by using materials at hand. They must construct the curriculum they use to meet the needs of those whom they are teaching, and efforts are made to take the education out of the classroom and into the community. Many of these volunteers coach various types of sports, organize bands, build school libraries, teach adult literacy classes, lead community discussions, and start village newspapers. They are all working toward the same goal: an international educational program to help all peoples to fulfill their destinies.

It is gratifying to note that a large percentage of those returning from the Peace Corps do continue in the educational field. It would be well if the enthusiasm that they bring with them, as well as the dedication to the service of young people, would in some way spark enthusiasm and dedication in teachers at home in our traditional schools, secure, but often dissatisfied and unchallenged.

> For every prospective teacher who enrolls in the Peace Corps, two teachers emerge. Corpsmen are asked when they volunteer to give their career choice; when they conclude their enlistment a check is made of who does what. Twice as many take teaching posts as had planned to do so. School boards compete to obtain these fledgling teachers. California grants special waivers, offers higher starting salaries. New York State has a Director of Peace Corps Affairs, whose job is to recruit corpsmen as teachers.[32]

One of the very encouraging changes taking place in the training programs of the Peace Corps is their removal from the college campus, too often in an isolated college town away from the main stream of daily life. An example of this is the placing of a group of

40 of the volunteers in the basement of a three-story brownstone house in Boston's South End, a poverty area where Negro, Puerto Rican, Chinese, Lebanese, Irish, and Italian families live. These volunteers, who are on their way to Colombia, are learning through first-hand experience what it means to move into a neighborhood, learning to "fit in," to be accepted. There is ample opportunity to assist in small projects, even though the volunteers spend the majority of their time in studying. The conditions of living may not be similar to those in Colombia, and a new language must be learned for Colombia, but the process of learning to become involved is similar and can be helpful to the volunteer and to the community.[33]

VISTA. Included here will be a brief discussion of Volunteers In Service To America (VISTA), which has been termed our domestic Peace Corps. When the first VISTA volunteers reported for training in January, 1965, they were told by President Johnson that their pay would be low and the conditions of their work would often be difficult. He assured them that they would have the ultimate reward that does come to those who are willing to serve their fellow men. These volunteers represent a cross section of this country, coming from every state and from every segment of our society. They represent every educational level from those who have not graduated from high school to those who hold advanced degrees, for there are no specific educational requirements, although it has been found that a high percentage have at least some college education. Within this group there are representatives of labor and of the professions, housewives and social workers, and retired military personnel. When they sign up they go where they are invited and serve under the direct supervision of a local agency to which they are assigned. They work for a monthly stipend of $50 with an allowance for living expenses. The stipend is not paid until their service is ended. It is most encouraging to note that the number of volunteers is increasing and that some are coming now from the ranks of the poor, bringing with them knowledge of poverty and a commitment that is strong because it represents their own personal struggles. The work is termed "community development," and VISTA workers are found in the rural areas, the city slums, among the migrant farm workers, on Indian reservations, with the mentally ill and the retarded, and in conservation centers where they cooperate with the Job Corps.

VISTA volunteers are trained at universities, settlement houses, and social action agencies, and by foundations and camps. In their six weeks of intensive training they learn the realities of poverty by being in the poverty stricken areas. They learn the effects of it and the methods of combatting it, and discover their own skills and abilities as they are tested on training assignments. Their training is not formal, but one state university does give both graduate and undergraduate credit for its successful completion. The programs in which they participate develop as they work and communicate with the poor, so they in turn motivate those who need to be helped to carry on to help themselves. The one common purpose is to put VISTA out of business eventually. The volunteers of VISTA and the Peace Corps have one strong point in their favor in preparing to work with the deprived — in both cases they live among those whom they serve. Much would be gained if our teachers of the deprived could do this. VISTA may prove to be another source of the fine type of person needed as an image for the deprived child and youth as they learn to find themselves.[34]

National Teacher Corps. The National Teacher Corps was established by the Higher Education Act of 1965 for two purposes. The first was to improve education at what had been called its weakest point, in the slum and rural schools where there is the highest rate of turnover of teachers and there are the most deprived of the children and youth. The second was to form through high quality special training a large group of willing and excellent teachers who would stay within these areas. The National Teachers Corps died as of June 30th, 1967. It died because it was born too soon. Too few saw its value. The cost was thought too high. A description of the program is included here in recognition of its value and with the hope that some will have the courage to see that it gains the support needed to revive it and that our deprived children and youth have teachers who are properly trained. Can we afford to lose this source of qualified teachers?

The literature concerning the National Teacher Corps stated that it offered dedicated men and women teachers a challenge and an opportunity to share their talents where they were needed most — in the schools of city slums and rural poverty. Through the National Teacher Corps, able Americans with perception and warmth, patience and energy, were to add a new dimension to teaching the nation's disadvantaged children.

As a salaried member of the National Teacher Corps the volunteer was invited by a local school system to join the regular staff of a poverty school, where he was able to pioneer special classroom, extracurricular, and neighborhood projects. Working with teachers, parents, and community agencies, he helped make education come alive for slum youngsters by relating school to their everyday lives. Some Corps members were assigned to schools near their homes; most moved to other parts of this country.

Career teachers in the National Teacher Corps used their experience and gifts where they are crucially needed — to bolster, not replace, regular poverty school staff. Experienced teachers were recruited for one or two years of service from among men and women with a master's degree plus five years of teaching or three years of work with the disadvantaged. Those without the degree needed eight years of teaching experience or three of teaching and three of poverty work. A few National Teachers Corps career teachers served alone, but most led teams of one to five teacher-interns. Salaries were at local pay scales, plus more for extra responsibility. Tenure, retirement, health and other benefits were protected within their home school districts. Other benefits were: travel, relocation costs for the volunteer and family; injury, disability and death benefit coverage; and a readjustment allowance at the end of the service.

Teacher-interns in the National Teacher Corps could launch a rewarding career in teaching the disadvantaged. They were selected from among outstanding college seniors and graduates with little or no teaching experience. They were recent college graduates and older graduates moving from jobs in offices and the home to the challenge of teaching. Teacher-interns served in the National Teacher Corps for two years, combining part-time teaching and community service with two years of tuition-free part-time graduate study leading to a master's degree. The pre-service tuition-free university program — which preceded National Teacher Corps service — trained teachers by highlighting the sociology of poverty and ways to teach the culturally deprived. Other benefits included salaries at local rates, stipends during pre-service training, travel and relocation expenses, and injury, disability and death coverage. These were the challenges and the opportunities offered by the National Teacher Corps when such a program was endeavoring to be appreciated and supported.

In following the story of the National Teacher Corps — an excellent program because it was national with goals for excellence — it is hard to realize that such a worthy program could be permitted to die as such by Congress, a group that apparently had little knowledge of its worth and chose to affect the lives of deprived children to the extent of possible further deprivation. Why must a program of this nature have to lobby in Washington or anywhere else? It was the "best bargain" for the most worth among the federal education endeavors. Those who served can now well identify themselves as deprived by the government along with those they served. As a recognized federal program, 50 universities and 111 school systems in 29 states were training 965 teacher-interns at a time of teacher shortage. The interns were dedicated students studying subcultures and ghetto sociology. They were becoming acquainted with the people in their homes. School systems bid for them. In one school system a principal noted that because of the contribution of these national corpsmen, ". . . we're all doing a better job."

The Teacher Corps. In the summer of 1967 the teachers corps "went local," stripped of its national importance, and turned over to "local control" for recruiting, training, and assigning. This action cut its significance in American education and put it at the mercy of those who have failed in the management of other "local" programs. It has become ". . . a local program designed and carried out by local authorities to meet local needs." As yet the relation of the present teacher corps to the Education Professions Development Act is not clear. There is an extension of the program for three years, but can there be any guarantee of uniformity in the high caliber of the recruits and in the quality of training? No longer do the recruits need to be college graduates. They are on a weekly salary, not on the salary of a teacher in the school system. They can be used to work with groups inside or outside of the school. Will the corps now reach and draw intelligent, creative individuals? Will they now become substitute teachers, aides, or assistants? Will the trained teacher hold them in the same high regard? It is one thing to serve a small community, another to serve a national need. Is there hope that before the last shreds of enthusiasm for the National Teacher Corps are lost in the mire of local politics Congress will see its value, restore its status, and give it the funds it merits? Can the Office of Education and the NEA convince Congress of its worth?

Talent Search Programs. In the past few years, considerable interest has been shown in the development of differentiated education for talented children at both the elementary and secondary school levels. There is evidence that considerable work has been done at the local, state, and federal levels towards the preparing of programs for talented children. Much of the information on the programs had not been distributed for general use and a need was expressed for a compilation of information on all programs and practices so that there might be an exchange of thought. As a result of this demand, a bibliography was published as a joint enterprise between the Council of State Directors of Programs for the Gifted and the Talent Development Project of the United States Office of Education. The Council consists of those individuals in state departments of education who are responsible for stimulating, directing, and coordinating state action on behalf of talent development. It was established in 1963 to improve communications within and among the states regarding research efforts, effective programs, and legislation for talented students and to publicize the need for full educational opportunity for them.

A nationwide college scholarship program for talented Negro students was established in 1964 by the National Merit Scholarship Corporation under a seven million dollar grant from the Ford Foundation. This program, known as the National Achievement Scholarship, provides for 200 four-year scholarships each year to promising Negro high school graduates at the colleges of their choice.

The Independent Schools have had considerable interest in the talented student over a long period of time, and several interesting programs have developed because of this interest. One of the traditional concerns was that the gifted student have the opportunity to move ahead at his own rate. This was evidenced in the Eight-Year Study of the 1930's and the Three School, Three College study of the 1950's.

In the late 1950's summer programs were established that were planned specifically for able students. This broke the traditional pattern of using summer programs for either make-up work or remedial work. The Advanced Studies Program at St. Paul's School initiated for capable boys and girls from the public and parochial schools in New Hampshire, the Liberal Studies Program at Mount Hermon School, and the Institute for Oriental Studies at Thayer Academy are all examples of advanced study summer projects that have drawn students from all types of schools. One of the factors that has influenced the development of such programs as the summer enrichment is the growing effort on the part of Independent Schools to involve themselves and their students more directly with their own communities. The majority of these schools are boarding schools drawing students from other sections of the country, and it is felt essential that these students, while working in intensive study programs, must relate themselves to the community by becoming involved in community affairs.

The Independent Schools have been concerned with the severe lack of opportunities available to the talented children within the poverty areas. Phillips Exeter Academy opened a program entitled SPUR, which brought to its regular summer school groups of students accompanied by guidance counselors or teachers from schools in five widely separated cities. A similar venture began in 1964, when six Independent Schools in the vicinity of Boston organized themselves into a group known as the Educational Research Program. They received assistance from the staff of the National Association of Independent Schools, and were sponsored by the New England Association of Colleges and Secondary Schools in cooperation with the Boston Public Schools and Action for Boston Community Development, the community action agency in that city. Summer schools for children from various city schools were opened at three of the Independent Schools, and the other three contributed funds, teachers, and teacher aides. Some 250 students from the elementary and junior high schools of the Boston Public Schools took part in that program.

One effort on the part of the Independent Schools has been the formation of the Independent Schools Talent Search Program (ISTSP), which has merited considerable recognition. In February, 1963, representatives from 21 Independent Schools convened at Phillips Andover Academy to consider ways and means of helping promising students who, because of a lack of resources or cultural advantages, were unable to realize their apparent ability. It was felt that at least two years at an Independent School could assist materially in preparing such students for successful college entrance. As a result of this meeting this program was organized for the purpose of seeking out promising students from disadvantaged circumstances and placing them in independent boarding schools, under major scholarship grants, for the final two to four years of their high school education. In the summer of 1964, Dartmouth College began an eight-week course, Project ABC (A Better Chance), to prepare some of the boys who had been accepted through ISTSP for the difficult curriculum and for the different way of life at the boarding school. In the summer of 1965, Dartmouth's program was complemented by a similar program for girls at Mount Holyoke College. During the summer of 1966 programs were operated in three additional colleges.

The Independent Schools make possible for these children a small pupil-teacher ratio, close attention from instructors, and excellent classroom, library and laboratory facilities, and place them with classmates who will stimulate and challenge them. Most of the schools have broad programs of physical education and extracurricular activities that complement work in the classroom. Every effort is made to cultivate academic ability, extracurricular interest, and character. The initial number of Independent Schools in this program has grown considerably. About 400 of these students were placed in the fall of 1966, 100 to be funded by the member schools, 300 by the Office of Economic Opportunity.

Project ABC at Dartmouth College included in its curriculum intensive work in English, reading, and mathematics. In English, help was given to the student to develop skills in composition, in the reading of mature literature, and in class discussion. In reading, all of the boys took part in a developmental study skills program and the average and poor readers were tested diagnostically and grouped into small classes for intensive corrective and remedial instruction. In mathematics two courses were given, one in pre-algebra and a first course in algebra. In the ABC program at Mount Holyoke College, the student had nine periods each of mathematics and English literature and composition a week, and six periods of reading instruction, which included study skills and remedial sessions for those who were suffering from similar problems. Both programs offered, in addition to the academic, experiences in sports, creative dramatics, music, and social activities — all of which were intended to give the students the opportunity to become accustomed to group living in a residential school.

A cutting of funds has limited this program and left it dependent primarily on scholarship funds from independent schools.

Upward Bound. A program initiated through the Office of Economic Opportunity during the summer of 1965 for the purpose of salvaging what was termed "talent waste" is known as Upward Bound. This is a pre-college program for secondary students, beginning with a full-time summer session, with follow-up meetings during the following school year to keep the students on the road towards college. Programs like this give full indication that it is never too late to help the deprived. It is an excellent plan to catch them when they are three years old or five, but the deprived children and youth are salvageable regardless of their ages or background situations, and even as failures at the elementary and secondary levels.

Over two thousand youngsters took part in the first Upward Bound program. They attended pre-college centers at colleges and universities across the country. The range was from ninth grade through high school and all students were of poor families and with mediocre school records. Initially Upward Bound had as its first goal the Talent Search, looking for those who gave some evidence of potential that might be developed at the college level; the second purpose was to give a chance for making up past deficits, of which these students have many; the third purpose was to salvage talent for society. This program in essence is a rescue operation. The students must be redirected, potential must be discovered, and the individual student must be motivated, and then his ability and talent, which become evident through his own endeavors, must be applied in a constructive manner. If his abilities and talents and energies are not directed constructively toward society, there is every possibility that they could be directed against society, which he has felt has been against him.

The selection of the students is made by the college or the university running the program. Information is gathered from welfare agencies, school records, teachers and principals, and often from juvenile court counselors and parole officers. Following a summer of intensive work these students are placed either in college or in special high schools or preparatory schools where they study as special students and combine some of the regular work with remedial help. During the regular school year they attend special classes held by the colleges concerned to aid them by tutoring and, secondly, to maintain identity with the college-bound group.

Following the preliminary success of this program, new guidelines for 1967–1968 have now been prepared. These help to sharpen the purposes and procedures, and every indication points to this program as an excellent means of remedying poor academic preparation and stimulating personal motivation at the high-school level and thereby increasing a deprived youngster's promise for acceptance and for success at the college level. It is hoped that this program will not only discover many who would never have considered college but will also hold out a promise to those adolescents who might easily have become dropouts before completing their work for a high school diploma. This program also offers an excellent opportunity for a close-working relationship between the secondary schools and the colleges or universities, and an opportunity for outstanding, imaginative teachers to work closely with the deprived at the adolescent age and to find the success and satisfaction that come from redirecting good ability and excellent talent.

Programs that provide for flexibility and adaptability in the learning process, in scheduling, and in interpersonal relationships are by far superior. How well this relates to the very same basic framework that works best for the preschool child, the intermediate school child, and the preadolescent! Grants can be applied for by recognized community action agencies associated with accredited academic institutions, by any accredited four-year college or university, either private or public, by a grouping of accredited colleges or universities provided the administrative responsibility remains with one institution, by any accredited public or private school that can provide the residential facilities for the summer program, and by any accredited two-year college, public or private, that can provide residential facilities.

The Upward Bound student now is designated as a young person with academic potential who, coming from a poverty background, has not had the motivation or the preparation either to use or to demonstrate his potential. He may be apathetic or even hostile, or he may have shunned possible meaningful educational experiences because of previous inadequate school experience. Post-secondary education might be possible for him if he were provided with instruction and the basic experiences necessary for overcoming the earlier obstacles. Ninety percent of these students must be from families whose annual incomes meet the poverty criteria. If the participating institutions wish to enroll additional students whose income levels are above those designated, funds must be obtained from other public or private sources. It is felt that such additional students would help to provide a diversity of backgrounds and enhance the programs.

The content of the curriculum is determined by the educational institution, and includes the concentrated summer phase as well as that within the academic year. It must be planned to promote the intellectual qualities and attitudes that are deemed necessary for success in post-secondary education. These are stated as being critical thinking, effective expression, and positive attitudes towards learning. In addition to the academic phase of the program, the institutions applying for grants must propose activities that will enhance the students' personal effectiveness as they relate their learning experiences to life experiences. Suggested activities are self-government, a student newspaper, tutoring of younger children or other neighborhood activities, and cultural programs including field trips to nearby places of historical, artistic, or cultural value. It is very important that recreational and physical activities be a part of each project. Group activities and the development of individual skills will introduce the students to recreational pursuits that they can continue on their own.

The faculty must include teachers from both the college and the secondary school, with a significant number from the regular teaching staff of the institution proposing the program. Every effort should be made to include, as additional staff, specialists in certain fields of learning needed by the students, and volunteers such as Peace Corps returnees, VISTA, undergraduate and graduate students, and youth workers. If some of these are drawn from the racial or ethnic groups represented by the students it is found that the rapport within the groups is markedly improved.

The Office of Economic Opportunity is very desirous of imaginative and effective proposals that will further the purposes of the Upward Bound program. At the present time Educational Projects, Inc., is under contract to assist in the development and evaluation of programs. The introductory statement to the guidelines made by Sargent Shriver, Director of the Office of Economic Opportunity, is as follows:

> One of America's greatest wastes occurs when capable young people who could succeed in college never attend because of the psychological, social, and physical conditions of poverty backgrounds. This waste is especially cruel when we remember that more than ever before, higher education holds the key to so many jobs in the future.
>
> No one knows how much talent is lost to the nation because of poor performance during the formative years of a youngster's education. Upward Bound is designed to cut into this waste and to see if substantial numbers of potentially successful youngsters can profit from a real chance at a higher education.
>
> We invite your ideas and your proposals on how best to provide that chance.[35]

In programs such as Upward Bound, where success seems to have repaid the effort expended, the difficulties encountered in the beginning steps are soon forgotten. It is well to review them at times in order that either progress is evidenced if they do not repeat themselves or, as new programs are launched, these same difficulties may be anticipated and overcome more easily.

Early in the program it was felt that ". . . the very smallest minority of youths in Upward Bound would benefit; that perhaps a half dozen of the first 75 tried to go on to college; few had special talents and most just didn't have the I.Q. no matter how it might be measured. . . . We may be perpetuating a colossal fraud on them by making them believe they are college material." Only one college would guarantee to take students from the program. In some areas teachers were threatened with the loss of their jobs if they participated in the summer program of Upward Bound. "Upward Bound has definite limitations. To many, its goal will always seem absurd."[36]

When the project was two years old and still a federal anti-poverty program, it was learned that it had taken 20,000 high school students whose marks did not signify their ability and sent them to 220 college campuses for summer remedial work. One survey shows that 80 percent of the first group (1965) did enter college and only 23 percent failed to finish the first year—an average freshman loss. Many in the group discovered for themselves their abilities and their talents. Some met with bitter disappointment.[37]

During the second summer (1966), another 20,000 students found themselves on 216 campuses. They represented city slums and rural poverty areas. Few were high school graduates. About half were Negroes; one out of every 15 was Spanish American; about 4 percent were Indians. Although it is too early to make judgments, Dr. Frost now reports with more pride that these students were "better than the colleges thought they'd be and better than the high schools said they'd be." Upward Bound can provide for a small percentage of our deprived youth the "critical difference." How long will it be before our educational program will provide this "critical difference" for the vast majority of all?[38]

Dropouts. Throughout the previous discussion there have been occasional references to the problem of dropouts, which ordinarily occurs at the high school level. This problem concerns educators at all levels, for it destroys future educational prospects for the student who leaves school and, secondly, it is evidence of conditions that begin far earlier than in the high school.

In 1963 a special summer program to combat school dropouts was financed from the President's Emergency Fund. It was considered a "crash program." $250,000 was given to 63 communities in 23 states and the District of Columbia, and the following federal agencies assisted: Welfare Administration, National Institute of Mental

Health, Vocational Rehabilitation Administration, and the United States Department of Labor under the Manpower Development and Training Program. There were 1,375 counselors and other professional workers, whose salaries were paid from a special fund and who identified 59,301 young people as dropouts or potential dropouts. These students were characterized by low reading ability, irregular attendance, marked disinterest, unhappy family situations, strong antagonism toward teachers, poor discipline, and a general purposelessness. These students were contacted by the workers by telephone, letter, mass media announcements, home visits, conferences, and interviews in the counselor's office. The students gave these reasons for dropping out of school or wishing to do so: disinterest, poor marks, rejection, a poor school program, poor parental attitude, lack of parental concern, home responsibilities, and the general lack of anyone who stressed the importance of school to them. Special classes were organized, after-school study programs planned, and tutorial help and individual attention provided. These students were released from the general fixed regulations of the schools and permitted to take part-time jobs or to use part of the school time for remedial help in the special programs that were organized. Efforts were made on the part of the school to improve the course offerings to meet the needs of these students, and the school became more intimately involved with the community agencies endeavoring to help. Fifty-one percent of the total students contacted returned to school in September, and 92 percent of those who returned were still enrolled in school as of November first.

It is the teacher who sees the child as he develops and can be aware of tendencies that will eventually lead him to drop out of school. It is the teacher who is aware of irregular attendance, poor conduct, and lack of interest, and who has the responsibility for seeking help for the young person while he can be helped. It has been said that we need the courage to do early what we are obligated to do too late.

Kelley reports that valid research points out that the potential high school dropout can be identified early in the educational program. This is a problem for every phase of the school; there is little time to spend on accusing one branch or another. The beginning of this problem comes when the child first meets failure, when he must repeat and becomes over-age for his grade level. It starts when he feels rejected. There is evidence to show that he drops behind others in reading, arithmetic, and spelling, and is also slow in working with abstract concepts. He comes from a situation which leaves him with a low IQ, for intelligence tests measure ability that has been developed, and he has no chance to develop his. From a health point of view and with reference to living conditions he is behind from the very beginning. This child is damaged by deprivation, but the school has the opportunity to repair that damage. Instead, one label is attached more often than any other, and this label can cause damage to him from which he may never recover — "not up to grade level." This not only causes the damage of negation but also indicates to the full extent the poor quality of the school where the grade level is important and not the child. Now that we can identify this dropout earlier, will we tend to use this label further down the ladder, and will the teacher let this child, the potential dropout, remain in the background and further neglected until the day comes when he stays away for good? (44:61–64)

What can we say of the future of the dropout? Martin Deutsch expresses this clearly:

> School dropout and failure, apart from what they represent in lost potential to the individual and his community, mean that as adults, those who have failed or dropped out will be confined to the least skilled and least desirable jobs and will have almost no opportunity for upward social mobility. (5:50)

A quick look at the changes taking place in our economy show the truth of this statement. First, there are few jobs open now for which a person can apply expecting to learn on the job, especially if he has no skills at the beginning. Second, the picture shows that if a student has no skill and no experience when applying for work, he must at least present a high school diploma. Third, the chances for a youth to make it on his own without benefit of education or skills are almost nonexistent. Fourth, the label "dropout" travels with a youth. If he decides to return to high school he cannot shake it, and if he looks for a job and is successful in finding even the most menial work, he is still a dropout to those around him. The army is not happy with him, his home is no satisfaction to him, no one seems to care, and his most cutting comment can be an honest one: "There is no one to turn to."

Do we stop, having recognized the characteristics of the dropout? Does research on the dropout stop when it has determined the reasons? What can be done? Who should do it? The parents still have a role, for it is never too late for someone to explain to the parents of a child why he is a failure. Failure is never so deep that there is not one spark that can be flamed if those closest to a youth show that they understand and care. The teacher has a role. The teacher guides, directs, instructs, disciplines, takes attendance, makes referrals, and lives with this child or youth a minimum of five days a week, five hours a day. It costs nothing to show concern for a child who is unhappy. It can give one an inner feeling of warmth to help a child or youth solve a problem through just talking it over. It takes little effort on the part of an experienced teacher to change the curriculum and its content to interest a child. It takes little time to rearrange a student's schedule to fit his needs, and it takes little effort to arrange his program so that he has longer periods for study or part-time work. It does take a little thought to remove the boredom from the classroom, because it has to be removed from the teacher first. Perhaps we should ask the question, should a bored teacher be teaching children or youth? Will teachers have the courage to discover how far behind a child is, give him experiences in learning at the level where he can be successful, and give him commendation? The dropout will stay in school if someone can give him a reason, prove to him that he is worth helping and that he has something to develop that society wants.

> Educational preparation has come to play an increasingly important part in determining the work and careers of the population. This means that any serious deficiencies in the schools will have increasingly serious consequences for the productivity of the economy and the stability of the society. A significant minority of the population grows up in a family and community setting which fails to prepare them to profit from what the school has to offer. Hence, the school faces a special challenge to meet the needs of this disadvantaged minority.[39]

Dropping out of school is not always a withdrawal from unchallenging work, a sign of failure, nor is it always the end result of a series of psychological upheavals. For this deprived youth it may mean just another expression of his anger, hostility, rebellion, and hatred. He may continue to change his patterning throughout his life as he needs to give expression to these reactions. The consequences of his action of the moment may have little impact on him. Subsequently he may suffer a lowering of his own self-esteem and regret the finality of his act and its consequences for his future.

In cases of this type or that of the lonely or "lost" youth, can the school take direct action to be of help? Hughes makes the following general recommendations:

1. The practice of organizing around self-contained classrooms lends a stability to the life of the child. . . .
2. The use of varied and multilevel materials helps deal with the diversity of the youngsters. . . .
3. Teachers who use the integrative unit approach are able to provide opportunities for the free play of interests and abilities . . . with respect to their individual levels of achievement.
4. More and more schools are providing specialized personnel. . . .
5. Our school experiences are expanding into the community and involving the community more in the school. . . .
6. More individualization of instruction . . . [is used] to meet the individual child's needs.
7. Teacher-pupil planning . . . allows the child to identify with the learning tasks. . . .
8. Evaluation procedures are becoming more comprehensive and continuous.
9. Recent emphasis on ungrading is removing some of the psychological threats to the learning environment and is providing more opportunity for children to learn at their own pace.

Such measures as these can be used with the younger child and continue throughout his schooling, thus giving no time when he "loses contact or becomes uninvolved."[40]

Job Corps. A brief consideration of the Job Corps is included here in order to stress the point of view that runs throughout this discussion. It is true that a student who drops out of school may be depriving society of an undiscovered asset or talent, but, more important, he is depriving himself of the satisfaction of work well done, and is cultivating dissatisfaction with himself and the world around him. It would be easy to say that if our schools, in a new and vitalized form, had programs that were flexible and made to fit the individual student so that he might have success, there would be no dropouts. We could guarantee that the percentage would be cut considerably, but there are still those who, given every opportunity and consideration, can neither adapt to situations as they find them nor permit conditions to be adapted to them. And the solution is not always to convince each dropout that he should return to school. If this is not the solution, care must be taken to help him plan and carry out another program of endeavor. His education is not over when he leaves the school if we support the premise that education is a process that goes on throughout life. Not all is lost when he changes from one pattern of endeavor to another. There are still resources, opportunities for financial assistance, and other educational doors to open. He can still advance himself educationally in adult education or within one of the projects.

The first monies were appropriated for the Job Corps in October, 1964, and in January, 1965, the first Job Corpsmen met at one of the new Corps Conservation Centers. This is a youth program organized as a part of the War on Poverty, which has as its purpose basic education and work-skill training for those who are either out of school or out of work. Young men and women from 16 through 21 years of age are eligible. This program in particular reached down to the deprived who presented a common background pattern of substandard housing and families at the poverty level, many receiving public assistance. About half had completed eighth or ninth grade, and more than half had a reading level below the sixth grade.

The Job Corps has won the interest of the business community, the colleges, and the social agencies. Corpsmen have been active in contributing to national benefit, particularly in the conservation of natural resources. They are learning occupational skills in areas where there is current and future need for trained workers.

The Centers are operated under contract to those companies or organizations that can use the help of these young people and in turn grant them proper training. Job Corpsmen can be found working for the Agriculture Department's Forest Service, for various Bureaus of the Interior Department, improving national forests and parks, helping out in disasters, at the Space Center, and in Washington offices. Young men who have a better grasp of mathematics and reading also go to the Training Centers under contract by major corporations. Upon graduation from the Job Corps most of them find full-time employment, but some choose one of the armed services and some return to high school or go to college. Not all have graduated, but the problems encountered by this program are being solved.

The concept of this program is good, but it has had its troubles. Discipline and cost have created heated discussion and time is needed to clarify and rectify mistakes. This is a program urgently needed by many deprived youngsters who are eager to make a way for themselves. For many it is the only possible opportunity.

Adult Basic Education. The Adult Basic Education program has had less publicity than some of the other major programs, but the extensiveness of its operation, its apparent success, and the apparent need for it warrants recognition. In all 50 states and territories there is now opportunity for persons over 18 years of age who have completed fewer than six grades of school to attend classes. Many persons are using the classes to help them prepare for a better job, and some are interested in education because they have been deprived of it in the past. Some participants are Puerto Ricans, and many of the Latin American countries are represented. This program is financed by the federal government as part of the Adult Education Act of 1966. It is possible to take courses at three levels: first, second and third grades, fourth through sixth grades, and seventh and eighth grades. A state participating in the program must contribute a minimum of 10 per cent of the cost of the program, but some are contributing more than the minimum.[41] The target of this program is the 25 million of all adult men and women unable to read or write beyond the sixth grade level.

It may be that if this program continues, a demand for the extending of its services through the high school level may be made by those who could not see the need for education previously, but have the desire now to return to some type of formal education to better themselves even while working. The title of the program could give to these young people a certain feeling of prestige, for it would be far easier to face being considered an adult learner than an over-aged high school returnee.

Children in Migrant Families. The despair of the migrant is felt in these words:

> It is not to die or even die of hunger that makes a man wretched. Many men have died. But it is to live miserably and know not why, to work more and gain nothing, to be heart-worn, weary, yet isolated and unrelated.[42]

Changes in agriculture in this country have produced a sharp demand for seasonal workers to harvest particular crops, and mechanization has intensified the demand for these workers for shorter periods of time. The seasons are comparatively short and frequently there are miles between one harvest and the next. A man does well to start in April and find enough harvesting to last into October. It is necessary for his family to travel with him, and at best his earnings are unpredictable. These frequent moves constitute the greatest single hazard to the migrant child's opportunity for an education. As one learns of the types of living arrangements available, of the mother working beside the father in the field, of the hazards that exist in the fields, one is fully aware that the migrants are among the most deprived groups in the country.

When the migrant family, white, Negro, or Puerto Rican, settles in for a brief time for a harvest, it does not mean that the children will be going to school. Many times the older children must stay in the barn, the shack, or the car where they are living to take care of the younger children. Thus education is denied to the children even for the short time when they may be in a community. Provision for the care of children is handled by some states through day care centers. This varies from state to state as does the cost of the care, which must come from state funds or from the grower. In some states child welfare services are available. In others, these services are provided in only one or two communities. Too often lack of knowledge concerning these services, or the family's belief that their stay is too short for them to take advantage of them, is the deterrent. Generally speaking, child care services available to residents of the state are also, by law, available to children of migrant workers.

What are the future prospects for the migrant and his children? Before solving the problems of education for this group it is essential first to provide the essentials for living that are basic to any form of satisfactory education. The migrants are the poorest of all of our poverty people. Their housing is the worst, and they are not protected at all by labor laws, for they are excluded from minimum wage coverage, unemployment benefits, and social security. There is, however, hope. The federal government is offering grants to school systems where migrants are to be found during their traveling to provide school supplies, food, clothing, and remedial teaching for the children. In the fall of 1967, schools in California began to teach Mexican American children in Spanish through the third or fourth grade; English is taught as a second language. It is hoped that this will promote better understanding as well as remove the children's feeling that their own language is unacceptable.[43]

Under the Economic Opportunity Act, a program has been authorized for improved housing, sanitation facilities, and projects for education and day care. The assistance given to these people and the organizing of projects for them must be initiated by the several states. Portable housing that can be put up on state-owned land is one possibility. Two approaches being taken would appear to make the endeavors successful in reaching and helping them. First, the migrants themselves were involved in planning the beginning projects so that their actual needs and thinking helped determine the direction taken. Second, although immediate help is essential to these people, another purpose within the projects is to plan for long-range assistance as well. Both are necessary because of the rapidly changing demands upon the workers, requiring new skills and also requiring that the migrants begin to prepare to develop skills in other lines of work as mechanization takes from them the meager farm responsibilities in the crop areas. Some communities are including educational programs for basic education, homemaking and health education. Ideally, as communities begin to work for the migrant it is hoped that the migrant and his family will be better accepted into a community and become involved in its activities even for the short period of time that they may reside there. Assistance in these basic concerns will lead not only to day care centers and summer programs of education for the children but also to more basic educational planning.

Six states, Arizona, California, Delaware, Florida, Oregon, and Washington, are now participating in a three-year project designed to improve the opportunities for education for the migrant child and supported by a grant from the United States Office of Education under the Elementary and Secondary Education Act of 1965. California will administer the program and it will be directed by school representatives from each of the states.

The project has these goals:

To develop methods of identifying the educational needs of migrant children, of keeping track of the children's movements, of transferring pupil records from school to school, and of planning coordinated educational programs for children as they move from State to State.

To develop educational materials and guidelines for teaching migrant children, and to provide supplemental inservice training for teachers to help them understand the problems of migrant children.

To help selected schools develop model educational programs for migrant children.[44]

Texas has undertaken a federally financed program, through a grant under the Economic Opportunity Act, that is designed to educate the farm workers during that part of the year when they are not traveling with the crops. It is planned that the trainees will attend classes to learn basic reading, arithmetic skills and writing. During this six-month program it is hoped that some workers can reach the educational level required to enter the Manpower Retraining Program. Others will continue with some form of vocational education or further adult education. This is a small beginning toward helping these people but certainly a worthy one, and it will be interesting to watch for the outcomes of programs such as these for they will determine further steps to be taken.

Closely related to the poverty experienced by the migrant is the poverty of rural America. The basic needs of the people in both groups are the same, for they are the very basic essentials for living. As the migrant travels through the rural areas there is little there to encourage him to better himself as he identifies with the poor rural farmer. The migrant can leave the situation when the harvesting is over, but the poor in the rural areas must stay, facing in addition to their basic lacks an isolation that so often destroys the last vestiges of hope or endeavor. This isolation prevents any form of cooperation among the people that might engender the possibility of banding together to help each other.

Here also, the Office of Economic Opportunity, in recognizing the seriousness of the rural conditions, has provided means of helping through several programs. Again, it is hoped these people will learn how to help themselves to build anew or to rebuild some form of social organization and find new possibilities for holding their people against migration to the larger communities or to the cities.

Where programs for migrant workers have gotten underway, assistance has been brought in to help meet the needs for mental health, a public health nursing program has been initiated, a home management aid program has been used for training women in managing on low incomes, and day care centers have been organized, with the mothers themselves helping. A rural environmental sanitation program was started and the neighborhood Youth Corps helped in the unemployment situation. All of these are Community Action Programs. The greatest success is found when the several programs are initiated at much the same time in order to meet the needs and fight the problem on all fronts. Thus good attitudes, good health, cleanliness, child care, employment, skill learning, and small loans as common and interwoven goals can help to make our rural areas a good place to live. Rural America must be aroused, organized, challenged, and productive. Its product can be an attractive countryside, a golden rippling field, sturdy children, and ambitious youth who find satisfaction in caring for and using the soil, which is the source of the food needed not only in this country but around the world.

Tutorials. One of the most important challenges to face the schools in regard to the education of the deprived has been the formation of what are termed tutorials. These are found chiefly in the urban areas, where it has become a status symbol chiefly for white, middle-class college students to take upon themselves as a part of community service the tutoring of disadvantaged students who need additional help to meet the demands they face in the schools. The tutees are usually Negro, lower class, and either elementary or high school students who meet with their tutors outside of school for small-group or individual teaching.

The tutorials have developed because of the urban schools' apparent lack of responsiveness to the needs of the minority group, because much of the form and content of the educational program in the urban school is geared to the skills and the aspirations of the middle class, and often because the middle-class teacher places value upon verbal learning and verbal competition, which the minority-group children find most difficult.

At present there is little contact between the tutors and the teachers in the schools, although this is being emphasized more. Ordinarily the tutors are free to experiment with the material that they are teaching, and many of them are finding the experience a rewarding one. The children are also finding it rewarding because the tutor has a personal interest in them, is closer to their age, and, in addition to the academic, shows an interest in their personal and social growth and emphasizes cultural enrichment.

Educators are concerned because these young college students are teaching with no formal training and generally under no supervision. This is indeed a challenge which the schools must accept and answer. There is room for teacher appreciation for what the tutor is doing, room for cooperative planning between the teacher and the tutor to increase the advantages of the tutorial, and room on the part of the educators to recognize what the tutors are doing in relation to building better self-pictures and better values.

An example of a more organized program, the "Tutor Corps," was sponsored by the Program of Action by Citizens in Education (PACE) in Cleveland, in which approximately 1,000 high school and college students participated as tutors during the summer. The tutoring students represented some 83 public, parochial, and independent schools of Cleveland, and 15 colleges, and tutored some 3,500 elementary public and parochial school children in the city, from grades three, four, and five. The tutors received no compensation except for transportation expenses, the program was free, and the children were recommended by their classroom teachers as likely to profit from such a program. The tutoring sessions took place four days a week for six weeks; each tutor conducted two sessions of one and one half hours per day. Sixty-one professional, mostly elementary school, teachers were employed to serve as advisers to the tutors. The four objectives of the program were to improve the validity of the tutorial concept, to provide personal attention and individualized instruction to every child to stimulate his desire to learn, to help the children overcome their weaknesses and improve their performances in reading, spelling, and arithmetic, and to develop in the tutors an interest in education as a profession. This program has been considered most successful.

Another advantage of the tutorials has accrued to the tutors themselves who, in certain situations, find that by helping those less fortunate or less able they in turn are learning about the subject which they are teaching. This was recently shown in an experiment in Flint, Michigan, where a group of sixth graders who were below average in reading and lacked motivation were assigned as tutors to slow fourth graders. Both groups, it is reported, showed a spurt in academic interest and progress. The younger children immediately accepted their tutors and looked up to them for their "superior" knowledge. The older children learned as they taught and, flattered by their tutorial post, worked harder in their own classes.

Tutoring projects can be funded through the United States Office of Economic Opportunity. The Albuquerque public schools received such a grant for a well organized program. A Comunity Action Program, on a volunteer basis, was planned so that those students who were handicapped by deprivation could receive help in the basic school subjects to increase their achievement. The tutoring was done after regular school hours. A campus coordinator recruited students from the high schools, university and college nearby and provided for their training, orientation and transportation. Supervising teachers were appointed at each of the tutoring schools to help the tutors, giving about six hours a week on the project. Good planning and cooperative supervision can make a volunteer program of tutoring successful. The school that takes the time for this benefits in its program, and its children benefit in both personal and academic progress.

Survey reports indicate that previous doubts concerning the value of tutorials can be erased in favor of very evident positive results — increased interest in education; the presenting of "models" of learn-

198 · *Deprivation and Compensatory Education*

ing that have raised the educational aspiration of students, parents, and communities; the discovery of creative approaches to the presenting of ideas; the making of effective teaching aids from materials at hand; the demonstrating of the importance of personal involvement in learning; the recognition and appreciation of cultural differences with a concurrent realization of the similarities of human beings in feelings, desires, fears, hopes, and sensitivities.

What special qualities do effective tutors need? These are suggested by Eleanor Fitzpatrick:

> . . . firmness without scolding; a sense of urgency which is not inflicted on the child; compassion without sentimentality; enthusiasm for learning, for striving, for the job well done, for things of the mind; contagious courage; a rich knowledge of many subjects; a love of teaching, a full "bag of tricks" for selling their wares; and imagination in using those "tricks."[45]

Not all the rewards are those gained by the child, especially the deprived child or deprived youth and his parents. There are rewards to the tutor who goes into the inner city, the deep South, the isolated rural area, who follows the migrant in his trek from field to field. At times these are difficult to put into words, but a few might include an appreciation of one's educational opportunities, a deepening of that education through working and living with those less fortunate, an opportunity to see some hope in the eyes of one who was "lost," an opportunity to narrow the gap in communication between peoples, and an opportunity to appreciate those of courage who have gained the values of good living without benefit of worldly goods or education.

The opportunities in Mississippi, in Texas, or at Rough Rock in the Navaho reservation, to name a few of the localities in need of personal encouragement, are open doors to volunteers who seek to serve here in the United States. Time and distance and the accumulation of evidence of the good that is done by these volunteers, who take the trouble to learn of the dire needs of their fellow citizens and help to carry their loads of despair for a short distance, will create another American story of courage and selflessness for our historical records.

All those who are interested in the possible solutions to our current social, economic, and educational crises, and who are interested in the evidence that is forthcoming from studies, surveys, and reports from many collection points, now may begin to have at hand information that can serve as a guide for further planning. Some of this evidence is regional, and necessarily so, for our poverty and deprivation are regional, with special problems in each region.

One should be acquainted with the Coleman Report and the Moynihan Report, both made early in the current attack on education and on poverty. These have been referred to previously. An example of the many health reports is the study made for the Munfred Foundation by Dr. Richard Eggleston, based on the breakfast patterns in deprived homes of 12 large cities.

A report by the Massachusetts State Advisory Committee to the United States Commission on Civil Rights, "The Voice of the Ghetto," issued in July of 1967, is representative of the descriptions now becoming available of conditions as they are in our cities. Challenging recommendations are made to the federal government, but the solutions of many of the problems lie with the people of the city and the state. Reports will be made on the several riot-torn cities, such as the ones on Watts and Newark, not only of the extent of damage but of the aftermath of cleanup, rebuilding, changes in attitudes and the analysis of the reasons behind these outbursts.

In 1967 the annual report of the Committee for Economic Development with *Saturday Review* was entitled "Changing Directions in American Education." This is another effort to keep the American public generally, and American business specifically, informed.

Research reports are also becoming available from centers of study across the nation. A listing of representative centers and further sources of information are given in Chapter VI.

What will the American people do in response to this continuing flow of evidence? How will it influence our Congress? How will it affect the lives of the deprived children and youth?

The United States Government is faced with certain facts that demand some form of immediate action. Both poverty and inequality must be fought. The government has confronted the situation and the fight has begun. Must trial and error be the method of testing and procedure? Can we take time for further trial and error while change is rebuffed by the *status quo* and revolution builds, when resolution is possible with leadership, statesmanship, honesty, humanity, and humility?

REFERENCES

[1] Arthur Bestor, *How Should We Educate the Deprived Child?* (Washington: Council for Basic Education, 1965), p. 2. (Occasional Papers: Number Seven.)

[2] See *The New York Times* (March 6, 1966), p. E9.

[3] Harold Howe II, "Parity in Schools Urged for Nation," *The New York Times*, Special Educational Survey (January 11, 1967), p. 27.

[4] "The Equal Educational Opportunity Act of 1967," *Saturday Review* (December 17, 1966), pp. 66, 86.

[5] Robert Sherrill, "It Isn't True that Nobody Starves in America," *The New York Times Magazine* (June 4, 1967), p. 22.

[6] C. Vann Woodward, "What Happened to the Civil Rights Movement?" *Harper's Magazine* (January 1967), pp. 29–37.

[7] See *The Independent School Bulletin* (February 1967), p. 62.

[8] Editorial, *Life*, 63:9 (September 1, 1967), p. 7.

[9] "Education as Public Investment," *Saturday Review* (January 14, 1967), p. 43.

[10] Education Policies Commission, *American Education and the Search for Equal Opportunity* (Washington: National Education Association, 1965), p. 27.

[11] Educational Policies Commission, p. 37.

[12] "Toward National Assessment," *Time* (January 27, 1967), p. 61.

[13] William Brickman, "Racial Isolation in Public Education," *School and Society*, 95 (April 1, 1967), p. 209.

[14] Harold Howe II, "The Need for Entangling Alliances," *The Independent School Bulletin* (May 1967), p. 18.

[15] Eugene S. Wilson, "The 'Fair Education Practice Act' is Dead," *Saturday Review* (September 16, 1967), pp. 85–86.

[16] James A. Turman, "Decisions from the Field," *American Education* (July-August 1967), pp. 20–21.

[17] Sam M. Lambert, "News Front," *The Instructor* (May 1967).

[18] "Talent Search," *School and Society*, 94 (December 10, 1966, pp. 441–442.

[19] See "News Front," *The Instructor* (May 1967), p. 6.

[20] See "News Front," *The Instructor* (August/September 1967), p. 6.

[21] John Brademas, "View from Capitol Hill," *Grade Teacher* (September 1967), pp. 15–16.

[22] Keliher, Alice V., "Project Head Start: What Have We Learned So Far?" (Lecture presented to American Association of School Administrators, Atlantic City, New Jersey, February 16, 1966), mimeographed.

[23] *Ibid.*

24 Theodor Schuchat, Washington Correspondent, "The Education scene," *Grade Teacher* (May–June 1966), p. 6.

25 Robert B. Semple, Jr., Special Reporter, "Head Start Value Found Temporary," *The New York Times* (October 23, 1966), p. 1.

26 Hartford Board of Education, "Child Development Program Pre-School Curriculum" (1965–1966), p. 1, mimeographed.

27 Hartford Board of Education, pp. 10–11.

28 See *The Journal of Educational Research*, 60 (February 1967), p. 287.

29 Nolan Estes, "Follow Through," *American Education* (September 1967), pp. 13–14.

30 Hartford Board of Education, p. 13.

31 Alfred Balk, "Western Man at His Best," *Saturday Review* (April 23, 1966), p. 15.

32 Bert Mills, *Instructor* Washington Réporter, "Washington Assignment," *The Instructor* (December 1966), p. 139.

33 Charles A. Ball, "South End: Training Ground for Peace Corps," *The Sunday Herald Traveler* (August 27, 1967), p. 24.

34 Office of Economic Opportunity, *A Nation Aroused*, First Annual Report (1965), p. 27–29. (Excellent summary of salient facts on federal projects.)

35 Community Action Program, *Upward Bound Guidelines, 1967–1968* (Washington: Office of Economic Opportunity, October, 1966). In introductory statement.

36 Mark Levy, "Upward Bound: A Summer Romance?" *The Reporter* (October 6, 1966), pp. 41–43.

37 "A Break for Lonely Losers," *Time* (May 26, 1967), p. 40.

38 Paula Dranov, "A Taste of College," *American Education* (April 1967), p. 25–27.

39 Committee on Education and the World of Work, "Jobs, Dropouts and Automation," *Education Age* (March–April 1966), p. 45.

40 Larry W. Hughes, "Dropouts Aren't Just a High School Problem — They're Ours, Too," *Grade Teacher*, 84 (January 1967), p. 24.

41 "Adult Education," *School and Society*, 94 (December 10, 1966), p. 445.

42 Thomas Carlyle, "Past and Present" in Book III: *The Modern Workers*, Chapter XIII: "Democracy" (New York: Harper Brothers, 1843).

43 "School Grants for Migrants," *Saturday Review* (July 15, 1967), p. 64.

44 "For Migrant Children," *Children*, 13 (September–October 1966), pp. 202–203.

45 Eleanor Fitzpatrick, "Tutoring — Baby-Sitting or High Art?" *The Independent School Bulletin*, 26 (February 1967), p. 50.

V

Representative School Programs

Poverty is a chief concern on the home front of our country. The challenge that it presents has caused concern on the part of those who could help our economy and lead us in improving our social environment, and on the part of those capable of guiding us toward the new education for all through a program of compensatory education so needed now as a temporary measure. This challenge can be met only through the cooperative efforts of all leaders, attacking all aspects of poverty and its resultant conditions in all phases of American life. The challenge requires redefining and re-establishment of our democratic objectives and values, with a revamping of our organizational agencies so that their purposes become these objectives and these values.

In the revitalizing of our educational process we need the help of people from every field of knowledge, the concern and support of every American citizen, and the equitable distribution of our tax money to provide this education, which is the basic enemy of poverty. We have made a good start, and although much of what we have done has been on a trial basis and the mistakes stand out sharply, the positive accomplishments outweigh them. It was impossible in Chapter IV to give consideration to all of the many ways in which our large problem has been attacked through the legislation enacted in the past few years. The same holds true in the consideration of the many programs and innovations that have been brought about in our schools by the stimulated interest in those who are deprived and by a renewed interest on the part of those who see the need for the improvement of our total education for all. In choosing those programs which might also be described as exemplary, we must remember that there are numerous others that deserve recognition and comment. Fortunately the recent literature in the field of compensatory education includes more complete referral to the many positive approaches being taken.

The discussion here will be limited to a consideration of types of programs that appear to realize the objectives that have been set up in defining the quality of education so needed by our deprived children and youth. It will also be, therefore, a consideration of steps taken toward the revitalizing of all education. Although the statements of the purposes of the programs vary, as do the formats, there does appear to be a set of broad objectives toward which all are working to some degree. They are all determined to discover the more basic abilities and talents of the deprived children and youth and give opportunity for their development, to help each learner to become motivated by his own desire to learn and to do well, and to raise the levels of both achievement and aspiration on the part of the young by inspiring better self-images, higher degrees of self-respect, and a larger measure of success.

If these programs are to be successful in achieving their purposes there are certain necessary aspects. They include well trained and sympathetic teachers, additional personnel to assist these teachers in meeting the broader problems that the child brings to school with him, a flexible school program that permits learning at all levels to take place simultaneously to meet individual differences, emphasis upon the various language arts, the building of experiences that the child lacks, and a plan for working closely with the parents, the community, and the various agencies that provide additional counseling. All programs express the need for additional financial assistance, which can be forthcoming in a limited amount from the school system itself, from local and national private groups or foundations, and from the federal government. The differences in the programs lie in the emphasis, the desired depth of the study, the nature of the program, research or functional change, the duration, and the type of evaluation.

How shall these new programs be evaluated? A survey of the current literature on deprivation and compensatory education shows little discussion on evaluation. Generalized suggestions are being presented as an outgrowth of some of the completed programs and these are listed for use in further programming. It is easy to cite the many failures in general education and in current compensatory programs and to say that a new program is successful if it corrects one or more of these faults. This approach, however, is a negative one, and evaluation on this basis would lead to just another *status quo* level, which we can no longer afford. This approach would not recognize the strengths in existing programs or give positive accomplishments as a basis for further growth. Few school administrators and teachers would be inspired to move ahead in meeting the challenge if the correction of current ills were the only purpose to which new effort would be put. The strengths of our general and compensatory education at this point are inconclusive, but they indicate the positive approach to meeting the challenge for change that must grow out of positive attitudes and a positive basic philosophy. If the positive approach is adopted by the total public down to the youngest child, improvement will follow — and hence this determines the broad base for evaluation.

Before endeavoring to put down stated recommendations for the evaluation of the education required for living successfully in today's world, before applying these statements to any specific programs that have grown out of the need for change, we must keep in mind that a comparatively short time has passed since Sputnik I awakened us to our deficits, some of long-standing, and that the need for improvement and change is still not universally accepted in our country. In relation to our broad problems and more specifically to education, the introduction of early programs did not begin until 1959 and 1960, and much of the research and the more finely designed programs were begun around 1962 and 1963. There has been little opportunity for a long-range study of the results, and the short-range view often puts too much emphasis upon the newness of the ideas and the inclusion of many techniques and procedures that could not realistically be undertaken by many school systems.

We must consider also the purpose for evaluating programs. If evaluation is limited to compensatory education, a crash program for immediate correction of the worst in the deprived areas, then the evaluation becomes narrow and must be made, not on the amount of money received or on the excitement engendered in its spending, but on a careful statement of the purposes and procedures to which attention is drawn within the light of the specific school or school system, the particular condition of the environment, the people, and the specific needs that brought about the program in the first place. The evaluation would be in terms of the degree to which the purposes of a specific program were met and in terms of specific gains that are clearly observable for that particular situation at the time that the study was carried on. A question immediately arises as to the ways in which even these specific gains can be adequately measured. Do we have the evaluative techniques or the appropriate forms of measurement to use on these innovations?

There are those in the research field who hold firmly to the conviction that the only valuable type of investigation is the isolating of a clearly defined problem that can be studied in such a way as to be able to compare an experimental and a control group. Also, there are those who would still rely strongly upon evidences of change in the exact measurement of the intelligence quotient as indicating potential, and in a child's score on a reading test stated in terms of grade level accomplishment. These approaches to research have been used for many years in the public schools, and, by gearing them to the average middle-class child, norms have been developed and children judged. It is sincerely hoped that some of the current studies will indicate new ways of evaluating the potential, development, growth, and overall progress in achievement of deprived children in the light of their backgrounds and their deprivations, and beginning from the point at which positive learning began to have its effect. This presents a real challenge to those in the research field, for here also there is a need for change in philosophy, in attitude and in procedures. A change in the area of measurement of growth will do more for the success of the teaching and of the learning, not only of the deprived child but of all children, than any other single change.

Evaluative Considerations

Until we have better defined measures to relate to our philosophy of the total new educational approach, the following would seem to be appropriate at least as tentative bases for any evaluation of the programs being initiated under compensatory education for the deprived child and the deprived youth:

1. Is the background of the study stated clearly in terms of facts? These facts, concerning the average income, housing, employment, family organization, literacy, language, education level, and parent and community attitudes in the setting of the school or school system, should provide the basis of understanding for the needs of the program.

2. Are the purposes of the study, program or project clear and definitive in terms of the desired results? The philosophy as pre-

viously stated gives generalized statements of broader and more inclusive results that good education should produce, but these can be realized only as more specific improvements and changes are spelled out as purposes of the program to be undertaken. The breadth and the length of the program would determine the number of closely related purposes.

3. Does the program include in the statement of its purposes not only an indication of the immediate desired results, but also the important idea that all progress forward must be open-ended, showing that the changes are to do far more than serve the immediate — that the realization of these purposes as stated will serve as steps for further change and further improvement as needed?

4. Is a clear picture presented of the actual changes that will take place within the school itself in order to open the way for fulfilling these purposes? All will be lost if fine sounding goals are set for the children within the framework of rigid lock-step procedures and arbitrarily stated expectations. If we are to take these children where they are in their development, growth, and achievement, the statement of the program will show new points of view, changes in requirements, and new understandings of terminology, evidencing that the school itself has faced its need for change and has made the change, and that its philosophy, curriculum, procedures, and teaching and learning process have been made flexible enough to fit each deprived child or youth.

5. Are the specific purposes translated into terms of rich experiences to be provided for the children, showing these in a sequential pattern beginning with those needed immediately, but also indicating the direction to be taken in further planning?

6. As these needed experiences of all types are expressed and become the curriculum for these particular children, are they planned in such a way as to be of value in the total life picture of the child, thus aiding him to use these experiences for the interpretation and understanding of himself within his home, his school, and his community?

7. Are all procedures, techniques, special materials, basic knowledge and information that are a part of this program discussed within the framework of the teaching-learning process to be employed? This consideration must clearly evidence the purposes as stated, the changes within the school, the broad experiences planned, and the reasons why this process will proceed in the manner designated. All of these should implement the flexible curriculum, putting emphasis

on guiding the child in gaining related information, building basic concepts, and incorporating these concepts within experiences, and, through the child's recognition and understanding of his own abilities and his own goals and values, lead him to desire and achieve continuously higher levels of reasoning and of creative thinking. The description of the teaching-learning process must be expressed in terms of the positive and challenging meaning of the readiness and the total maturity of the child as he is, and of the level of expectations for him. No program is complete without the setting of the expectations of the program — which can only be the goals of the individual child taking part. If these are stated, one can quickly tell whether the school itself has become the environment in which they can be realized. There can be no preconceived notions or preset limits for this child no matter how poor his background, no matter how few his experiences. The teacher's attitudes, the school, and the curricular organization must all be of an open-ended, flexible nature allowing each child to move along in his learning at his own pace, with satisfaction, with goals set ahead and reset as they are reached, and with a desire and determination to seek knowledge that he can use because he sees the reason for it. As yet we cannot measure a child's potential, and nothing can be more exciting than to witness a child discovering for himself previously unrealized abilities. There can be guidelines to the expectations, but no limits to either depth or breadth. The statement of the specific purposes, together with each step in the development of the program, determines for that specific program open-ended expectations that can be stated in terms of (1) the enriching of learning, knowing, and thinking; (2) the deepening of the learning and the thinking; (3) the developing of the dynamic potential and the freeing of the learner to work toward his own level; (4) the development of positive attitudes, creative thinking, and a creative spirit toward life and its many challenges based on enduring interests and proven abilities; (5) the building of enduring personal values from a healthy, positive, imaginative and thoughtful approach to living.

8. Does this program for compensatory education, leading toward a new education, include a statement of the ways in which the successful achievement of the purposes set can be determined? Whether it be through comparison, through measurement, or through observation, it must be clear from the beginning of the program how the successes can be recognized and why outcomes that are less than successful are to be recognized as steps towards further

exploration and endeavor. The important aspects will be those steps forward that have been taken towards the purposes and goals set, which can lead beyond any compensatory form of education to the ideal of that which is vital for all children. And suggestions should be given for a follow-up study so that the point at which the children, the program, and the school have arrived as a result of this endeavor becomes clear.

9. If a program evaluated in these terms proves helpful to one or more of our deprived children or youth, a step in the right direction has been taken. Ideally, schools and school systems will be able to see the possibilities of incorporating this type of evaluation into the regular daily classroom. As the changes are made the values should be in terms of the quality of education possible without expenditure of vast amounts of additional funds, *but* with sufficient funds to permit the pre-service and in-service training of teachers, the revitalizing of the thinking, operation and organization of the school, and sufficient teachers to keep the student-teacher ratio small enough so that all of the experiences, the total curriculum, the teaching, and the learning can be judged excellent through this type of evaluation. The time should come when this is not a picture of something extra being done but of our good educational system as it is.

With the use of such an evaluative scheme as this, it would be possible for those in the field of education for the deprived to read through the description of a program and the statements of results and be able to interpret them in such a way as to enrich their thinking toward further possible steps that might be taken either in the form of other projects or programs or in terms of ways to help these children in the school's everyday program. In reviewing the results of many such programs, the school that is desirous of change would have the opportunity to gain much from the thinking of those who have carried out previous programs, but we must remember that the interpretation has to be made by those who are "in tune" with the thinking, attitudes, and aspirations for the new and vital education. Our final goal is the rich educational experience as the opportunity for every child, with the freeing of the child to work toward and through this experience, thus becoming a dynamic person, a creative person, and the responsible citizen of his community and country. This is the final goal for all compensatory education and for all education.

Reports on the numerous programs and projects are becoming more available as annotated listings appear. Those who have had wide experience with the deprived child and youth are devoting considerable time to the preparation of the literature in the form of individual descriptive writings, or sections within the excellent compilations being issued. Funds are also available for the collection and processing of data concerning the programs. For interested readers there is included here a sampling of descriptions of programs that seem pertinent and that offer a sound groundwork on which to build. In choosing these, there is no intent to negate the value of certain others. Those who are interested in this exciting and challenging movement toward a better education must keep abreast of the materials being prepared and published and, through their own experience, extract the values from the ones that to them, within their own experiences and situations, seem most pertinent and applicable.

Speaking generally, the programs have proved successful in helping the child to overcome many of his deficits as the emphases have been placed on the development of listening and language skills, concept formation, and further readiness skills. It would appear that the deprived child who has had the opportunity of taking part in one of the preschool experimental programs is more nearly ready for some success in the conventional elementary school. It would be best if this child could continue on into experimental or improved programs at the elementary level so that his process of education would be a continuous one within an educational organization especially designed for him. Experimental programs at the elementary school level and above have reported success in improving the school performance of the deprived child by providing opportunity for the experiences needed and for the gaining of the skills necessary within a curriculum and within the use of materials again especially adapted to this child's readiness and need.

The deprived child is not new to us in education. In the 1930's the schools were attempting to work with the children who, because of limited language skills and poor background, were failing to learn to read. Before World War II teachers in the large cities and those working with poor farm children were looking for ways of helping the deprived who, because of their difficulty in learning to read and write, were lagging behind the other children in achievement.

Nor should the emphasis upon the need for change in our educational program imply that this need exists in every instance.

There have always been outstanding creative teachers who have quietly gone their ways providing an enrichment of the school experiences, fitting these to the specific needs of specific children and deriving satisfaction from seeing deprived children succeed and move on through an educational system toward good personal accomplishment.

The Demonstration Guidance Project

This pioneer project began in 1956 in one of the junior high schools of New York City and has served as a model for many other projects. This six-year program began with an experimental group of 717 seventh, eighth and ninth grade pupils, chiefly Negro and Puerto Rican, from disadvantaged homes, and was continued through 1962, when these three classes of children were graduated from high school. The success of this program was claimed because of the improvement of reading ability and school marks, increased school attendance, increased IQ figures, reduction in discipline problems, and an increase in parent participation.

The children selected for this project were thought to have latent academic aptitude, although they ranked low in school achievement and in IQ. Within the program special emphasis was placed on the improvement of basic reading skills, and all teachers in the several subject matter areas were responsible for the teaching of reading, while special remedial reading groups were organized when necessary. Children were stimulated to read through book fairs and circulating libraries of paperbacks, and the ones who read a given number of books wore badges that said, "Readers are Leaders." Within the classroom the children were surrounded with pictures of successful Negroes and Puerto Ricans to motivate them to further effort and to improve their self-concepts. The school remained open after school hours to provide places for quiet study, and counseling was given to provide guidance in further education and career planning. The "cultural sights" of the children were raised through a program of listening to good music, going to plays, and attending other cultural events within the area. Each of these opportunities was preceded by a careful study of what they were to hear or see, and was followed by a discussion of the occasion upon their return to school. These cultural experiences were extended to include bus trips to historic sights, visits to museums, hospitals, laboratories, and factories, and attendance at operas and movies.

This project was considered a compensatory program. As many services as possible were provided these pupils. Curricular changes were made, classes were small, and although the major emphasis was upon the improvement of reading through remedial instruction, stress was also placed upon speech and arithmetic. It was considered a successful project by the participating students and by the teachers.

The evaluation was made on the basis of comparisons between the three project classes (1960, 1961, and 1962) with those students from the same junior high and senior high school in the classes of 1956, 1958 and 1959. Comparisons were made on the number of earned academic diplomas from high school, on the number completing high school with no failures, on grade averages, on rank in class, on the number being admitted to institutions for further study or higher education, and on the dropout rate. Those taking part in the project showed gain in each of these areas and, in addition, the teachers saw additional gains in their self-images, in their aspirations for the future, and in their personalities. There could not be exact duplication of circumstances or of the characteristics of the students, and it would appear that this was not taken into consideration, but the percentages on the comparisons were significant enough to prove the value of introducing compensatory services at that time.[1]

Higher Horizons Program

The extension of the Demonstration Guidance Project became known as the Higher Horizons Program in New York City. It began in the fall of 1959 in selected elementary and junior high schools within depressed areas, and was later extended to the senior high schools. This was the first of the major educational programs designed to help disadvantaged children. Its prime objective was to seek out, uncover, and develop human talent in the schools. Every effort was made to work on the problems of wasted potential among these children of lowered achievement and the increasingly large numbers of dropouts at the secondary level. In order to improve the school program, each junior high and elementary school within the experiment received an additional allotment of teachers who served as curriculum assistants, teacher trainers, and teacher-training specialists in reading, mathematics, social studies, and science. The major emphasis, again, was in reading. As the program progressed most schools received three additional especially trained teachers, two for academic stimulation and improvement of program and one to plan the cultural enrichment. Each group of 10 schools had an additional teacher of science and an additional teacher of library. Within the junior high these specialists organized small classes in reading, mathematics, and foreign language study, with about half of these corrective and remedial services going to children with greater academic potential.

The Demonstration Guidance Program dealt only with those who were academically able. With the extension of this program to the Higher Horizons, all children were included within the schools used. The schools represented various degrees of deprivation and differed also in the make-up of the population of the school, some being predominately Negro and others Puerto Rican or Portuguese and Italian. Since the schools represented two different districts and different school programs, the use of the additional personnel was determined by need. After the assignments to the schools, the responsibilities were determined by the principals of the buildings. As a result, not all of the schools had all of the services, but all schools had some.

This program was based upon the premise that the change that is desired in an individual child can be best brought about by directly influencing the child himself, then the teacher, and then the parent. As it has been stated, the desire was to raise the aspiration levels. This had to be accomplished first within the child as his key to better self-motivation and achievement. The teacher was considered the important element within this program, for he necessarily also had to believe in the child and in the program itself. The program was deemed successful because of the faith that teachers did have in the pupils and the opportunities that were given to see that faith materialize. Some 14 specific objectives or purposes were cited for this program, and its operation fell into nine categories: inspirational, guidance, curriculum enrichment, curriculum adaptation, remedial, teacher training, cultural, parent education, and record keeping and evaluation.

It is interesting to note that the evaluation of this particular program was conducted by the United States Bureau of Education Research because it was felt that those within the program who were responsible for its operation ought not to be in charge of judging its effectiveness. As the studies have been released, by comparing the children from the Higher Horizons schools with those not involved in the program, it has been seen that gains were made, particularly on reading scores and verbal IQ scores. In the subjective evaluation by those involved in the program itself, enthusiasm was expressed and there was a general feeling that significant improvement had been made not only in reading but also in the interest and participation of the children within the schools, in a better identification of potential, improved attendance, morale and behavior, in an enrichment of the background of the pupils, in parent participation and teacher morale, and in the guidance and follow-up of individual cases.

The gains shown in this program should warrant its adoption in the school system. It has meant a change in attitudes and in school programming, and as other schools look to this program as a guide they can learn much through a study of the analysis, questioning, and recommendations that have resulted from it. The fact is that school programs in other cities are now using the phrase "Higher Horizons" to identify either the school itself or the program being maintained, thus giving evidence of the influence that this major endeavor is having.

One of the outstanding features of this program has been the carefully planned evaluation and questioning that has gone on. Questions have been asked and every effort made to find satisfactory answers. The final evaluation comes from an intensive experimental-control study using tests, reading scores, personal evaluations, record cards, questionnaires, and check lists. Statistical analysis is applied to the evaluation of the growth and development of those participating. Where no form of measurement could take place, samplings were taken of opinions. Perhaps one of the weaknesses (which also could be said of every program) is the inability to state or to weight which of the many variables being considered in a program as extensive as this have more or less influence on the results.

The following statement is made by Jacob Landers:

> Higher Horizons is an organized effort to effect a major breakthrough in the education of those who need special help to be able to make their maximum contribution to our American democracy. It has established the basic philosophy and indicated the major areas of operation. It inspires hope and supplies the personnel to translate that hope into reality. What might formerly have been done sporadically or in isolation is now part of a total program, with far greater impact upon the child. If Higher Horizons has done nothing else, it has provided a rallying point in the fight for our disadvantaged children, and a peg upon which all — supervisors, teachers, parents, and pupils — might hang their hopes. (93:98)

An Early School Admissions Project

A project for young deprived children in Baltimore was initiated in the fall of 1962 as a three-year educational program and has been financed jointly by the Baltimore City Public Schools and the Ford Foundation. This was an experiment to determine whether early admission to school can overcome any of the barriers to learning that environmental factors seem to impose. The basis for establishing this program was the belief that the patterns of learning and of personality development are fairly well established for most individuals before the end of the earliest years of school. If this is true, foundations for attitudes, habits, and knowledge originate in the preschool experiences of children. This program was planned to develop in the children a wholesome self-concept, to help them to acquire a drive to learn and, at the same time, to develop interests and capabilities. In order for a child to succeed in this, the belief was that he should be assured of security and affection, be involved in experiences that would arouse curiosity and extend his horizons, and be guided in developing his interests and his abilities.

In the *Progress Report of 1964* is given this list of factors in the home environment that might damage developmental patterns:

1. Illness in the home.
2. Large number of siblings.
3. Death.
4. Separation.
5. Divorce.
6. Illegitimacy.
7. Poor family relationships.
8. Emotional disturbances.
9. Migration.
10. Limited education of parents.
11. Limited social and economic circumstances.

The educational aspect of the program was planned to enrich the lives of four- and five-year-olds, ordinarily not in school but requiring educational services of a compensatory nature. In addition, it was a research project designed to discover ways to accelerate the achievement of children limited in their development by environmental factors beyond their control, to increase parental understanding of the values of education and the degree to which parents accept the responsibility for the education of their children, and to facilitate communications between the school and community agencies as they work together to assist children and adults in depressed areas to raise their aspirations and improve their levels of competency.

Prior to the initiation of the project, five factors were used to identify an area of disadvantaged population:

1. High rate of housing — low rental, low value, dilapidated or deficient.
2. High rate of density of population.
3. High rate of adult and juvenile delinquency.
4. Low family income.
5. High rate of unskilled or semi-skilled workers.

Two schools or centers were used at the beginning of the project, and two others were added later. Children who took part in the project had to be four years of age on or before December 31. Parents had to signify interest in their child's entering the project by coming to the school for an interview, permitting home visits by those connected with the project, and permitting medical checks on the children. These children were also tested with the Columbia Mental Maturity Test and a Verbal Maturity Test that was designed by the Division of Educational Testing of the Baltimore Schools.

The instructional program was based on two objectives — one, to help children from depressed areas overcome those academic handicaps that otherwise would confront them upon their entrance to regular elementary school programs, and two, to determine those learning experiences needed to overcome limitations imposed by factors in the environment of the children. The school environment offered sensory-rich learning to arouse interest, stimulate thinking, and provoke questioning, and was warm and accepting in order to dispel fear and enable these children to develop feelings of "belongingness," self-confidence, adequacy, and security. Every effort was made to incorporate into the learning activities the significant components of experience at any developmental level of the child as needed.

Each center had a team of four adults: the senior teacher, assistant teacher, teacher aide, and volunteer. The senior teacher was selected from the Baltimore City Public Schools and qualified as a competent and experienced teacher of children of this age and one who had proven skillful in working with deprived children and their parents;

the assistant teacher was also trained to work with young children and had had experience but was selected for this project from outside the Baltimore Schools in order not to deplete their existing staff. Some of these assistant teachers came from private nursery schools, private kindergartens, or parochial schools. The teacher aide assisted with duties in the center that did not require teacher training, and was also responsible for maintaining the clerical work and the records. The volunteer placed with the group was recruited from the membership of three community agencies, and in some instances lived in the community where the project center was located.

The guidelines for the curriculum development for the project were as follows:

1. Develop communication skills.
2. Develop ability to understand quantitative relationships.
3. Develop aesthetic values through experiences in art, literature, and music.
4. Foster good health and further physical development.
5. Develop an understanding of self and a wholesome self-concept.
6. Develop an awareness and an understanding of the environment.

Since the major goal of the program was to develop a positive self-concept on the part of the child, it was thought necessary to help the child to establish habits of cleanliness and care of property, to communicate and to relate to others, to share with others in the enjoyment of music, art, and literature, and to develop an awareness of the world around him through a wide range of experiences. The content of the curriculum was based on an organizational plan within each area that would show the concepts to be formed, the ideas to be gained leading to the development of that particular concept, and the learning experiences that should be provided.

Record keeping was a very important aspect of this project and included the pupil's personal history and a check list for progress in vocabulary and language development, in number understandings, in visual and auditory discrimination, and in the use of materials. An anecdotal record was kept when there was need to make note of any particular aspect of the child's growth or development while in the situation. In addition to these an Index of Growth was used, which is an Evaluative Scale for Four-to Seven-Year-Olds developed by the Elementary Division of the Baltimore Public Schools, which contains 31 items to guide the teacher in estimating the level of maturity of the child in relation to various aspects of physical, mental, social, and emotional development.

In addition to these formal records, samples of the children's work were filed as were the teachers' own record of the educational experiences. This included daily summaries, details that appeared most significant, tape recordings of happenings, movies, still pictures or slides that were used with the children, and a class activity log, which gave the step-by-step picture of the day with any records of trips or visits taken.

Considerable detail has been given concerning this project because it was planned as a program that might be used as a model for other cities. It was designed for children who would go on into the public schools. It was hoped that such a program would prepare these children for success within the regular educational plan. A final report on this project will soon be available, as will the results of the research that has accompanied the project.[2]

The teachers in these centers have reported observing gains on the part of the children in the understanding and use of language, in the development of skill in auditory and visual discrimination, and in becoming more independent, following directions, using materials, and taking part in new activities. These gains could be identified from the records and the check lists, which proved to be a valuable means of noting progress. The parents also indicated that they were aware of progress on the part of the children in using more words, in using materials, and in getting along better with other children. These ideas would have come from the questionnaires. The kindergarten teachers who admitted children from this project the following year noted a good adjustment at the beginning of school and ease in adjusting to routine procedures, eagerness to participate in new activities, and the ability to express themselves more easily and in better form than the other entrants from that community who had not attended that project. Credit is given in some of the evaluations of this project to the fact that the senior teacher has had previous experience with disadvantaged children and enjoys being with them and working with their parents.

This has been a program, carefully planned, well organized, and fitting to the children in the situation, that can well serve as a model for the type of compensatory education highly desirable.

Experimental Nursery School Program

The Experimental Nursery School Program was operated by the School District of Philadelphia in cooperation with the Philadelphia Council for Community Advancement. The target area chosen for the location of this program was North Philadelphia, which has the following characteristics:

1. Negroes constitute 71 percent of the population in the target area as contrasted with 27 percent of Negroes in the total city population.
2. The dwelling units are smaller. . . .
3. 27 percent of the housing is classified as "deteriorated" or "dilapidated" in comparison to 13 percent. . . .
4. The median value of dwelling units in 1960 was assessed at $6,915 as compared to a median assessment of $8,700. . . .
5. The median income in 1960 was $3,383 in comparison to a median of $4,189. . . .
6. The median amount of education in 1960 was 8.7 years as contrasted to 9.6 years. . . .[3]

The range of these figures on the lower side of the median was much greater in the target area and, hence, the range of problems was very wide.

The nursery schools were located in public schools in this target area and were considered an integral part of the elementary school program within each school. The children were to be three years and seven months to four years and six months old when the program began. These children were to be without serious physical or mental handicaps, living with their families in low-value and low-standard housing with the family on public services or mothers working, or living in broken homes. A random sample of 30 children was chosen for the experimental group in each school and selected from a total group whose interested mothers were interviewed previously. An additional sample of 15 children was selected for the control group.

This program was also based on the assumptions that these deprived children would require intellectual, social, and cultural enrichment in advance of school age, that a preschool program would afford the opportunity to work closely with the parents of these children, and, in addition, that an early childhood program would provide an opportunity for community agencies to relate themselves to the development of children in a preventive sense.

Each school had a morning and an afternoon group of 15 children, each with one head teacher who was fully accredited and selected from the staff of the Philadelphia Public Schools because she had had previous early childhood teaching experience, and one assistant teacher who was a liberal arts graduate with no teaching experience. The selection of a non-trained assistant teacher was deliberate. The intention was to encourage persons with teaching potential to enter the teaching field where the challenge is apparent. In addition, both senior and sophomore students from Temple University observed and participated in the group, and other volunteers were used whenever possible. The classes operated four days a week; on the fifth day the teachers were engaged in continuing their in-service training program, making home visits, or conferring with parents, home-school coordinators, the social worker, or other school personnel.

This program continued through the school year 1965–1966. The in-service training of the staff continued with more emphasis on seminars on the development and evaluation of curriculum guidelines for providing the kinds of learning experiences needed to help the disadvantaged child. The staff had the opportunity to observe other centers and to work closely with the social service staff. Experimentation and identification of materials and techniques that had been effective were continued throughout. The staff worked on curriculum guidelines, but as this project ended, only suggestions were available concerning this curriculum, which it was felt should be based on extensive research. There had also been strong opposition to developing a "packaged nursery school curriculum for disadvantaged children" since all teaching should be individualized for particular children, for the particular city as well as the particular community in which they live.

During 1965–1966 the teaching staff considered the following questions in their planning:

1. How can what has been learned about child development and good education for young children during the past 25 years be retained in the face of the present crash preschool program hysteria?
2. What are the capabilities, limitations, and present needs of the children in . . . Program?
3. What can the children be reasonably expected to achieve in one year?
4. How can a program that pressures children to such a degree that it compounds their problems rather than helps them be avoided?
5. How can making the child over to fit the school's image be avoided?

6. How can the effectiveness of any instructional materials or teaching procedures be evaluated without objective measures?
7. How effective can teachers be if parents are often severely limited, unmotivated, and hostile?[4]

The *Progress Report* on this experimental program for the year 1964–1965 contains considerable information helpful to anyone interested in planning such a nursery school program and includes, in an appendix, samples of the materials used for the building of the guidelines of their program.

It is interesting to note, in the discussion of the educational program in this *Report*, that exception is taken to the idea that programs need to be new and different or future-oriented, which could "conceivably result in throwing the baby out with the bath." This would seem to contradict some of the expressions in this book concerning a new education. If the attitudes of the teacher and the programs of a school are changed from a rigid and formal organization of subject matter to be taught to a flexible curriculum made up of stimulating and rich experiences made to fit the child, even the deprived child, that particular school and school program becomes "new." There is justification, however, for the comment in this report, for all of us are fully aware of the fact that the good preschools of today come more closely to the stated ideal type of program planning than do the schools beyond — the elementary, the junior high, senior high, and the college. The preschool has been interested in *the child*, and although the trend is to introduce, as a part of a spiraling curriculum, the beginning of each of the subject matter areas with the three-, the four-, and the five-year olds, all of these learnings are planned at the child's level and fitted to his present needs. It is also stressed that this program is built on the child's need at his present stage of development. And again, this is correctly spoken, for not until the child's needs are met where he *is* can he move forward in development and in learning.

The emphasis in the Experimental Nursery Program was on a proper balance between activities that are self-initiated and those that are structured, thus permitting from the first opportunities for self-expression, for the exercising of the child's ideas, and for experiences that are used to extend his knowledge of the world around him and help him to build the skills that will serve as a foundation for his later learning. This program also identified a deprived child's deficits as being in the areas of language facility, visual and auditory discrimination, concept building, self-esteem, listening and attending, learning good motor control and coordination, and gaining information about the world around him. These were the skills with which this program was concerned. This is another excellent example of a program that followed the pattern of evaluation previously set.

In the reporting of some of the research findings of this program, those in the experimental group gained some six points in the Stanford-Binet IQ scores, and eight points as compared with children who had no nursery school experience. Gains were also noted on the Peabody Picture Book Vocabulary Test and The Philadelphia Verbal Abilities Test, but no consistent difference was shown in the Goodenough-Draw-A-Man Test. The experimental group was also rated as more casual, expressive, and flexible in its reactions to tests and learning situations in the kindergarten following the nursery school program. It is hoped, however, that in preschool programs now under study there will be forthcoming some new measures of the behavioral and more basic personal gains on the part of these children, which could very well exist with little gain in test results as they are now used.

Enrichment Program of the Institute for Developmental Studies

Another program was initiated in 1962 in New York City by the Institute for Developmental Studies as an enrichment program for young children from the economically deprived sections of the city. The Institute was founded at Downtown Medical Center in Brooklyn in 1958, moved to New York Medical College in 1960, and then moved to New York University School of Education in July, 1966. Its first interest was in research relating to children from varying environments, particularly in the verbal and linguistic skills that these children brought to school with them.

In 1962, following a conference at Arden House that was attended by members of the Institute and representative educators, a co-operative plan developed between the Institute and the New York Board of Education for the introduction of an enrichment program. This program, as described in the 1965 *Annual Report*, from which the following information was gleaned and again in *Proceedings* of November 1966, is still in progress, is serving children from preschool through grade three, and is located in selected public schools in the Harlem area. It has also been recognized as a research as well as a demonstration program that, through providing for early intervention for these young children, is attempting to reverse the effects of social deprivation through the designing of special curricula. This program exemplifies one of the major evaluative points in that its specific purposes have to do with the study of the immediate effects of such an enrichment program presented through intervention. At the same time the long-range aspect of the program is designated for a study of its effects on later learning and possible learning problems.

The more specific and immediate purposes to be served by the Experimental Enrichment Program are to study the responsiveness of the children, their ability patterns, and their improvement in specific skills as these are related first to the patterns of environmental deprivation and then to the "therapeutic" curriculum that has been planned for them in the areas of language, mathematics, reading skills, science, and concept formation. In addition to these, the modification of the intellectual performance and the academic achievement of these children will be studied to determine the effects of this special program as they enter the regular public school classes. Since this program is based upon the provision of successful experiences, efforts will be made to determine whether this opportunity will promote the desired positive attitudes on the part of each child toward himself and his society and raise his aspirations. Parent-school interaction is being encouraged from the beginning of this program so that through understanding and involvement the parents may be encouraged and helped to both supplement and reinforce the goals and values set by this school program.

The children taking part were selected from those whose parents had applied for their children's admission following the announcement of this program in the community. They were carefully selected on the basis of specific criteria requiring that the child be in good physical condition and free of unusual physical difficulties and severe emotional or behavior problems, that the child and the parents must be English-speaking and the family must come from a lower socio-economic class level defined by an index prepared by the Institute, based on the amount of education and the occupational status of the family's supporting member, that the child be of proper age for admission to the kindergarten as of September for the following year, and that the parents be prepared to assume the responsibility for the child's regular attendance in the program. These children were then randomly assigned to the experimental group in the ratio of approximately one control to two experimental.

A three-stage sequence of learning is used as a basis for the program, the sensorimotor, the perceptual, and the ideational-representational. Emphasis is placed upon creating a climate receptive to learning, enhancing the self-identity and self-value of each child, improving language usage through listening, labeling and conversing, using carefully chosen books that meet the standards themselves, training auditory and visual perception, and conceptual training. One of the innovations within this program is the emphasis on the use of field trips, the taking of photographs by the classes, the providing of listening centers using tapes, the use of games for the purpose of learning the rules, presenting new learning to small groups and using tutorial instruction when necessary, and experimentation with many of the exciting new materials such as the Cuisenaire Color Rods and prepared materials from a Science Materials Center. Each new procedure is carefully planned to provide the greatest benefit to the child and to permit evaluation of its worth. For example, the field trips serve several purposes.

> Before, during, and after trips, the children have an opportunity to differentiate the real from the symbolic, to organize and classify material, to develop number concepts . . . and to strengthen expressive language skills through discussions and by drawing pictures of the trip.[5]

It is stressed that these innovations are not yet permanent features of the curriculum, but are being evaluated for their effectiveness. Several years of experimentation must follow before this program will commit itself to any particular curriculum, method, or type of teaching material.

The evaluation techniques set up in this program include the giving of a battery of individually administered standardized tests, which include the Stanford-Binet, the Peabody Picture Book Vocabulary Test, and the Columbia Mental Maturity Scale. All subjects are retested with the same instruments toward the end of the school year. In addition, interview techniques are used with both the child and the parent as well as a series of observational techniques, and the eventual reporting of the results of this study will show the relationships between the material collected from the interviews and observations and the achievement on the standardized tests.

In a paper that presents initial findings drawn from some of the data collected during the first two years by Goldstein it is interesting to note that only those children who had experienced the enriched curriculum were able either to maintain or to increase their achievement levels, while there was evidence of a decline after both the first and second years in the mean IQ of the control groups. Further indications point to the fact that the emphasis on language development in the enrichment curriculum has resulted in significant gains. In the early statements of the parents it is noted that the children, by introducing attitudes gained in the classroom, had brought about a variety of behavioral changes in the members of their families and that both the quality and the degree of interaction between child and parent and child and sibling had been enhanced.[6]

This program should be followed carefully by those with an interest in compensatory education, for it is set up in such a manner that the evaluation possible can be most valuable not only to the children, their parents, and the community, but to all who would be concerned in the initiating of similar programs. When there is a publication or an issuing of recommended curricula and procedures as an outgrowth of this program, it will be interesting to note the recommendations. Will the purpose be the application of these to all deprived children or will those who have developed the curricula and the procedures warn those who are working with deprived children that once again it must be said that curricula and procedures used must be determined in the light of the specific situation and the specific children concerned so that suggestions made must be adapted? There can be no doubt as to the value of this program to all in terms of the analysis of the results and the guidance and inspiration that it will provide toward the development of excellent guidelines for outstanding compensatory education and in turn for outstanding general education. This program is built on substantial research and no doubt will produce equally substantial research results.

An additional contribution being made through this program is the provision for teacher training for both enrichment and non-enrichment staff teachers. Seminars are held and there is opportunity for active participation in the program itself. The enrichment teacher is not only trained to be a highly competent classroom teacher, but is also a researcher as she prepares curricular materials, evaluates her experimental enrichment techniques, takes part in conferences, and represents the Institute in numerous ways to extend the information to others about the work going on.

The Great Cities Program for School Improvement

Concern about the urban school resulted in a meeting of representatives of 10 of the major city school systems in 1956 for the discussion of possible programs for vocational education. As a result of this meeting the Research Council of the Great Cities Program for School Improvement, a nonprofit educational organization, was formally incorporated in February of 1961. Membership now includes 15 major cities, and the chief purpose of the organization is to conduct studies of unique problems that are faced by these great cities in their efforts to meet the comprehensive public school needs of their citizens and to plan for the continuing development of improved educational opportunity for all children. As was stated, the first concern was the development of programming in the vocational education field, which began in 1956. Following the study, recommendations were made in 1959 by the Council for changes in this field. In 1957, this group prepared one of the first documents calling attention to the special educational needs of urban children and youth whose background and environment differed from the prevailing culture. As a result, experiments in the education of the culturally deprived began in 1960 in the urban areas of Chicago, Philadelphia, Detroit, Pittsburgh, Cleveland, Buffalo, Milwaukee, St. Louis, San Francisco, and Washington. These programs were assisted by grants from the Ford Foundation and organized under the title of the Great Cities School Improvement Program. The Research Council has initiated further studies dealing with fiscal policies for education, the preparation of teachers for the disadvantaged, the modernization of outmoded schools, instructional materials designed particularly to meet the needs of urban youth, and the exchange of information as it is received concerning various interests between its members and interested persons at all governmental levels. It recognizes the importance of cooperative efforts in the planning and executing of worthwhile educational advances.[7]

The individual programs that have grown out of this larger improvement program differ in detail, but there are certain common factors. Four of these are:

Awareness that the culturally deprived student is usually poor in communication skills and that this inability causes failure in other subjects;

Willingness to experiment with a broad range of teaching materials

such as filmstrips, records, and television, and with administrative
approaches such as team teaching and flexible programing;

Strenuous efforts to search out and use community help, such as
various public health and welfare services or private philanthropic
organizations and business and industry;

Preparation both in teaching skills and in attitudes of teachers involved in the great cities programs and, happily, the concern, devo-
tion, and enthusiasm which ordinarily result from that involvement.[8]

Some of the programs that have been an outgrowth of this larger
project are described below.

Baltimore. The Early School Admissions Project, as previously
discussed, experimental in nature, was planned to attempt to establish a foundation for the continuity of experience, to promote
parental understanding of the growth and development of children
and the roles of parents, to augment and increase the effectiveness
of the project's staff through the involvement of volunteer personnel,
and to better coordinate their work with community agencies.

Buffalo. In the development of a program adapted to the needs
of the culturally different, the emphasis was placed upon the raising
of the academic achievements of the pupils in five of the elementary
schools, particularly in the area of reading, by introducing necessary
services through additional personnel, among whom were reading
specialists, special reading teachers, and speech therapists.

Chicago. A special project here was planned for the development
of an improved program for boys and girls over 14 years of age who
had not graduated from the eighth grade, through the planning of
an in-school and an out-of-school program; the in-school phase has
grown into Educational and Vocational Guidance Centers where
these children may be grouped in nongraded classes for intensive
help.

Cleveland. The phases of the public school program which have
received attention and considered successful because of their more
promising practices are: An intern program for prospective teachers,
transition classes for pupils entering from elementary schools, the
organization of dropout prevention program classes through the industrial arts and the home economics departments involving the
"least likely" pupils. Other satisfactory innovations were the pre-
orientation for new teachers, and programs for secondary reading,
home visitation, after-school and Saturday recreation, and a summer
camp.

Detroit. The promising practices here related to the reinforcement of the teaching of reading in the classroom, the encouragement of reading for pleasure and information, the development of an "integrated," urban environment reading series for grades one, two, and three, the organization of a summer school program, and the use of the project school as a community agency.

Houston. An effective practice emerged from the Talent Presentation Project as a back-to-school drive conducted during the month of August when twenty teachers were employed to screen the records of incoming seventh grade students, and to visit homes of the students enrolled in the project classes and of those who would be eligible for the incoming class. In the effort to create interest on the part of the community, the results were excellent. A large percentage returned to school rather than dropping out, and 200 who had previously dropped out of school returned, some after an absence of two years. As a part of the larger school community opportunity project in education (SCOPE), the student tutorial education project (STEP) was an experiment in which volunteer college students tutored educationally disadvantaged high school students and, although the program was short there were indications that a tutoring program such as this was valuable. "Workreation," a pilot program, designed to provide work, study, and recreation activities for high school dropouts promised to be successful.

Milwaukee. School Orientation Centers were established for the culturally deprived children of in-migrant and transient parents to help them to adjust to the community, to provide remedial help, and to prepare them for regular classwork.

New York. In addition to the Demonstration Guidance Project, the programs for dropouts, for junior high school career guidance classes, junior guidance classes, and teacher recruitment for "special service" schools have been most successful.

Philadelphia. This city added a bilingual coordinator for its project to work with Spanish-speaking parents and help them to establish a stronger bond with the schools, and has put special emphasis upon pointing out the importance of the language arts teacher's responsibility in providing for the improvement of communication skills and the structuring of the reading program.

Pittsburgh. Team teaching and flexible programming have been points of interest in the planning of education for the deprived children, with special emphasis upon the "more able pupils."

St. Louis. A combined academic and vocational program was set up which was aimed at the economic independence for students who would otherwise join the army of dropouts, and this group has received special counseling and assistance from both the school and the employer.

San Francisco. The need was felt to provide extra services to be of particular help to the teacher of culturally deprived pupils in order to extend their practice of individualized instruction. This has been promoted through their School-Community Improvement Program, Superintendent's Compensatory Program, the State Compensatory Education Program, Youth Opportunity Center and the Drama Demonstration Projects.

District of Columbia. The emphasis here was also on the language arts, and the practice was established to assign one language arts special teacher to work with the primary children in a school which served the deprived; the direction here points to the development of a curriculum innovation with the teaching of our standard English to these children as a second language.[9]

This listing by no means includes all of the many efforts made in these cities, but it does give an indication of the direction that efforts have taken and, through the pooling of the results of these and many others which also deserve comment, will continue to be of help in future planning. Good descriptions of these programs can be found in the reference given as well as in other sources.

The programs that have been discussed here can be viewed, in general, as total projects or total programs, thus giving all those interested an opportunity to gain both distance and perspective, making it possible for some to choose those aspects that they can consider directly applicable in their own situations, and others that can be used as guidelines. These programs have been criticised at times because they do not present enough statistical evidence of values gained. Perhaps the time has come, as has been mentioned before, when we must decide whether we are going to use as bases for judgment of further endeavors of compensatory education only those specific gains that can be statistically measured and compared, such as the increased points in the IQ and increased grade level accomplishment in the subject matter areas, or whether the actual changes that take place in the behavior, the speech, and the attitude of a deprived child or a deprived youth as observed by competent teachers, by parents who have discovered the value of an education, or by the child himself in his willingness to come to school and in his desire to communicate and cooperate with his peers, have some place in evaluation. Perhaps we have three figures to choose from at this point: the statistically significant correlation or score arrived at through perfectly controlled conditions; the figure of speech within the academic language of the educator, the psychologist, the sociologist, or the anthropologist, which sounds well in speech and reads well in the latest article but seldom reaches a state of reality; and the man or woman to be, a human being, one who is unique and has gifts that if developed will contribute to the society in which he lives — a figure that cannot be duplicated but one that may have an inestimable value. This is indeed a choice for us to consider carefully.

In reviewing carefully the many current programs, there appear to be different forms of organization in which they may be grouped as to purpose and emphasis. This is particularly noticeable in the literature that is available at the present time concerning the variety of compensatory activities going on. It would pay the reader to look at more than one of these, for the nature of the listings at times affects not only the choice of the programs used as examples, but also the interpretation of the program as well as the choice of the aspects described. There are, in the majority of them, enough of these aspects or factors to make this possible.

One may approach a study of these current activities by viewing the broad national programs, such as the Head Start Program or the current endeavor to lower the level of entrance into schools to include the four-year-old to permit intervention at an earlier age. Then the state programs can be considered, such as The Compensatory Education Program of California, which was authorized by its legislature with passage of the McAteer Act, thus permitting the organization of pilot programs that would represent the state geographically and operate through a state advisory committee.[10]

We can then study the county projects such as one finds in Florida under the program "PRIDE," which provides for identification and solution of the problems dealing with school desegregation through the furthering of Personal Responsibility for Individual Development through the Education of teachers.[11] The city programs are of course the most numerous, although many concern a single area rather than being totally city-wide in nature and purpose. The St. Louis Banneker District project is an excellent example of a program designed to meet the specific needs of an area. It is proving successful because of the high interest of the community and the excellent leadership of Dr. Samuel Shepard, Jr., assistant superintendent of schools, who clearly states the reason:

> Mainly we ask our teachers to do four things: (1) we ask them to
> quit teaching by I.Q.; (2) we ask them to quit their attitude of con-
> descension in work with these youngsters; (3) we ask them to assign
> home work; (4) we ask that they visit the homes of the parents.[12]

Another excellent example of a city program is the Three-Year Experimental Project on Schools in Changing Neighborhoods in Wilmington, Delaware. The emphasis was on the development of language skills through the planning of experience units that stressed the opportunity for role playing, thus allowing the deprived children to extend their knowledge and information and their sensitivities in actual human relationships. The written discussion of this program should be helpful for those in education who would find this method appropriate and helpful to them in their planning. (100:46–47)

Another approach that one can take in the review of the programs is through the progression from those serving the preschool child to those in the elementary and secondary schools, and then to the attempts being made at the college level. Surveys can be found either in booklet form or combined in book form and either covering this total range[13] or a satisfactory partial range[14] of these levels.

There are to be found discussions of individual programs designed for the single levels, with more of them, such as the ones in Dade County, Florida, New Haven, and Hartford, examples of extensions of the Head Start Program. The Early Training Program in Murfreesboro, Tennessee, the Pennsylvania Environment Enrichment Program, The Pilot Kindergarten Program in Racine and the Ypsilanti Program, entitled The Intervention in the Cognitive Development of the Culturally Deprived and Functionally Retarded Negro Preschool Child, are also others endeavoring to provide a compensatory program for the young child. An example of an elementary school program that promises to be well worth careful consideration is New York City's program More Effective Schools. Pittsburgh and Tucson are using teams of teachers, each teacher representing a different subject area. These teams work in blocks of time dividing the groups of children on the basis of remedial and enrichment needs. Many of these programs prove to be short-lived, some being terminated temporarily for further study, some because of cost or matters of organization and management. One of the issues in the New York City teachers' most unfortunate strike was purported to be the question of the continuance of More Effective Schools, one of the intensive experimental programs for educational excellence. This was agreed upon as part of the final negotiations.

The endeavors at the secondary level tend to show that efforts are being made to vary the curricular programs of the schools to maintain interest, to prevent dropouts and to provide basic remedial instruction such as is being done in San Francisco where the pupils may transfer to more flexible scheduling following an intensive developmental reading program. Others programs at the secondary level include those for the foreign-speaking students, and those geared to improving specific subject matter areas such as the social studies, science, and mathematics in addition to reading and language usage.

Emphases are also being placed upon the value of the school library and on the importance of subject matter oriented projects that begin with the younger child and are being developed over a long age range. In this case, not only are the basic subject matter areas being studied within the projects and reports,[15] guides, and curricula being produced, but the areas of citizenship, economics, and the several arts are receiving attention. Work-study programs are planned at the upper secondary level, particularly for those deprived youth who will not be able to extend their education past the secondary level. Summer programs, after-school study and guided enrichment projects, and guided tutoring are now found to be of value as there seems to be a desire for extending the school day and week, and also the school year. Summer schools are being initiated at all levels of education, not only for remedial assistance, but for further exploration in learning, in enrichment, and in the search for talent.

Part of the more recent planning has been that of the new educational programs to be included in broader Model City plans. This permits the consideration of the educational provisions in relation to the social and economic considerations. This thinking may prove to be most productive.

It is encouraging to note that there is evidence now of the extension of the development of compensatory programs and practices to the college level. It has been stated that a larger proportion of the higher education institutions are now involved than is found at the elementary and secondary levels within the public schools. These include Berea College in Kentucky, Oberlin College in Ohio, Tuskegee Institute in Alabama, and Hampton Institute in Virginia, all of which have been offering programs of outstanding service for some time. Both junior and community colleges across the country have taken an interest in providing for the deprived youth. The College Discovery Program in New York City, begun in two of the community colleges, should be one to watch and study for the trend in public education is not only downward to extend a sound education to the four-year-old, but it is also upward with every indication that public schooling will, before too long, extend beyond the secondary school to the junior and the community college as a part of our free system of education.

Yale is setting an excellent example of involvement by its 1967 summer program, in which 225 high school and college students from across the country were on campus for six to eight weeks of summer learning. In addition, some 240 New Haven students from the sixth to twelfth grades attended various activities. This represents Yale's ". . . commitment of its human and physical resources to the aid of able students whose limited financial resources prevent them from taking full advantage of their educational potential." Of the 50 who taught in the programs, more than 20 teach in Yale College. Most of the students will never matriculate in a college at Yale. However, "through each of these efforts, Yale hopes to open to young people with talent doors to institutions which have the capacity to develop it to the full."[16]

Thus we see several trends emerging from the results of a combination of serious and dedicated effort to meet the need for educational change and the rush against time to gain and to spend monies available for other quickly planned efforts. The major positive trends are forward-looking and are concerned with providing more than an adequate education; indicating a willingness to recognize the deficits within the current education and those within the lives and experiences of the deprived; proposing to make the changes that will help to eradicate these deficits and to determine the philosophy, the curriculum, the teacher preparation, the process of teaching and learning; and the evaluating of these in terms of a new and vital education, one that will not only meet the need for change but will be planned in such a manner that it will continue change as it is demanded, thus eradicating a *status quo* condition. The individual is important and we are beginning to want him to be more than an average citizen, for we are willing to recognize that as yet we have not provided the educational means by which he may realize his values and his strengths. All children and youth must educate themselves to face today and live today in such a way as to prepare for tomorrow, to meet tomorrow with satisfaction as the preparation for still another tomorrow. The American people have reason to be proud of the efforts being made in this direction.

REFERENCES

[1] Henry T. Hillson and Florence C. Myers, *The Demonstration Guidance Project: 1957–1962* (New York: Board of Education of the City of New York, 1963).

[2] Baltimore City Public Schools, *An Early Admissions Project: Progress Report 1963–64* (Baltimore City Public Schools, September 1963).

[3] *1964–1965 Progress Report of the Experimental Nursery School Program* (School District of Philadelphia), pp. 4–5.

[4] *Ibid.*, p. 45.

[5] *Annual Report 1965*, (New York: Institute for Developmental Studies, Department of Psychiatry, New York Medical College), p. 60. The Institute as of the fall of 1966 associated with the School of Education, New York University.

[6] Leo S. Goldstein, "Evaluation of an Enrichment Program for Socially Disadvantaged Children" (New York: Institute for Developmental Studies, School of Education, New York University, June, 1965), mimeographed.

[7] Research Council of the Great Cities Program for School Improvement, *The Past is Prologue* (Chicago: 5400 North St. Louis Avenue, 1966).

[8] Dorsey Baynham, "The Great Cities Projects," *NEA Journal*, 52 (April 1963), pp. 1–2 (From a Ford Foundation Reprint).

[9] Research Council of the Great Cities Program for School Improvement, *Promising Practices for the Culturally Deprived* (Chicago: 5400 North St. Louis Avenue, April, 1964).

[10] Advisory Committee on Compensatory Education, *Progress Report on Compensatory Educational Programs in California* (Sacramento, California; January, 1965).

[11] Volusia County Board of Public Instruction, *Program "PRIDE": Revised County Project and Budget* (DeLand, Florida, April 16, 1965), mimeographed.

[12] Samuel Shepard, Jr., *How Should We Educate the Deprived Child?* (Washington: Council for Basic Education, 1965), pp. 21–22. (Occasional Papers: Number Seven.)

[13] Edmund W. Gordon and Doxey A. Wilkerson, *Compensatory Education for the Disadvantaged* (New York: College Entrance Examination Board, 1966); *Education: An Answer to Poverty* (Washington: U.S. Office of Education and Office of Economic Opportunity, 1966).

[14] *Disadvantaged Children Series:*

    No. 1: *Educating Disadvantaged Children Under Six,* 1965,

    No. 2. *Educating Disadvantaged Children in the Primary Years,* 1965,

    No. 3. *Educating Disadvantaged Children in the Middle Grades,* 1965,

    No. 4. *Administration of Elementary School Programs for Disadvantaged Children,* 1966,

    No. 5. *Educating Disadvantaged Children in the Elementary School* (An Annotated Bibliography), 1966, (Washington: Office of Education).

[15] Richard Corbin and Muriel Crosby, co-chairmen, *Language Programs for the Disadvantaged,* The Report of the NCTE Task Force on Teaching English to the Disadvantaged (Champaign, Illinois: National Council of Teachers of English, 1965).

[16] Joel Fleishman, "Providing Education — and Opportunity," *Yale Alumni Magazine* (June 1967), pp. 38–41.

VI

Centers of Study and Sources of Information

What one knows is, in youth, of little moment; they know enough who know how to learn.
— Henry Adams, *The Education of Henry Adams*[1]

This quotation is most timely, both for the concluding of a consideration of deprivation and compensatory education and for an approach to education in today's world. We are fully aware now of the force and the speed of change with which we must deal. The adult of today can clearly see that the schooling of his youth bears little relationship to the intellectual demands now being made on each person if he is to understand the world around him. What today's child and youth learn today in their effort to understand their world will be of little moment in their adult world. This is true to an even greater degree for today's deprived child.

What then will be of moment to them? In the process of continuing education, what is of moment to any of us today regardless of age? If we recognize the need for a new and vital approach to education for each person, and if we accept the fact that this does mean change in our attitudes, in our conception of education, in what we teach and how we teach it, in how we guide those who are to teach, and in how we evaluate what has been taught and what has been learned, what is our single unifying goal? And what is our single need in order to reach this goal?

To state this goal is to summarize the consideration that has been given to education. Equality of educational opportunity is not the goal, for it is not enough. This goal must be one of dynamic guid-

237

ance for each individual so that he may discover for himself that his greatest gift is the ability to think, that his personal goal is to use the total of his abilities to think creatively, and that to think creatively is to learn how to learn. It is true that we must open the door for this educational opportunity to all, but the guidance given varies with the individual and his environment. The guidance through teaching and the teaching through guidance must be individual, for the learner is unique in his pattern of growing, developing, and learning. He alone, as a result of this guidance and his discovery of the power of creative thought and learning, must be the one to evaluate his success, for success can come only as he reaches the goals that he has set for himself and as he reaches the levels of aspiration that he has determined by his own personal values. He then will know enough because he knows how to think and how to learn, and he recognizes this as a continuous process, his process of living a rich and rewarding life. The guidance upon which he depends is the education we permit him to have. The quality of this guidance will determine for him the degree to which he can learn to think and what he can learn — it determines whether or not he will have learned enough to know how to learn.

What is our greatest single need in the providing of this education — a program of guidance to free this individual to think and to learn? There can be only one answer to this: It is the need to know more in order to know how to learn more continuously. We can build an educational program only as we have the knowledge about the learner as a person, and about the way he learns. We must know what approach to teaching will be the best for his guidance and how to guide him in the building of his own personal values that he may evaluate his own success in the continuous learning process that will be built not on the *facts* he learns today, but on the way he learns how to learn today. This knowledge must come to us through study and through research. The current questioning in education, evidenced by the attempts to do something about it, shows that there has been some good study and research and that this *is* the way in which we will continue to learn more about the most interesting process of all, that of the interchange of teaching and learning which, in its broadest sense, is the active process of living. We do know enough to realize now that we must learn a great deal more.

We need to know more about the learner but we need to study him in context, for we can determine how he is learning and thinking only by the way in which he responds to the everyday experiences in the light of the conditions and the atmosphere of his surroundings. We need to know more about thinking. The deprived child offers to us an excellent case for study, for his responses, his ideas, and the process of his thinking are temporarily impeded by the environmental circumstances. This affords us the opportunity for study as he demonstratively moves from his very simple responses, which can be easily observed and understood if we know him well enough, to more complex, abstract, and creative thinking.

What do we know about potential? How do we recognize an upper level of ability? We must know about these if we are to be at all successful in a guidance program that assumes as one of its goals the fullest development of the potentials of the individual. What do we know about successful learning? How can we evaluate successful guidance and successful teaching? This evaluation cannot be made out of the context of the individual learner and the individual teacher, out of the context of the process of teaching and learning, or out of the particular environment. The total picture must be considered if the knowledge we gain is to be interrelated and have meaning. The measures we have now do not suffice and the challenge is cast to those with the ability to understand and to discover new measures as they work closely with those who teach as well as those who learn. What do we know about values? How are values discovered, determined, and used by an individual? Knowledge is our need that we may guide, that the child may think and learn, for himself, independently and creatively.

Our concern for the deprived learner has stimulated not only a recognition for the need for research but also the desire to carry on meaningful studies so essential at this time. Research in the area of deprivation and its effect upon human beings is not a specialized or narrow field, for what we learn in this study will aid us in knowing what we need to know about all children. All are human, all are persons, all are worthy of study. Only the environments and the opportunities differ. Systematic study is essential, for it is the basis of sound research and it is possible to approach current problems in a systematic manner if we do not lose sight of the individual who is to profit from this study.

Both projects and programs for the improvement of education must be based upon sound research. In many instances projects and programs should be the means by which investigations can be increased, for their planning can be of the nature of inquiry, controlled yet realistic and sound. We are just as close to the beginning of research on the deprived child and his education as we are to the beginning of our concern about him. Hence, we must allow time for those who are conducting the type of research that will be helpful in further understanding. Research, to be of value, must be verified. In spite of this shortness of time, however, reports on some excellent studies on certain aspects of deprivation and the resultant deficits in the life and education of the child are becoming available. These studies are concerned with the characteristics of deprived children,[2] the effects of environmental deprivation on learning and learning skills,[3] the effects of certain types of training and remedial approaches to learning,[4] language development,[5] the communication of information,[6] maternal behavior,[7] and conceptual styles. Representative studies on these aspects give an indication of the areas of interest and the areas of assistance for furthering our understanding of the deprived learner.

With the renewed interest in research and the recognized need both for further study and for the compilation of evidence from studies in process, there have grown up certain centers for this study and centers that will serve as sources of information. Again, this consideration of deprivation and compensatory education must remain open-ended, trusting that those who are vitally interested in the changes taking place will continue to be stimulated and challenged to review the studies, research projects, and other evidences of the further knowledge we need. The opportunities for research have been considerably increased through grants, through support by the cooperative research program of the Office of Education, through centers and laboratories now established for the screening and launching of research projects, through institutes within our colleges and universities, as well as through the granting of funds for actual research in the field — in the inner city, in the rural area, and with the migrant. Reports are also available on the activities of research councils from such as the National Institutes of Health, and The National Science Foundation and other Government agencies, and from conferences on research as it relates to education and deprivation. Many of the centers are now making available periodic reports of studies and research that are either underway or are completed. It is possible to find some evidence of research on many phases of almost any of the larger problems which have been given consideration. Some of this evidence is in mimeographed form, some in pamphlets, or as reprints of recent articles, in current journals and books, and as films, all of which are meant to keep those who are interested, informed of what is occurring.

As a concluding section to this chapter there is presented a listing of some of the study and information centers with representative materials available or produced through them.

There are supplementary lists of books, articles, and other materials which have been made available since the beginning of the preparation of this consideration. The text references are from materials not included in the basic bibliography, thus extending the listing of valuable material. Such listings cannot be comprehensive, but it is encouraging to know that one of the services now being established at the various centers of information is the preparation of bibliographies of new materials as they are received.

Such a consideration as this on the topic of deprivation and compensatory education cannot be concluded for it has only begun. At this particular time of uncertainty, the following words spoken by President Johnson on January 26, 1967, as a part of his text of the Economic Report (as taken in part from the photographically reproduced text in *The New York Times* on January 27, 1967, on pages 14 and 15) are pertinent:

Combating Poverty
We will continue to attack poverty and deprivation through such weapons as
— Community Action and Head Start;
— rent supplements and child nutrition;
— aid to elementary and secondary education in poverty areas and the Teachers Corps;
— the Manpower Development and Training Act, the Job Corps, the Neighborhood Youth Corps; Medicare, Medicaid, and neighborhood health centers;
— measures to end discrimination in jobs, education, and public facilities;
— the expanded coverage enacted last year for a higher minimum wage.
I am proposing that our attack be reinforced with new weapons in 1967.
Yet, with old weapons and new, the war on poverty will not be won in 1967 — or 1968. There is no wonder drug which can suddenly conquer this ancient scourge of man. It will be a long and continuing struggle, which will challenge our imagination, our patience, our knowledge, and our resources for years to come. Our

capacity to stay with the task will be a test of our maturity as a people. . . .

HELPING THE DISADVANTAGED

The United States is the first large nation in the history of the world wealthy enough to end poverty within its borders. There are many fronts in the War on Poverty. We are moving forward on them all.

There must be full employment so that those qualified and able to work can find jobs. . . . The unemployment rate last year was the lowest in 13 years. Those not now fully qualified must be given the education and training, the health and guidance services which will enable them to make their full contribution to society. . . . We have greatly increased our aid to education and enlarged our training programs, and we will expand them further.

For those who will be unable to earn adequate incomes, there must be help — most of all for the benefit of children, whose misfortune to be born poor must not deprive them of future opportunity. . . . We have increased our income support, and we will increase it further.

Wherever the poor and disadvantaged are concentrated, intensive and coordinated programs to break the cycle of deprivation and dependency must continue and be reinforced. . . . We have instituted these programs in hundreds of cities and rural areas; we are expanding them and designing others. . . .

EDUCATION AND HEALTH

Individually and collectively, Americans have insatiable appetites for more education and better health. Education and health contribute both to individual well-being and to the Nation's productivity. But far too many of our urban and rural poor are denied adequate access to either. The efficiency of our methods of education and of providing medical care can and should be strengthened.

History will record these years as the time when this Nation awoke to its needs — and its limitations — in education and health. The Elementary and Secondary Education Act, Head Start, the Teachers Corps, Medicare, Medicaid, and the Partnership in Health will be landmarks in our social and economic development.

I shall propose

— an expanded Head Start program; a Follow-Through program in the early years of school; and the opening of other new educational opportunities for children;

— both legislative and administrative changes to accelerate re-

search and development on more efficient and effective ways
of providing health resources;

— an expanded child health program, including early diagnosis
and treatment, a pilot program of dental care, and the training of additional health personnel to provide services to
children.

Also pertinent are these excerpts from the Johnson Poverty Message
sent to Congress on March 15, 1967 (from *The New York Times*,
March 15, 1967, p. 32):

. . . I recommend that the Congress appropriate $2.06-billion for the
Office of Economic Opportunity for fiscal 1968 — a 25 per cent
increase over fiscal 1967.

I have asked the director of the Office of Economic Opportunity
to strengthen these efforts and to expand the services available to
smaller towns and rural areas.

I have asked the director of the Office of Economic Opportunity, in
cooperation with the Secretary of Housing and Urban Development
and other Federal Departments, to expand and strengthen the development of neighborhood multiservice and multicounty centers in the
coming fiscal year.

The director of the Office of Economic Opportunity, in cooperation
with the Secretary of Health, Education and Welfare, will encourage
local communities to establish additional health centers in the coming
year, so that up to 50 will be in operation by the end of fiscal 1968.

My budget includes sufficient funds for Upward Bound to benefit
more than 30,000 young men and women in fiscal 1968.

The director of the Office of Economic Opportunity, in cooperation
with the Secretary of Health, Education and Welfare, will expand this
(foster grandparents) program next year.

. . . I have recommended the Head Start follow-through program.
My budget recommendations to the Congress include $472-million
for Head Start, including funds for the new head start follow-through
program to sustain the progress Head Start has made.

My budget recommendations include $295-million for the Job
Corps program in fiscal 1968 — to educate, train and renew the
hopes of some 50,000 young men and women.

My budget recommendations for fiscal 1968 include $31-million
for the VISTA program. . . .

I also recommend legislation to expand the provisions of the
existing loan programs to permit farm owners or their tenants to
shift the entire use of farm land with adequate recreation potential
from agricultural production to income-producing recreation enter-

prises, as part of comprehensive land-use plans for rural and neighboring urban areas.

I recommend a five-point program for these forgotten Americans:

1. Legislation to provide 90 percent Federal reimbursement for vocational rehabilitation services for disabled migratory farm workers.

2. Amendments of the public assistance law to authorize pilot projects to provide temporary public assistance and other welfare services for migratory farm workers and their families, who are now barred by residence requirements from receiving these services.

3. A 25 per cent increase — from $28-to $35-million — in funds to provide:

   Special educational services for more than 10,000 migrant children.

   Health services for about 280,000 migratory workers and their families.

   An expanded self-help housing program for the construction of 2,000 housing units.

4. Amendment of the unemployment insurance laws to provide benefits for workers employed on large commercial farms.

5. Extension of Social Security benefits to 500,000 farm workers by reducing from $150 to $50 the amount which must be earned from a single employer each year.

REFERENCES

[1] Quoted by Lance R. Odden, "They Know Enough Who Know How to Learn," *The Independent School Bulletin*, 26 (December 1966), p. 55.

[2] Vera P. John, "A Brief Survey of Research on the Characteristics of Children from Low-Income Backgrounds" (Prepared for the U.S. Commissioner on Education, August, 1964), mimeographed.

[3] Vera P. John, "2. The Intellectual Development of Slum Children: Some Preliminary Findings," *The American Journal of Orthopsychiatry*, 33 (October 1963), pp. 813–822; Cynthia P. Deutsch, "Effects of Environmental Deprivation on Basic Psychological Processes: Some Hypotheses" (Presented at the Annual Meeting of the American Educational Research Association in Chicago, Illinois, February 1965), mimeographed; Cynthia P. Deutsch, "Learning in the Disadvantaged" (Paper presented at the Conference on Analyses of Conceptual Learning at the Research and Development Center for Learning and Re-Education, University of Wisconsin, Madison, Wisconsin, October 1965), mimeographed.

4 Shirley C. Feldmann, Dorothy E. Schmidt, and Cynthia P. Deutsch, "A Study of the Effects of Auditory Training on Remedial Reading" (Paper read at American Educational Research Association, Chicago, Illinois, February 17, 1966), mimeographed.

5 Martin Whiteman, Bert R. Brown, Martin Deutsch, "Some Effects of Social Class and Race on Children's Language and Intellectual Abilities" (Revision of paper read at the Biennial Meeting of the Society for Research in Child Development, Minneapolis, Minnesota, March 1965), mimeographed.

6 Martin Deutsch, Alma Maliver, Bert Brown, Estelle Cherry, "Communication of Information in the Elementary School Classroom," Cooperative Research Project No. 908 (Office of Education, U.S. Department of Health, Education, and Welfare), 1964.

7 Robert D. Hess and Virginia C. Shipman, "Early Experience and the Socialization of Cognitive Modes in Children," *Child Development*, 36 (December 1965), pp. 869–886.

STUDY AND INFORMATION CENTERS

Anti-Defamation League of B'nai B'rith
315 Lexington Avenue
New York, New York 10016

Publications and Films on Education and the Disadvantaged for Pre- and In-Service Teachers

Publications 1965–1966

Mack, Raymond W., and Troy S. Duster. *Patterns of Minority Relations* (a Freedom Pamphlet).

Raab, Earl, and Seymour M. Lipset. *Prejudice and Society* (a Freedom Pamphlet).

Reprints

Asbell, Bernard. "Not Like Other Children" from *Redbook*, October 1963.

Dunbar, Ernest. "The Negro in America Today" from *Look*, April 10, 1962.

"Guidelines for Testing Minority Group Children" from *Journal of Social Issues*, April 1964.

Noar, Gertrude. "The Times Call for Courage" from *The Journal of Teacher Education*, December 1964.

Silberman, Charles E. "Give Slum Children a Change — A Radical Proposal" from *Harper's Magazine*, May 1964.

Stevenson, Ian (M.D.). "People Aren't Born Prejudiced" from *Parents' Magazine*, February 1960.

Films

"As the Twig is Bent" (Volunteer service for summer preschool program for disadvantaged children).

"Felicia" (Social conditions of a teen-age Negro girl living in Watts area of Los Angeles, California).

"Incident on Wilson Street" (Documentary — 5th grade involvement in an All-Day Neighborhood School education program. Program is designed to provide an enriched curriculum for underprivileged children).

"I Wonder Why" (Negro child's feelings about prejudice).

"The Non-Violent" (". . . white college student 'bears witness' to a civil rights demonstration . . . focuses attention on the grave injustices and denial of freedom meted out to American Negroes").

"Segregation Northern Style" (CBS Documentary of Negro couple's search for a home in a middle-income northern community) Actual taping.

"Watts: Riot or Revolt?" (CBS Reports, documentary on the Watts, Los Angeles riot during the summer of 1965).

"A Chance at the Beginning" (Documentary which demonstrates preschool training [for deprived, etc.]. "Provides a sound foundation for the fullest development of each child's potential throughout the school years." Focuses on Dr. Martin Deutsch's project, Institue for Developmental Studies).

"A City Decides" ("True story about integration of the public schools of St. Louis. . . .").

"A Morning For Jimmy" (True story of a young Negro boy's search for employment. He encounters discrimination and discovers through his teacher that a proper education will help him discover his proper place).

"All the Way Home" (Integrated communities can work with the help of responsible community leadership).

"The Burden of Truth" (Problems and prejudices faced by young Negro) Sponsored by United Steelworkers of America.

"Cast the First Stone" (Documentary: "Features interviews on location with Americans whose lives have been affected by prejudice and discrimination").

"Crisis in Levittown" ("Interviews with residents, both for and against the integration of the first Negro family to move into Levittown, Pa.").

"Epitaph for Jim Crow" (Focuses on the history and current situation of the Negro American).

"For White Christians Only" (Housing discrimination against minorities).

"The New Girl" ("The pro and con arguments in hiring a Negro girl in an all-white company . . .").

"No Hiding Place." One of CBS' series "East Side-West Side" ("Traces the events in a neighborhood into which a Negro family has just moved").

"To Find a Home" (Experiences of Negro families trying to rent apartments.)

"Study in Color" (A trilogy of films consisting of "Boy," "The Job,"

and "Study" ("A group of three plays which represent a strong indictment of racial prejudice").

"Wanted — A Place to Live" ("A Negro is rejected when he answers
an ad to share a room with three other university students").

"Walk in my Shoes" (Documentary: "Explores the innermost feelings of the Negro as he reacts to prejudice and discrimination in
America").

"The Other Face of Dixie" (Integration achievement in Clinton,
Little Rock, Norfolk, Atlanta) "CBS Reports."

Bank Street College of Education
69 Bank Street
New York, New York 10014
Dr. Gordon J. Klopf, Dean of Faculties
Dr. Garda W. Bowman, Coordinator of Special Projects

"Bank Street College Survey," Sponsored by OEO Survey indicated
that most educational programs for disadvantaged pupils are not
benefiting from current research findings related to the impact of
environment on learning and development. Survey cites 52 recommendations and suggestions for their implementation for improving teacher-training programs related to meeting the educational
needs of disadvantaged children and youth.

Publications

Teacher Education in a Social Context. New York: Mental Health
Materials Center, 1967.

Center for Research & Development on Educational Differences
Harvard University
Cambridge, Massachusetts 02138
Theodore R. Sizer, Chairman

Focus: Programs concerning preschool, elementary-secondary, and individual and cultural differences.

Mimeographed material

"Harvard Clearinghouse on Educational Differences Acquisitions List"
(September–October 1966).

"Bibliography on the Culturally Disadvantaged."

"Bibliography on Urban Education" (Supplement to bibliography on
disadvantaged — April 1966).

"Bibliography on Juvenile Delinquency" and "Supplement."

"Bibliography on Dropouts" and "Supplement."

"Bibliography on Racial Imbalance and *De facto* Segregation" and
"Supplement."

"Bibliography on School Performance of Working Class Children"
(Compiled by Marjorie Elias).

Center for Urban Education
33 West 42nd Street
New York, New York 10036
Robert A. Dentler, Director

> Organized in 1965 by eight institutions of higher education in New
> York City "to contribute strategic knowledge and resources to the
> strengthening, improvement, and reconstruction of educational
> services of all kinds and at all levels within urban society:
>> By providing consultative services for research and development
>> already in progress, both in member institutions and in the pub-
>> lic school systems of the New York metropolitan area, and in-
>> itiating additional research where required;
>> By providing facilities, expert personnel, and dollar support for
>> new research and innovation;
>> By giving maximum dissemination to the results of this research;
>> By serving as a center of coordination between the academic
>> community and the world of urban educational and other com-
>> munity services."

Mimeographed material

> Mackler, Bernard. "A Report on the '600' Schools: Dilemmas, Prob-
> lems, and Solutions."

Publications

> Dentler, Robert A., and Mary Ellen Warshauer. *Big City Dropouts
> and Illiterates.*
> Koblitz, Minnie W., *The Negro in Schoolroom Literature* (A Center
> Bibliography).
> Shapira, Rina, *Attitudes Toward Israel Among American Jewish
> Adolescents.*
> Gittell, Marilyn, *Participants and Participation: A Study of School
> Policy in New York.*
> Randolph, Helen (compiled and annotated by) *Urban Education
> Bibliography.*
> Dentler, Robert A., Bernard Mackler, and Mary Ellen Warshauer,
> eds., *The Urban R's.*
> *The Urban Review* (A Bi-monthly publication published only during
> the school year).

Cornelius J. Drew Foundation, Inc.
211½ West 141st Street
New York, New York 10030

> "The Drew Foundation program . . . attempts to evaluate the educa-
> tional performance of the Negro poor when actually given equal op-

portunity for preschool, starting at age three, with peers from white middle-class families."

Mimeographed material

"Action Oriented Experimental Study of the Educational Needs of the Urban Child."

"Towards Correcting the Educational Failures in the Negro Ghetto Among the Poor."

Ford Foundation
477 Madison Avenue
New York, New York 10022

Publications

Brown, Dyke. *Ford and Other Foundations in Public Affairs.*
Bundy, McGeorge. *Action for Equal Opportunity.*
Jones, Edgar L. *Early School Admission Project.*
Meade, Edward J. Jr. *Foundations, Schools, and the Public Good.*
Metropolis.
Stirrings in the Big Cities: The Great Cities Project.
The New Teacher.
Winnick, Louis. *Housing and Urban Development: The Private Foundation's Role.*
Ylvisaker, Paul N. *Community Action: A Response to Some Unfinished Business.*

Independent Schools Talent Search Program
P.O. Box 1051
Hanover, New Hampshire 03755

Mimeographed material

"A Description of the Independent Schools Talent Search Program — Its Students and Operations"

Publications

A Better Chance — An Educational Program (Sponsored by Mount Holyoke College) 1965, 1966.
A Better Chance — An Educational Program (Sponsored by Dartmouth College) 1965.
The First Two Years of the Independent Schools Talent Search Program — September 1965.
The Independent Schools Talent Search Program (Information bulletin).

Reprints

* Berkeley, William D. "For Talented Young People, Alternatives to Poverty," from *Southern Education Report*, January–February 1966.

250 · *Deprivation and Compensatory Education*

Information Retrieval Center on the Disadvantaged
Graduate School of Education
Yeshiva University
55 Fifth Avenue
New York, New York 10003

Joshua A. Fishman, Dean of Graduate School of Education

Publications

> IRCD *Bulletin*, a Bi-Monthly Publication from the Eric Information Retrieval Center on the Disadvantaged.
> IRCD *Bulletin Supplements*, a series addressed to problems of concern to educators of disadvantaged pre-school children.

Mimeographed material

> Wilkerson, Doxey A. "Some Practices and Theoretical Issues in the Education of Socially Disadvantaged Children and Youth" (Paper given at the meeting of the Western Regional Membership of the College Entrance Examination Board, Colorado Woman's College, June 17, 1964).
> "The Education of Socially Disadvantaged Children and Youth: A Brief Introduction and Bibliography" (March 1965).
> "Teachers' Attitudes Towards Socially Disadvantaged Children — A Brief Bibliography."
> "Project Beacon Training Program" (October 22, 1965).
> "Some References on Preschool Curricula" (Not including Project Head Start).
> "Some References on Program Evaluations Measuring Student Change."
> "Accessions Lists."

Reprints

> Fishman, Joshua A. "Project Beacon: A project addressed to the needs of the socially disadvantaged" from *Pioneer Ideas in Education* (Committee on Education and Labor, House of Representatives, 88th Congress — 1st Session) September 1963.
> Gordon, Edmund W. "A Review of Programs of Compensatory Education" from *American Journal of Orthopsychiatry*, Vol. 35, No. 4, July 1965.

Films

> "No Man Is An Island" produced by CBS in cooperation with the National Council of Churches. (Theme: Human Relations. Friendship of two people (white and Negro) is tested by the fears and prejudices of a community.)
> "Our Race Problem" (Various points of view are expressed.)

Institute for Developmental Studies
New York University
547 West Broadway
New York, New York 10016
Martin Deutsch, Director

Publication

Proceedings of a Presentation to the Division of Early Childhood and Elementary Education (November 28, 1966).

Mimeographed material

Beilin, Harry and Lassar G. Gotkin. "Psychological Issues in the Development of Mathematics Curricula for Socially Disadvantaged Children" (Revision of address to Conference on Mathematics Education for Below Average Achievers — School Mathematics Study Group, Chicago, Ill., April 10–11, 1964).

Deutsch, Cynthia P. "Brief Partial Review of Activities Related to Urban Education," November 1964.

Deutsch, Cynthia P. "Education for Some Special Groups," 1965.

Deutsch, Cynthia P. "Effects of Environmental Deprivation on Basic Psychological Processes: Some Hypotheses" (Paper presented at the annual meeting of American Educational Research Association in Chicago, Ill., February 1965).

Deutsch, Cynthia P. "Learning in the Disadvantaged" (Paper presented at the conference on Analyses of Conceptual Learning at the Research and Development Center for Learning and Re-education, University of Wisconsin, October 1965).

Deutsch, Cynthia P. and Martin Deutsch. "Brief Reflections on the Theory of Early Childhood Enrichment Programs" (Prepared for the Social Science Research Council Conference on Early Childhood Education, Chicago, February 7–9, 1966).

Deutsch, Martin. "Some Elements in Compensatory Education."

Deutsch, Martin, Alma Maliver, Bert Brown, and Estelle Cherry. "Communication of Information in the Elementary School Classroom" (Cooperative Research Project No. 908).

Feldmann, Shirley C., Dorothy E. Schmidt and Cynthia P. Deutsch. "A Study of the Effects of Auditory Training on Remedial Reading" (Read at the American Educational Research Association, Chicago, February 17, 1966).

Goldstein, Leo S. "A Partial Overview of Process Research at the Institute for Developmental Studies" (December 1964).

Goldstein, Leo S. "Evaluation of an Enrichment Program for Socially Disadvantaged Children" (June 1965).

Gotkin, Lassar G. "Some Implications of Programed Instruction Research for Urban-Teacher Education."

Gotkin, Lassar G. "The Teaching Machine and the Child."

John, Vera P. "A Brief Survey of Research on the Characteristics of

Children from Low-Income Background" (Prepared for the U.S. Commissioner of Education, August 1964).

Weiner, Max and Shirley Feldmann. "Measurement of Reading Skills in Lower Socio-Economic Status Children" (Read at American Psychological Association Conference, Philadelphia, 1963).

Whiteman, Martin, Bert R. Brown and Martin Deutsch. "Some Effects of Social Class and Race on Children's Language and Intellectual Abilities" (Revision of a paper read at the Biennial Meeting of the Society for Research in Child Development, Minneapolis, Minn., March 1965).

Brown, B.R. "The Assessment of Self-Concept among Four-year-old Negro and White Children: a Comparative Study Using the Brown-IDS Self Concept Referents Test," 1966.

Gotkin, L.G. "Simon Says: A New Look at an Old Game," 1967.

Reprints

Deutsch, Cynthia P. "Auditory Discrimination and Learning: Social Factors" from the *Merrill-Palmer Quarterly of Behavior and Development*, Vol. 10, No. 3, 1964.

Deutsch, Cynthia P. "Breaking Through to Learning" from *Council Woman*, February 1965.

Deutsch, Martin. "Social and Psychological Perspectives on the Development of the Disadvantaged Learner" from *Merrill-Palmer Quarterly*, Spring 1964).

Deutsch, Martin, et al. "Selected Papers from the Institute for Development Studies — Arden House Conference on Pre-School Enrichment of Socially Disadvantaged Children" from the *Merrill-Palmer Quarterly*, Vol. 10, No. 3, July 1964.

Deutsch, Martin. "What We've Learned About Disadvantaged Children" from *Nation's Schools*, April 1965.

Deutsch, Martin. "Some Psychosocial Aspects of Learning in the Disadvantaged" from *Teachers College Record*, Vol. 67, No. 4, January 1966.

Gotkin, L.G. "A Calendar Curriculum for Kindergarten Children from Disadvantaged Backgrounds" from *Teachers College Record*, February, 1967.

Graff, Virginia A. "Testing and Reporting Procedures For an Intensive Tutoring Program" from *The Reading Teacher*, January, 1966.

Institute for Research on Exceptional Children

University of Illinois

Urbana, Illinois 61801

Samuel A. Kirk, Director

Mimeographed material

Bereiter, Carl. "A Beginning Language Program for Disadvantaged Children" (Paper presented at the American Educational Research Association, Chicago, February 19, 1966).

Reprints

Bereiter, Carl and Siegfried Engelmann. "Observations on the Use of Direct Instruction with Young Disadvantaged Children" from *Journal of School Psychology*, 4:55–62; Spring 1966.

Institute of Urban Studies
Teachers College, Columbia University
New York, New York 10027
Prof. Robert A. Dentler, Executive Officer

Study: Urban problems of 131 cities. Social Security Administration financing the project.

Mimeographed materials

Mackler, Bernard, Thelma P. Catalano, and W. Dana Holman. "The Successful Urban Slum Child: A Psychological Study of Personality and Academic Success in Deprived Children" (Progress Report and Prospectus, March 1965).

National Association of Independent Schools
4 Liberty Square
Boston, Massachusetts 02109
John Chandler, Jr., President

Publications

Mallery, David. *Negro Students in Independent Schools*, December 1963.
Yeomans, Edward. *And Gladly Learn — Summer Enrichment Programs for Urban Children*, November 1965.

National Education Association
1201 Sixteenth Street, N.W.
Washington, D.C. 20006

Publications

A *Statement on the National Teacher Corps* (April 4, 1966).
Educational Policies Commission of the N.E.A. and American Association of School Administrators. *The Central Purpose of American Education*, 1962.
Educational Policies Commission of the N.E.A. and American Association of School Administrators. *American Education and the Search for Equal Opportunity*, 1965.
Goslin, Willard E. *Learning to Plow on a City Street* (Department of Rural Education, 1963).
Strom, Robert D. *The Tragic Migration* (Published by the Depart-

ment of Home Economics, N.E.A., 1964) (Pamphlet related to school dropouts).

Films

"A Desk for Billie" (Influence of good schools and teachers on a migrant child) Listing 903.

"A Chance to Learn" (Filmed to show the needs of education which the ESEA of 1965 hopes to meet) Listing 900.

"Right Angle" (Newspaper reporter finds the public school doing a good job educating all children, regardless of family backgrounds or abilities) Listing 912.

"Mike Makes His Mark" (Impact of good junior high school on a potential delinquent) Listing 909.

"Segregation in Schools" (Civic leaders, teachers, parents, students — Negro and white — debate and discuss the most recent facet of an old problem).

"Children Without" (Shows children without parental love and care, and the basic requisites of daily living, helped by teachers and counselors in a Detroit public school).

National Association for the Education of Young Children
3700 Massachusetts Avenue, N.W.
Washington, D.C. 20016

Mimeographed material

"Criteria for Selection of Institutions for Head Start Orientation Programs," Summer 1966 (Criteria developed by members of the Governing Board of the National Association for the Education of Young Children, March 1966).

Publications

Preparing Teachers of Disadvantaged Young Children (Summary of a Conference of N.D.E.A. Institute for Teachers of Disadvantaged Youth, 1966).

Office of Economic Opportunity
Washington, D.C. 20506

Mimeographed material

"Head Start and Pre-School Summer Orientation" (a notice).
"The War on Poverty — A Hometown Fight," 1965.
"Head Start Newsletter."

Publications

Upward Bound.
Summer Volunteer Service in the War on Poverty (Spring 1966).
The Nonprofessional in the Educational System (July 1966).
Job Corps Conservation Centers Program (A guide for teachers, youth workers, counselors, neighborhood and community leaders).

An Invitation to Help Head Start Child Development Programs.
Project Head Start

1. The Staff	6. Parents
2. Medical Guide	7. Daily Program II
3. Nutrition	8. Social Services
4. Daily Program I	9. Equipment and Supplies
5. Volunteers	10. Points for Parents.

How to Apply for Head Start (September 1966).
Selected Lists of Children's Books and Recordings (Prepared by The Children's Services, Division of the American Library Association, 1966).
Migrant Worker Programs in Rural Community Action.
Remedial Reading in Rural Community Action.
OEO–CAP Summer Training Programs — 1966 Workbook for Neighborhood Centers, Manpower Development, Education and Health Programs, 1966 (August 1966).
Education — An Answer to Poverty (School programs which may be eligible for federal aid).
A Nation Aroused (First Annual Report).

Office of Education

Washington, D.C. 20202

Research and Development Centers (RDC) (Presently in operation at eight universities for eight specific areas of pure research).

1. University of California at Berkeley
   "A study of the purposes, organization, outcome and direction of American higher education with a view to assisting individuals and organizations concerned in improving the quality, efficiency and availability of such education."
2. Stanford University, Palo Alto, California
   "A study designed to improve the theory, practice and quality of U.S. teaching and teacher education."
3. Harvard University, Cambridge, Massachusetts
   "An investigation of the wide range of critical psychological, social, cultural, ethnic and other differences among individuals that affect the learning process and an effort to develop means that will make schools more responsive to these differences."
4. University of Georgia, Athens, Georgia
   "A study to determine the learning potential of children age three to six and teaching programs that take these children at the earliest possible age and advance them as far and as fast as they can go."
5. University of Texas, Austin, Texas
   "Development of a program for students and in-service teachers focusing on such innovations as may be found appropriate."
6. University of Pittsburgh, Pittsburgh, Pennsylvania
   "Development of programs and/or methods that will expedite

fruitful interaction between learning research in the behavioral sciences and instructional practices in U.S. schools."

7. University of Oregon, Eugene, Oregon
"A study of school organization and educational administration in the U.S."

8. University of Wisconsin, Madison, Wisconsin
"A broad study designed to improve the efficiency of learning, both formal and informal, in children, youth, and adults."

Educational Research Information Centers (ERIC) (Each center deals with a specific subject area, collecting, collating and disseminating RDC and EDLAB and other findings, results and conclusions in its subject area).

Clearing Houses for ERIC:

1. City University of New York: Preparation of Urban School Personnel
2. University of Oregon: Educational Administration
3. New Mexico State University: Small Schools and Rural Compensatory Education
4. University of California: Junior Colleges
5. University of Michigan: Counseling and Guidance
6. Ohio State University: Science Education
7. Indiana University Foundation: Reading
8. Yeshiva University: Disadvantaged Children and Youth
9. Modern Language Association of America (New York, N.Y.): Teaching of Foreign Languages
10. Center for Applied Linguistics (Washington, D.C.): Linguistics and the Uncommonly Taught Languages
11. National Association for Exceptional Children (Washington, D.C.): Exceptional Children
12. Ohio State University: Vocational and Technical Education

Consortium Research Development (CORD) (A program which enables six groups of small colleges to work in the area of educational research). Projects scheduled are as follows:

North Carolina: Developmental program for entering college students from disadvantaged backgrounds

North and South Dakota: New media for the improvement of colleges in sparsely populated areas

Oregon: Development of new biology curriculum

Tennessee and Mississippi: Methods of enabling students to compete academically on a national rather than a regional scale

Virginia and New York: Studies of today's college freshmen

Wisconsin: Inter-institutional study of the college dropout

Mimeographed material

"Educational Research Document Summaries" (Prepared from material issued by ERIC). Volumes I and II. Reproduced by Bell & Howell Company, Cleveland, Ohio 44112, 1966.

Publications

Equality of Educational Opportunity.
A *Chance for a Change: New School Programs for the Disadvantaged* (ESEA 1965/Title I).
ERIC (Information booklet 1966).
ERIC Catalog of Selected Documents on the Disadvantaged, 1966.
1. Subject Index
2. Author and Number Index

Psycho-Educational Clinic

Yale University
New Haven, Connecticut 06520

Seymour B. Sarason
Murray Levine
I. Ira Goldenberg
Dennis L. Cherlin
Edward M. Bennett

Purposes: To initiate services which did not exist in the community previously; to concentrate its efforts on that part of the urban population heretofore under-represented in mental health facilities; to develop a research program focused on the special problems of the inner city school and the processes whereby change is introduced into ongoing systems.

Publication

Psychology in Community Settings, New York: John Wiley and Sons, Inc., 1966.

Research Council for the Great Cities Program for School Improvement

5400 North St. Louis Avenue
Chicago, Illinois 60625

Benjamin C. Willis, President

Mimeographed material

"Currently Available Publications of the Research Council."
Mitchell, Charles. "The Culturally Deprived — Educating the Disadvantaged" (1964).

Publications

Promising Practices from the Projects for the Culturally Deprived (1964).
The Challenge of Financing Public Schools in Great Cities (1964).
Instructional Materials to Meet the Needs of Urban Youth (1965).
The Past is Prologue (1966).

Urban Child Center
School of Education
University of Chicago
Chicago, Illinois 60637
Robert D. Hess, Director

Mimeographed material

"Inventory of Compensatory Education Projects 1965."

"Condensed Inventory of Preschool Projects 1965."

Hess, Robert D., and Virginia C. Shipman. "Cognitive Elements in Maternal Behavior."

Brophy, Jere, Robert D. Hess, and Virginia C. Shipman. "Teaching Behavior of Mothers in Structural Interaction with Their Four-Year-Old Children: A Study of Frustration" (Paper presented at the 38th annual meeting of the Midwestern Psychological Association, Chicago, May 5, 1966).

Bear, Roberta Meyer, Robert D. Hess, and Virginia C. Shipman. "Social Class Differences in Maternal Attitudes Toward School and the Consequences for Cognitive Development in the Young Child" (Paper presented at the American Educational Research Association, February 19, 1966, Chicago, Illinois).

Shipman, Virginia C., and Robert D. Hess. "Children's Conceptual Styles as a Function of Social Status and Maternal Conceptual Styles" (Prepared for the American Psychological Association Symposium on "The Effect of Maternal Behaviour on Cognitive Development and Impulsivity," given September 5, 1965, in Chicago, Illinois).

Publications

Graham, Jory. *Handbook for Project Head Start.*

Reprints

Hess, Robert D., and Virginia C. Shipman. "Early Experience and the Socialization of Cognitive Modes in Children" from private circulation of *Child Development*, Vol. 36, No. 4, December 1965; copyright, The Society for Research in Child Development, Inc.

Modern Talking Picture Services, Inc.
1168 Commonwealth Avenue
Boston, Massachusetts 02134

Films available through the auspices of Project Head Start.

Films

"Vassar College Nursery School — A Camera Visit" Stone & Levens.

"A Pre-Kindergarten Program — A Camera Visit to New Haven."

"Los Nietas Kindergarten — A Camera Visit"

"Chance at the Beginning," Institute for Developmental Studies.

"Four and Five Year Olds: Part II of a Long Time to Grow."

"Little World — N. Y. City Day Care."
"When Should Grownups Stop Fights?" Vassar College Series.
"When Should Grownups Help?" Vassar College Series.
"The Child Development Center" Julius B. Richmond, M.D.
"Adapting the Curriculum to the Child" D. Keith Osborn.
"Educational Needs of Young Deprived Children" Barbara Biber, Ph.D.
"Impact of Deprivation on Young Children" Barbara Biber, Ph.D.
"Portrait of a Disadvantaged Child — Tommy Knight."
"Children Without" Detroit Public Schools.
"My Own Yard to Play In."
"Palmour Street" Georgia Department of Public Health — Butler & Mason.

New York University Film Library
New York University
New York, New York 10016
Films

"Brothers and Teachers" ("What happens when forty boys from disadvantaged areas join with the same number from a college preparatory school in an attempt to bridge the cultural gap that exists between them?") Produced by the Project in the film, Horace Mann School; George H. Bouwman, Director.
"Operation Head Start" (Home and classroom experiences of a child in the Head Start program).
"And So They Live" (". . . a gap between the every day needs of the community and the actual instruction in the schools of the particular area").
"The Dropout" (Problems of a dropout — flashbacks to elementary school days when problems in reading first developed. . . .")
"Portrait of the Inner City" ("Film examines the streets, schools, and living quarters of the inner city slums of a large, but nameless urban community in the United States").
"Portrait of a Disadvantaged Child — Tommy Knight" ("A day in the life of a slum child . . .").
"Portrait of the Inner City School: A Place to Learn" (". . . illustrates the over-all theme that the school can be a place for the inner city child to learn and grow or a place of confinement where the child is forced into failure and frustrations").

Supplementary Listing of Films

"The Dropout" (A film stressing hidden cause of "dropouts" and suggesting possible remedies). International Film Bureau, 332 So. Michigan Avenue, Chicago, Illinois, 60604.
"Harvest of Shame" (A film revealing the deplorable plight of millions of migratory workers who harvest America's crops). Audio-Visual

Center, Florida State University, Tallahassee, Florida; University of California, Berkeley, California, and others.

"The Pine School" (The portrayal of a research and demonstration project in work with low-income families and their mentally retarded children). University of Iowa, Extension Division, Ames, Iowa.

"Small Miracles" (A VISTA film, showing the work of volunteers involving the poor in poverty programs). VISTA, Washington, D.C. 20506.

"Superfluous People" (A CBS documentary telling the story of modern urban poverty, its major causes and effects). Audio-Visual Center, Pennsylvania State University, University Park, Pennsylvania; University of Illinois, Champaign, Illinois; Florida State University, Tallahassee, Florida; and others.

"When I'm Old Enough Goodbye" (A film portraying with sensitivity and depth, some of the behavioral dynamics associated with the needs of some adolescents to leave school and find work). State Employment Services, everywhere in the U.S.A.

"5½ — Reflections on an Age." Produced by Robert Newman for the United Church of Christ.

"The Neglected." Produced by the Mental Health Film Board, New York ("Portrays disadvantaged families whose children have come under the protection of community authorities as a result of parental abuse or neglect").

"A Chance for a Change" (Information concerning Head Start Center in Mississippi — Child Development Group in Mississippi). Inquiries should be sent to Friends of Children of Mississippi, 507½ North Farish, Jackson, Mississippi, 39200.

"The Captive." National Council of Churches of Christ ("The story of a man, a coal miner of Appalachia, struggling to escape from poverty"). Visual Instruction Center, Iowa State University, Ames, Iowa.

"Marked for Failure" ("The first of four consecutive 'America's Crisis' programs dealing with the state of education in America today. Film examines the profound handicaps to learning that affect children from depressed areas"). NETV Film Service, Audio-Visual Center, Indiana University, Bloomington, Indiana 47405.

"The Hard Way" (A motion picture dealing with one fifth of the population who may be cut off from the American ladder of opportunity and success). NETV Film Service, Audo-Visual Center, Indiana University, Bloomington, Indiana 47405.

Supplementary Listing of Books

Ackerman, Nathan W. *Treating the Troubled Family*. New York: Basic Books, 1966.

Bagdikian, Ben H. *In the Midst of Plenty: the Poor in America*. Boston: Beacon Press, 1964.

Berstein, Abraham. *The Education of Urban Populations*. New York Random House, 1967.

Brembeck, Cole S. *Social Foundations of Education — A Cross-Cultural Approach*. New York: John Wiley & Sons, Inc., 1966.
Brink, William, and Louis Harris. *Black and White*. New York: Simon and Schuster, 1967.
Cheynev, Arnold B. *Teaching Culturally Disadvantaged in the Elementary School*. Columbus, Ohio: Charles E. Merrill Books, Inc., 1967.
Coles, Robert. *Children of Crisis*. Boston: Atlantic-Little, Brown, 1967.
Conot, Robert. *Rivers of Blood, Years of Darkness*. New York: Bantam Books, 1967.
Corbin, Richard and Muriel Crosby (co-chairmen). *Language Programs for the Disadvantaged*. Champaign, Illinois: NCTE, 1965 (Report of the National Council of Teachers of English Task Force on Teaching English to the Disadvantaged).
Cowles, Millie, ed. *Perspectives in the Education of Disadvantaged Children*. New York: World Publishing Company, 1967.
Eddy, Elizabeth M. *Walk the White Line: A Profile of Urban Education*. Garden City: Doubleday and Company, Inc., 1967.
Elman, Richard. *The Poorhouse State: The American Way of Life on Public Assistance*. New York: Pantheon Books, 1966.
Fanon, Frantz. *Black Skin, White Masks*. New York: Grove Press, 1967.
Ferman, Louis A., et al. *Poverty in America: A Book of Readings*. Ann Arbor: University of Michigan Press, September 1965.
Galbraith, John Kenneth. *The Affluent Society*. Boston: Houghton Mifflin Company, 1960.
Ginzberg, Eli. *The Middle-Class Negro in the White Man's World*. New York: Columbia University Press, 1967.
Gladwin, Thomas. *Poverty U.S.A.* Boston: Little, Brown and Company, 1967.
Goldstein, Bernard. *Low Income Youth in Urban Areas*. New York: Holt, Rinehart and Winston, Inc., 1967.
Gordon, Edmund W., and Doxey A. Wilkerson. *Compensatory Education for the Disadvantaged: Programs and Practices: Preschool Through College*. Princeton, N.J.: College Entrance Examination Board, 1966.
Gordon, Margaret S., ed. *Poverty in America*. San Francisco: Chandler Publishing Company, 1965.
Goslin, David A. *The School in Contemporary Society*. Chicago: Scott, Foresman & Co., 1965.
Havighurst, Robert J. *Education in Metropolitan Areas*. Boston: Allyn and Bacon, Inc., 1966.
Havighurst, Robert J., Bernice Neugarten, and Jacqueline M. Falk. *Society and Education: A Book of Readings*. Boston: Allyn and Bacon, Inc., 1966.
Keach, Everett T. Jr., and others. *Education and Social Crisis: Perspectives on Teaching Disadvantaged Youth*. New York: John Wiley and Sons, 1967.
Keppel, Francis. *The Necessary Revolution in American Education*. New York: Harper and Row, 1966.
King, Martin Luther, Jr. *Where Do We Go From Here?* New York: Harper and Row, 1967.

Klopf, Dr. Gordon J., and Dr. Garda W. Bowman. *Teacher Education in Social Context.* New York: Mental Health Materials Center, 1967.

Kontos, Peter G., and James J. Murphy, eds. *Teaching Urban Youth — A Source Book for Urban Education.* New York: John Wiley and Sons, Inc., 1967.

Kvaraceus, William O., and others. *Poverty, Education and Race Relations.* Boston: Allyn and Bacon, Inc., 1967.

Lewis, Oscar. *La Vida: A Puerto Rican Family in the Culture of Poverty — San Juan and New York.* New York: Random House, 1966.

Liebow, Elliot. *Tally's Corner.* Boston: Little, Brown and Company, 1967.

Lowe, Jeanne R. *Cities in a Race with Time.* New York: Random House, Inc., 1967.

Lyford, Joseph. *The Airtight Cage: A Study of New York's West Side.* New York: Harper & Row, 1966.

Miller, Elizabeth W., compiler. *The Negro in America: A Bibliography.* Cambridge: Harvard University Press, 1966.

Miller, Harry L. ed. *Education for the Disadvantaged.* New York: The Free Press, 1967.

Miller, Harry L., and Marjorie B. Smiley, eds. *Education in the Metropolis.* New York: The Free Press, 1967.

Moore, G. Alexander. *Realities of the Urban Classroom: Observations in Elementary Schools.* Garden City: Doubleday and Company, Inc., 1967.

Ornati, Oscar A. *Poverty Amid Affluence; A Report On A Research Project Carried Out at the New School for Social Research.* New York: Twentieth Century Fund, 1966.

Passow, A. Harry, Miriam L. Goldberg, and Abraham J. Tannenbaum, eds. *Education of the Disadvantaged.* New York: Holt, Rinehart and Winston, Inc., 1967.

Pettigrew, Thomas. *A Profile of the Negro American.* Princeton: Van Nostrand, 1967.

Powledge, Fred. *Black Power, White Resistance.* New York: The World Publishing Company, 1967.

Ritz, Joseph. *The Despised Poor.* Boston: Beacon Press, 1966.

Roberts, Joan I. *School Children in the Urban Slum.* New York: The Free Press, 1967.

Sarason, Seymour, and others. *Psychology in Community Settings: Clinical, Educational, Vocational, Social Aspects.* New York: John Wiley and Sons, Inc., 1966.

Schorr, Alvin L. *Poor Kids: A Report on Children in Poverty.* New York: Basic Books, 1966.

Schrag, Peter. *Village School Downtown.* Boston: Beacon Press, 1967.

Segal, Bernard E., ed. *Racial and Ethnic Relations. Selected Readings.* New York: Crowell, 1966.

Swanson, Bert E. *The Struggle for Equality: School Integration Controversy in New York City.* New York: Hobbs, Dorman & Co., 1966.

Taba, Hilda, and Deborah Elkins. *Teaching Strategies for the Culturally Disadvantaged.* Chicago: Rand McNally and Company, 1966.

Tannenbaum, Abraham J. *Dropout or Diploma*. New York: Teachers College Press, 1966.
Terkel, Studs. *Division Street: America*. New York: Pantheon Books, Inc., 1967.
Thomas, Piri. *Down These Mean Streets*. New York: Knopf, 1967.
Webster, Staten W., ed. *Educating the Disadvantaged Learner*. San Francisco: Chandler Publishing Company, 1966.
————. *Knowing the Disadvantaged*. San Francisco: Chandler Publishing Company, 1966.
————. *Understanding the Educational Problems of the Disadvantaged Learner*. San Francisco: Chandler Publishing Company, 1966.
Witty, Paul A., ed. *The Educationally Retarded and Disadvantaged*. Chicago: University of Chicago Press, 1967. (National Society for the Study of Education, 66th Yearbook, Part 1).

Supplementary Listing of Articles

Anderson, C. Arnold. "The National Assessment of Educational Progress: Some Technical Deficiencies," *School and Society*, 95:48–50; January 21, 1967.
Antes, John M. "Implications for the Elementary School of the Oberlin College Special Opportunities Program for Culturally Disadvantaged Children," *Childhood Education*, 43:370; February 1967.
Blaug, Mark. "Literacy and Economic Development," *The School Review*, 74:393–418; Winter 1966.
Brazziel, William F. "Federal Aid and the Negro Colleges," *Teachers College Record*, 68:300–306; January 1967.
Bryan, Dorothy. "Education for the Culturally Deprived: Building on Pupil Experience," *Social Education*, 31:117–118; February 1967.
Carton, Aaron S. "Poverty Programs, Civil Rights, and the American School," *School and Society*, 95:108; February 18, 1967.
Clement, Rufus E. Book review of *The Predominantly Negro Colleges and Universities in Transition* by Earl J. McGrath, in *Journal of Higher Education*, 37:418–420; October 1966.
Cordasco, Frank M. "Puerto Rican Pupils and American Education," *School and Society*, 95:116–119; February 18, 1967.
Culligan, Glendy. "High School and the Cultural Illiterate," *American Education*, 2:1–5; November 1966.
Curran, Robert L., and Wilson H. Guertin. "The War on Poverty and the Social Origins and Training of Education Students," *Journal of Teacher Education*, 17:456–463; Winter 1966.
de Neufville, Richard, and Caryl Conner. "How Good Are Our Schools?" *American Education*, 2:1–9; October 1966.
Dlabal, John J., Jr., and Robert L. Hanson. "What Kind of Teacher for the Culturally Deprived," *The Elementary School Journal*, 67:218–223; January 1967.
Elliott, Delbert, Harwin L. Voss, and Aubrey Welding. "Capable Dropouts and the Social Milieu of the High School," *Journal of Educational Research*, 60:180–186; December 1966.

Fischer, John H. "Race and Reconciliation: The Role of the School," *Daedalus*, 95:24–44; Winter 1966.

Fowler, William, and Alice Burnett. "Models for Learning in an Integrated Preschool," *The Elementary School Journal*, 67:428–441, May 1967.

Fulton, Robert. "The Negro Child and Public Education," *School and Society*, 95:109–110; February 18, 1967.

Gardner, John W., and Harold Howe II. "What Are Americans Receiving in Return For Their Heavy Investment in Education?" *American Education*, 2:24–26; November 1966.

Getzels, J.W. "Pre-school Education," *Teachers College Record*, 68:219–228; December 1966.

Handlin, Oscar. "The Goals of Integration," *Daedalus*, 95:268–286; Winter 1966.

Hartog, Joseph. "The Mental Health Problems of Poverty's Youth," *Mental Hygiene*, 51:85–90; January 1967.

Hawk, Travis L. "Self-Concepts of the Socially Disadvantaged," *The Elementary School Journal*, 67:196–206; January 1967.

Hilliard, Asa G. "Cross-Cultural Teaching," *Journal of Teacher Education*, 18:32–35; Spring 1967.

Itzkoff, Seymour. "Cultural Pluralism in Urban Education," *School and Society*, 94:383–386; November 12, 1966.

Joyce, Bruce R. "Please Stop Beating the Textbooks!" *The School Review*, 74:319–322; June 1966.

Kahrs, Helga. "Teaching English as a Foreign Language," *The Educational Forum*, 31:303–306; March 1967.

Kaufman, Bel, et al. "NCSPS: Education and Social Change," *Teachers College Record*, 68:229–241; December 1966.

Keliher, Alice V. "Strength of Mutual Efforts for Children," *Childhood Education*, 43:379–381; March 1967.

Komisar, B. Paul. "The Paradox of Equality in Schooling," *Teachers College Record*, 68:251–254; December 1966.

Levey, Seymour. "Are We Driving Teachers Out of Ghetto Schools?" *American Education*, 3:2–4; May 1967.

Levine, Daniel U., Sharon Albers, and Robert H. Krieger. "The Community Context of School Desegregation in a Midwestern City," *The Elementary School Journal*, 67:113–121; December 1966.

Lincoln, C. Eric. "Color and Group Identity in the United States," *Daedalus*, 96:527–541; Spring 1967.

Mackler, Bernard. "The Civil Rights Movement: From Reflection to Heartbreak," *Teachers College Record*, 68:42–48; October 1966.

Marascuilo, Leonard A., and Kathleen Penfield. "A Northern Urban Community's Attitudes toward Racial Imbalances in Schools and Classrooms," *The School Review*, 74:359–379; Winter 1966.

Marlar, Mary A. "The Lights Are On and the Whole Family Goes to School at Night," *American Education*, 3:21–24; May 1967.

Moynihan, Daniel P. "Employment, Income, and the Ordeal of the Negro Family," *Daedalus*, 94:745–770; Fall, 1965.

Moynihan, Daniel P. "The Relationship of Federal to Local Authorities," *Daedalus*, 96:801–808; Summer 1967.

Olsen, Edward G. "Teacher Education for the Deprived: A New Pattern," *School and Society*, 95:232–234; April 1, 1967.

Reid, Robert D. "Curricular Changes in Colleges and Universities for Negroes," *Journal of Higher Education*, 38:153–160; March 1967.

Riessman, Frank. "The New Anti-Poverty Ideology," *Teachers College Record*, 68:107–119; November 1966.

Sandefur, J. T., and Jeanette Bigge. "An Investigation of the Relationship Between Recognized Problems of Adolescents and School Achievement," *Journal of Educational Research*, 59:473–474; July–August 1966.

Saxton, Regina H. "Three Years of the Neighborhood Youth Corps," *Children*, 14:156–161; July-August 1967.

Shaffer, Robert H. "Peace Corps: Antidote for Provincialism," *School and Society*, 95:261–263; April 15, 1967.

Shaftel, Fannie R., and George Shaftel. "Role-Playing as a Learning Method for Disadvantaged Children," *School and Society*, 94:494–498; December 24, 1966.

Shaw, Frederick. "The Changing Curriculum," *Review of Educational Research*, 36:343–352; June 1966.

Sonquist, Hanne D., and Constance K. Kanii. "Applying Some Piagetian Concepts in the Classroom for the Disadvantaged," *Young Children*, 22:231; March 1967.

Spalding, Keith. "The Relevance of Federal Programs to the Purpose of the Institution," *The Educational Record*, 47:138–147; Spring 1966.

Stein, Lisa S. "Techniques for Parent Discussions in Disadvantaged Areas," *Young Children*, 22:210–217; March 1967.

Strickland, Virgil E. "Current Priorities in Education," *School and Society*, 95:51–53; January 21, 1967.

Thatcher, David A. "Enter Funding—Exit Curriculum-Planning," *The Elementary School Journal*, 67:171-178; January 1967.

Thomas, Maurice J. "The 'Establishment' Needs No Defense . . ." *Teachers College Record*, 68:65–70; October 1966.

Thomas, Ruth. "Negro in the School," *The Clearing House*, 41:167–169; November 1966.

Thompson, Michael L., and Robert H. Nelson. "Twelve Approaches to Remedy the DROPOUT PROBLEM," *The Clearing House*, 41:238–242; December 1966.

Weltner, Hon. Charles L. "Pride and Progress," *American Education*, 2:23–25; October 1966.

Wernick, Walter. "Must Language Programs for the disadvantaged be different?" *The Instructor*, 67:46; October 1967.

Bibliography

BOOKS

1. Adams, Donald K. *Introduction to Education*. Belmont, California: Wadsworth Publishing Co., Inc., 1966.
2. Adams, Robert M. *The Evolution of Urban Society*. Chicago: Aldine Publishing Co., 1966.
●3. Auchincloss, Louis. *The Indifferent Children*. Englewood Cliffs, N.J.: Prentice-Hall, Inc., 1964.
4. Barclay, Dorothy. *Understanding the City Child*. New York: Franklin Watts, Inc., 1959.
●5. Beck, John M., and Richard W. Saxe, eds. *Teaching the Culturally Disadvantaged Pupil*. Springfield, Ill.: Charles C Thomas, Publisher, 1965.
6. Benson, Charles S. *The Cheerful Prospect*. Boston: Houghton Mifflin Company, 1965.
7. Bereiter, Carl. "An Academically-Oriented Preschool for Culturally Deprived Children," in *Preschool Education Today*, ed. Fred M. Hechinger. New York: Doubleday and Company, Inc., 1966.
8. Bereiter, Carl, and Siegfried Engelmann. *Teaching Disadvantaged Children in the Preschool*. Englewood Cliffs, N.J.: Prentice-Hall, Inc., 1966.
9. Biddle, William W., and Loureide J. Biddle. *The Community Development Process: The Rediscovery of Local Initiative*. New York: Holt, Rinehart and Winston, Inc., 1965.
10. Bloom, Benjamin S. *Stability and Change in Human Characteristics*. New York: John Wiley and Sons, Inc., 1964.
●11. Bloom, Benjamin S., Allison Davis, and Robert Hess. *Compensatory Education for Cultural Deprivation*. New York: Holt, Rinehart and Winston, Inc., 1965.
12. Bradford, Leland P., ed. *Human Forces in Teaching and Learning*. Washington: National Training Laboratories, National Education Association, 1961.

13. Brameld, Theodore B. H. *Cultural Foundations of Education: An Interdisciplinary Exploration.* New York: Harper and Row, Publishers, 1965.
14. Brickman, William W., and Stanley Lehrer. *The Countdown on Segregated Education.* New York: Society for the Advancement of Education, 1963.
15. Broudy, Harry S. *Democracy and Excellence in American Secondary Education.* Chicago: Rand McNally and Co., 1964.
16. Bruner, Jerome S. *The Process of Education.* Cambridge, Mass.: Harvard University Press, 1961.
17. Butts, Robert F. *American Education in International Development.* New York: Harper and Row, Publishers, 1963.
18. Cay, Donald F. *Curriculum: Design for Learning.* Indianapolis: The Bobbs-Merrill Co., Inc., 1966.
19. Cervantes, Lucius F. *The Dropout: Causes and Cures.* Ann Arbor: University of Michigan Press, 1965.
20. Chandler, B. J., Lindley J. Stiles, and John I. Kitsuse. *Education in Urban Society.* New York: Dodd, Mead and Co., 1962.
21. Clark, Kenneth B. *Prejudice and Your Child,* 2nd ed. Boston: Beacon Press, 1963.
22. ————. *Dark Ghetto.* New York: Harper and Row, Publishers, 1965.
23. Clift, Virgil, ed. *Negro Education in America.* New York: Harper and Row, Publishers, 1962.
24. Clinard, Marshall B. *Sociology of Deviant Behavior.* New York: Holt, Rinehart and Winston, Inc., 1965.
25. ————. *Slums and Community Development.* New York: Free Press of Glencoe, Inc., 1966.
26. Conant, James B. *Slums and Suburbs.* New York: McGraw-Hill Book Company, 1961.
27. Corwin, Ronald G. *A Sociology of Education.* New York: Appleton-Century-Crofts, 1965.
28. Crosby, Muriel. *Curriculum Development for Elementary Schools in a Changing Society.* Boston: D. C. Heath and Company, 1964.
29. ————. *An Adventure in Human Relations.* Chicago: Follett Publishing Company, 1965.
•30. Crow, Alice, and Lester D. Crow, eds. *Vital Issues in American Education.* New York: Bantam Books, Inc., 1964.
•31. Crow, Lester D., Walter I. Murray, and Hugh H. Smythe. *Educating the Culturally Disadvantaged Child.* New York: David McKay Co., Inc., 1966.
32. Davis, Allison. *Social-Class Influences Upon Learning.* Cambridge, Mass.: Harvard University Press, 1949.
33. Dentler, Robert A., and Mary Ellen Warshauer. *Big City Dropouts and Illiterates.* New York: Center for Urban Education, 1965.
34. Deutsch, M. *Minority Group and Class Status as Related to Social and Personality Factors in Scholastic Achievement* (monograph #2). Ithaca, N.Y.: Cornell University, 1960.

35. Dinkmeyer, Don C. *Child Development: The Emerging Self.* Englewood Cliffs, N.J.: Prentice-Hall, Inc., 1965.
36. Dukette, Rita, and Thelma Thompson. *Adaptive Resources of Negro Children.* New York: Child Welfare League of America, 1959.
37. Educational Policies Commission. *Education and the Disadvantaged American.* Washington: National Education Association, 1962.
38. Edwards, Newton, and Herman Richey. *The School in the American Social Order.* Boston: Houghton Mifflin Company, 1963.
39. Eells, Kenneth, and others. *Intelligence and Cultural Differences.* Chicago: University of Chicago Press, 1951.
40. Erikson, Erik H. *Youth: Change and Challenge.* New York: Basic Books, Inc., Publishers, 1963.
41. —————, ed. *The Challenge of Youth.* Garden City, N.Y.: Doubleday and Company, Inc., 1965.
42. Ferrer, T. *The School and Urban Renewal: A Case Study from New Haven.* New York: Educational Facilities Laboratories, 1964.
43. Fischer, Louis, and Donald Thomas. *Social Foundations of Educational Decisions.* Belmont, California: Wadsworth Publishing Co., Inc., 1965.
44. Frost, Joe L., and Glenn R. Hawkes, eds. *The Disadvantaged Child.* Boston: Houghton Mifflin Company, 1966.
45. Fusco, Gene C. *School-Home Partnership in Depressed Urban Neighborhoods.* Washington: U.S. Department of Health, Education, and Welfare, Office of Education, 1964.
46. Giles, H. Harry. *The Integrated Classroom.* New York: Basic Books, Inc., Publishers, 1959.
47. Ginzberg, Eli. *The Negro Potential.* New York: Columbia University Press, 1956.
48. Glazer, Nathan, and Daniel Moynihan. *Beyond the Melting Pot.* Cambridge, Mass.: M.I.T. Press, 1963.
49. Goode, William J., ed. *Readings on the Family and Society.* Englewood Cliffs, N.J.: Prentice-Hall, Inc., 1964.
50. Goodman, Paul. *Growing Up Absurd.* New York: Random House, Inc., 1960.
51. Gordon, Ira. *Children's Views of Themselves* (Bulletin 104). Washington: Association for Childhood Education International, 1959.
52. Gordon, Mitchell. *Sick Cities.* Baltimore: Penguin Books, Inc., 1965.
53. Gore, Lillian, and Rose Koury. *Educating Children in Nursery Schools and Kindergartens.* U.S. Department of Health, Educacation, and Welfare, Office of Education. Washington: U.S. Government Printing Office, 1964.
54. Gottlieb, David, and Jon Reeves. *Adolescent Behavior in Urban Areas.* New York: Free Press of Glencoe, Inc., 1963.
55. Gowan, John C., and George D. Demos, eds. *The Disadvantaged and Potential Dropout: Compensatory Education Programs.* Springfield, Ill.: Charles C Thomas, Publisher, 1966.
56. Graham, Jory. *Handbook for Project Head Start.* New York: Anti-Defamation League of B'nai B'rith, 1965.

57. Grambs, Jean D. *Schools, Scholars, and Society.* Englewood Cliffs, N.J.: Prentice-Hall, Inc., 1965.

•58. Greene, Mary Frances, and Orletta Ryan. *The School Children: Growing Up in the Slums.* New York: Pantheon Books, Inc., 1965.

59. Greene, Maxine. *The Public School and the Private Vision.* New York: Random House, Inc., 1965.

60. Greer, Scott A. *Urban Renewal and American Cities.* Indianapolis: The Bobbs-Merrill Co., Inc., 1966.

61. Gross, Ronald, ed. *The Teacher and the Taught.* New York: Dell Publishing Co., Inc., 1963.

62. Gross, Ronald, and Judith Murphy, eds. *The Revolution in the Schools.* New York: Harcourt, Brace and World Inc., 1964.

63. Handlin, Oscar. *The Newcomers: Negroes and Puerto Ricans in a Changing Metropolis.* Cambridge, Mass.: Harvard University Press, 1959.

64. Harrington, Michael. *The Other America: Poverty in the United States.* New York: The Macmillan Company, 1962.

65. Harris, Irving D. *Emotional Blocks to Learning: a Study of the Reasons for School Failure.* New York: Free Press of Glencoe, Inc., 1961.

66. Havighurst, Robert J., and others. *Growing Up in River City.* New York: John Wiley and Sons, Inc., 1962.

67. Havighurst, Robert J., and Bernice L. Neugarten. *Society and Education,* 2nd ed. Boston: Allyn and Bacon, Inc., 1962.

68. Hawkes, Glenn R. *Helping Children Understand Themselves.* N.E.A. Elementary Instructional Service. Washington: National Education Association, 1965.

69. Hechinger, Fred M., ed. *Preschool Education Today.* Garden City, N.Y.: Doubleday and Company, Inc., 1966.

70. Hellmuth, Jerome, ed. *The Disadvantaged Child.* Vol. I. Seattle Special Child Publications, 1966.

71. Henry, Jules. *Culture Against Man.* New York: Random House, Inc., 1963.

72. Hentoff, Nat. *The New Equality.* New York: The Viking Press, 1965.

73. ———. *Our Children Are Dying.* New York: The Viking Press, 1966.

74. Herriott, Robert E., and Nancy H. St. John. *Social Class and the Urban School.* New York: John Wiley and Sons, Inc., 1966.

•75. Hickerson, Nathaniel. *Education for Alienation.* Englewood Cliffs, N.J.: Prentice-Hall, Inc., 1966.

76. Hodgkinson, Harold L. *Education in Social and Cultural Perspectives.* Englewood Cliffs, N.J.: Prentice-Hall, Inc., 1962.

77. Hoffman, Martin L., and Lois W. Hoffman. *Review of Child Development Research, Vol. I.* New York: Russell Sage Foundation, 1964.

78. Humphrey, Hubert H. *Integration versus Segregation.* New York: Thomas Y. Crowell Company, 1964.

79. Hunnicutt, C. W., ed. *Urban Education and Cultural Deprivation.*

Syracuse: University Division of Summer Sessions, Syracuse University, 1964.

80. Hunt, J. McV. *Intelligence and Experience.* New York: The Ronald Press Company, 1961.

81. Hunter, David R. *The Slums.* New York: Free Press of Glencoe, Inc., 1964.

82. Hunter, Evan. *Blackboard Jungle.* New York: Simon and Schuster, Inc., 1954.

83. Inlow, Gail M. *The Emergent in Curriculum.* New York: John Wiley and Sons, Inc., 1966.

84. Janowitz, Gayle. *Helping Hands: Volunteer Work in Education.* Chicago: University of Chicago Press, 1965.

85. Jewett, Arno, Joseph Mersand, and Doris Gunderson. *Improving English Skills of Culturally Different Youth in Large Cities.* U.S. Department of Health, Education, and Welfare, Office of Education. Washington: U.S. Government Printing Office, 1964.

86. Johnson, Charles S. *Education and the Cultural Crisis.* New York: The Macmillan Company, 1951.

87. Kazamias, Andreas M., and Byron G. Massiales. *Tradition and Change in Education.* Englewood Cliffs, N.J.: Prentice-Hall, Inc., 1965.

88. Keniston, Kenneth. *The Uncommitted.* New York: Harcourt, Brace and World, Inc., 1965.

89. Kerber, August, and Barbara Bommarito, eds. *The Schools and the Urban Crisis: A Book of Readings.* New York: Holt, Rinehart and Winston Inc., 1965.

90. Klausmeier, Herbert J., and William Goodwin. *Learning and Human Abilities,* 2nd ed. New York: Harper and Row, Publishers, 1966.

91. Klopf, Gordon J., and Israel A. Laster, eds. *Integrating the Urban School.* New York: Bureau of Publications, Teachers College, Columbia University, 1963.

92. Kvaraceus, William C., and others. *Negro Self Concept.* New York: McGraw-Hill Book Company, 1965.

93. Landers, Jacob. *Higher Horizons: Progress Report.* New York: Board of Education of City of New York, 1963.

94. Landes, Ruth. *Culture in American Education.* New York: John Wiley and Sons, Inc., 1965.

•95. Lanning, Frank W., and Wesley A. Many, eds. *Basic Education for the Disadvantaged Adult.* Boston: Houghton Mifflin Company, 1966.

96. Leavitt, Jerome E. *Nursery-Kindergarten Education.* New York: McGraw-Hill Book Company, 1958.

97. Lesser, Gerald S., and others. *Mental Abilities of Children from Different Social Class and Cultural Groups.* Chicago: University of Chicago Press, 1965.

98. Levitan, Sar A. *Federal Aid to Depressed Areas.* Baltimore: The Johns Hopkins Press, 1964.

99. Lewis, Gertrude. *Headstart for Children in the Slums.* Washington: U.S. Government Printing Office, 1965.
*100. Loretan, Joseph O., and Shelley Umans. *Teaching the Disadvantaged.* New York: Bureau of Publications, Teachers College, Columbia University, 1966.
101. Mack, Raymond W. *Patterns of Minority Relations.* New York: Anti-Defamation League of B'nai B'rith, 1964.
102. Mackintosh, Helen K., Lillian Gore, and Gertrude M. Lewis. *Educating Disadvantaged Children Under Six.* U.S. Department of Health, Education, and Welfare, Office of Education. Washington: U.S. Government Printing Office, 1965.
103. ——————. *Educating Disadvantaged Children in the Primary Years.* U.S. Department of Health, Education, and Welfare, Office of Education. Washington: U.S. Government Printing Office, 1965.
104. ——————. *Educating Disadvantaged Children in the Middle Grades.* U.S. Department of Health, Education, and Welfare, Office of Education. Washington: U.S. Government Printing Office, 1965.
105. Manuel, Herschel T. *Spanish Speaking Children of the Southwest.* Austin: University of Texas Press, 1965.
106. McGeoch, Dorothy M., and others. *Learning to Teach in Urban Schools.* New York: Bureau of Publications, Teachers College, Columbia University, 1965.
107. McGurk, F. C. J. *Comparison of the Performance of Negro and White High School Seniors on Cultural and Non-Cultural Psychology Test Questions.* Washington: Catholic University of America Press, 1951.
108. Miller, Leonard M. *Dropouts: Selected References.* Washington: U.S. Government Printing Office, 1965.
109. Morgan, Arthur E. *It Can Be Done in Education.* Yellow Springs, Ohio: Community Service, 1962.
110. National Association for the Education of Young Children. *Teaching the Disadvantaged Young Child.* New York: Mental Health Materials Center, Inc., 1966.
111. National Council of Teachers of English. *Language Programs for the Disadvantaged.* Champaign, Ill.: National Council of Teachers of English, 1965.
*112. Ogletree, James R. *Teacher Education in Service.* Lexington: Bureau of School Service, College of Education, University of Kentucky, 1962.
113. Page, Charles H. *Sociology and Contemporary Education.* New York: Random House, Inc., 1964.
114. Passow, A. Harry., ed. *Education in Depressed Areas.* New York: Bureau of Publications, Teachers College, Columbia University, 1963.
115. Piper, Don C., and Taylor Cole, eds. *Post-Primary Education and Political and Economic Development.* Durham, N.C.: Duke University Press, 1964.

116. Purcell, Carl. *Teach Me!* Washington: National Education Association, 1966.

117. Rabb, Earl, and Seymour M. Lipset. *Prejudice and Society.* New York: Anti-Defamation League of B'nai B'rith, 1959.

118. Redfern, George B. *How to Appraise Teaching Performance.* Columbus, Ohio: School Management Institute, 1963.

119. Reiss, Albert J. *Schools in a Changing Society.* New York: Free Press of Glencoe, Inc., 1965.

120. Reissman, Leonard. *Class in American Society.* New York: Free Press of Glencoe, Inc., 1960.

121. Reuter, George S., and Helen H. Reuter. *Democracy and Quality Education.* Arlington Heights, Ill.: Paddock Publications, 1965.

122. Rickover, Hyman G. *American Education: A National Failure.* New York: E. P. Dutton and Company, Inc., 1963.

123. Riese, Hertha. *Heal the Hurt Child.* Chicago: University of Chicago Press, 1962.

124. Riessman, Frank. *The Culturally Deprived Child.* New York: Harper and Row, Publishers, 1962.

125. —————. *Alternative Strategies for the Education of the Disadvantaged.* New Brunswick, N.J.: Rutgers University Press, 1963.

126. —————. *Mental Health of the Poor.* New York: Free Press of Glencoe, Inc., 1964.

127. Ripple, Lillian. *Motivation, Capacity and Opportunity.* Chicago: School of Social Service Administration, University of Chicago, 1964.

128. Rose, Arnold, ed. *Human Behavior and Social Processes.* Boston: Houghton Mifflin Company, 1962.

129. Rousseau, Jean Jacques. *Émile.* Boston: D. C. Heath and Company, 1889.

130. Rudy, Willis. *Schools in an Age of Mass Culture.* Englewood Cliffs, N.J.: Prentice-Hall, Inc., 1965.

131. Russell, James E. *Change and Challenge in American Education.* Boston: Houghton Mifflin Company, 1965.

132. Schrag, Peter. *Voices in the Classroom.* Boston: Campbell and Hall, Inc., 1965.

133. Schreiber, Daniel, ed. *Guidance and the School Dropout.* Washington: National Education Association, 1964.

134. Seligman, Ben B. *Poverty as a Public Issue.* New York: Free Press of Glencoe, Inc., 1965.

135. Senior, Clarence. *The Puerto Ricans: Strangers — Then Neighbors.* New York: Anti-Defamation League of B'nai B'rith, 1965.

136. Sexton, Patricia C. *Education and Income: Inequalities of Opportunity in Our Public Schools.* New York: The Viking Press, 1964.

137. Sheldon, E.H.B. *Pupils and Schools in New York City.* New York: Russell Sage Foundation, 1965.

138. Silberman, Charles E. *Crisis in Black and White.* New York: Random House, Inc., 1964.

139. Silverman, Susan B. *Selected Annotated Bibliography of Research Relevant to Education and Cultural Deprivation.* Bibliography for Conference on Research Problems of Education and Cultural Deprivation. Chicago: University of Chicago, 1964.

140. Solomon, P., ed. *Sensory Deprivation.* Cambridge, Mass.: Harvard University Press, 1961.

141. Spodek, Bernard, ed. *Preparing Teachers of Disadvantaged Young Children.* Washington: National Association for the Education of Young Children, 1966.

142. Stone, James C., and Frederick W. Schneider. *Foundations of Education: Commitment to Teaching. Vol. I and II.* New York: Thomas Y. Crowell Company, 1965.

143. Strom, Robert D. *Teaching in the Slum School.* Columbus, Ohio: Charles E. Merrill Books, Inc., 1965.

144. —————. *The Inner-City Classroom: Teacher Behaviors.* Columbus, Ohio: Charles E. Merrill Books, Inc., 1966.

145. Sutton, Elizabeth. *Knowing and Teaching the Migrant Child.* Washington: National Education Association, Department of Rural Education, 1962.

146. Thomas, R. Murray, and Shirley M. Thomas. *Social Differences in the Classroom.* New York: David McKay Co., Inc., 1965.

147. Tiedt, Sidney W. *The Role of the Federal Government in Education.* New York: Oxford University Press, Inc., 1966.

148. Torrance, E. Paul, and Robert D. Strom, eds. *Mental Health and Achievement: Increasing Potential and Reducing School Dropout.* New York: John Wiley and Sons, Inc., 1965.

149. Ulich, Robert. *Education in Western Culture.* New York: Harcourt, Brace and World, Inc., 1965.

150. U.S. Department of Health, Education and Welfare, Social Security Administration, Children's Bureau, *Children in Migrant Families.* Washington: U.S. Government Printing Office, 1961.

151. —————. *Programs for the Educationally Disadvantaged.* Washington: U.S. Government Printing Office, 1963.

152. —————. *Twenty-nine Questions and Answers About Title III of the National Defense Educational Act of 1964.* Washington: U.S. Government Printing Office, 1964.

153. —————, Office of Education. *Contemporary Issues in American Education.* Washington: U.S. Government Printing Office, 1965.

154. —————. *Elementary and Secondary Education Act of 1965: Public Law 89–10; 89th Congress, H.R. 2362, April 11, 1965.* Washington: U.S. Government Printing Office, 1965.

155. —————. *The First Work of These Times. A Description and Analysis of the Elementary and Secondary Act of 1965.* Washington: U.S. Government Printing Office, 1965.

156. —————. *Guidelines: Special Programs for Educationally Deprived Children.* Elementary and Secondary Education Act of 1965/Title I. Washington: U.S. Government Printing Office, 1965.

157. —————. *A Chance for Change: New Programs for the Disadvantaged*. Elementary and Secondary Education Act of 1965/ Title I. Washington: U.S. Government Printing Office, 1966.

158. —————. *Equality of Educational Opportunity*. A Summary Report. Washington: U.S. Government Printing Office, 1966.

159. —————. *State and Local Provisions for Talented Students*. Washington: U.S. Government Printing Office, 1966 (an annotated bibliography).

160. —————. Office of Economic Opportunity, Community Action Program. *Education: An Answer to Poverty*. Washington: U.S. Government Printing Office, 1966.

161. Vassar, Rena L., ed. *Social History of American Education*. Volumes I and II. Chicago: Rand McNally and Co., 1965 .

162. Warren, Robert P. *Who Speaks for the Negro?* New York: Random House, Inc., 1965.

163. Weisbrod, Burton A. *External Benefits of Public Education*. Princeton, N.J.: Department of Economics, Princeton University, 1964.

164. Weller, Jack E. *Yesterday's People*. Lexington: University of Kentucky Press, 1966.

165. Weyl, N. *The Negro in American Civilization*. Washington: Public Affairs Press, 1960.

166. Yeomans, Edward. *And Gladly Learn*. Boston: National Association of Independent Schools, 1965.

167. Yeshiva University Graduate School of Education. *Guidance for Socially and Culturally Disadvantaged Children and Youth*. New York: The University, 1963.

ARTICLES

168. Abrahamson, Stephen. "School Rewards and Social Class Status," *Educational Research Bulletin*, 31:8–15; January, 1952.

169. American Council on Education. "College Programs for Disadvantaged," *Expanding Opportunities*, 1:1–8; December, 1964.

170. —————. "Anti-Poverty Group to Assist College Projects for Disadvantaged," *Expanding Opportunities*, 2:1–2; June, 1965.

171. Anastasi, Anne, and R.V. D'Angelo. "A Comparison of Negro and White Preschool Children in Language Development and Goodenough Draw-a-Man I.Q.," *Journal of Genetic Psychology*, 81: 147–165; 1952.

172. Anastasi, Anne, and I.A. Cordova. "Some Effects of Bilingualism Upon the Intelligence Test Performances of Puerto Rican Children in New York City," *Journal of Educational Psychology*, 44: 1–19; 1955.

173. Anderson, J.W. "Special Hell for Children in Washington," *Harper's*, 231:51–56; November, 1965.

174. Arnez, N.L. "Effect of Teacher Attitudes Upon the Culturally Different," *School and Society*, 94:149–152; March 19, 1966.

175. Asbell, B. "Not Like Other Children — Slum Children," *Redbook*, 121:64–65; October, 1963.

176. Austin, E.H. Jr. "Cultural Deprivation: A Few Questions," *Phi Delta Kappan*, 47:67–76; October, 1965.

•177. Ausubel, David P. "A Teaching Strategy for Culturally Deprived Pupils: Cognitive and Motivational Consideration," *School Review*, 71:454–463; Winter, 1963.

•178. ——————. "Effects of Cultural Deprivation on Learning Patterns," *Audiovisual Instruction*, 10:10–12; January, 1965.

179. Bagford, Jack. "Quality Teachers for Our Elementary Schools," *Journal of Teacher Education*, 17:307–311; Fall, 1966.

180. Barbe, W.B. "Who are the Educationally Retarded?" *Education*, 85:451–454; April, 1965.

181. Barber, Bernard. "Social Class Differences in Educational Life-Chances," *Teachers College Record*, 63:102–129; November, 1961.

182. Baum, E.L. "Washington University Campus Tutoring Project," *Liberal Education*, 51:551–557; December, 1965.

183. Becker, H.S. "Social Class Variations in the Teacher-Pupil Relationship," *Journal of Educational Sociology*, 25:451–465; April, 1952.

184. Becker, R.J., and S. Halperin. "A.B.C.'s of Implementing Titles I, II and III of Elementary and Secondary Education Act of 1965," *American School Board Journal*, 151:5–9; July, 1965.

185. Bender, Louis W., and William G. Sharpe. "Junior High School Course for Disadvantaged Students," *National Association of Secondary School Principals Bulletin*, 47:128–131; March, 1963.

•186. Berkeley, William. "For Talented Young People, Alternatives to Poverty," *Southern Education Report*, 1:21–25; February, 1966.

187. Berlin, Irving N. "Special Learning Problems of Deprived Children," *NEA Journal*, 55:23–24; March, 1966.

188. Black, Millard H. "Characteristics of the Culturally Disadvantaged Child," *The Reading Teacher*, 18:465–470; March, 1965.

•189. Blair, G.E. "Survival of the Disadvantaged," *New York State Education*, 53:12–15; December, 1965.

190. Bloomberg, C.M., and C.H. Troupe. "Big Brothers to Troubled Children," *NEA Journal*, 53:22–25; January, 1964.

191. Blumenson, G.T. "We Pay Less by Giving More," *California Teachers Association Journal*, 60:23–24; March, 1964.

192. Boutwell, William D. "What is the Higher Horizons Program?" *PTA Magazine*, 56:17–18; December, 1961.

193. ——————. "What's Happening in Education: Culturally Deprived Children," *PTA Magazine*, 57:11; October, 1962.

194. Bradley, Gene E. "A Thousand Partnerships," *American Education*, 2:1–4; June, 1966.

195. Brazziel, William F. "Higher Horizons in Southern Elementary Schools," *Journal of Negro Education*, 33:382–389; Fall, 1964.

196. Brickner, Balfour. "Differences are Vital," *Childhood Education*, 42:67–69; October, 1965.
197. Brieland, D. "Cultural and Social Change," *Young Children*, 20:223–229; March, 1965.
198. Broudy, H.S. "Schooling for the Culturally Deprived," *Teachers College Record*, 37:4; October, 1965.
199. Brown, W.M., and R.D. Russell. "Limitations of Admissions Testing for the Disadvantaged," *Personnel and Guidance Journal*, 43:301–302; November, 1964.
200. Brunner, C. "More Than An Ounce of Prevention: Early School Admission Project," *Childhood Education*, 42:35–43; September, 1965.
201. —————. "Deprivation: Its Effects, Its Remedies," *Educational Leadership*, 23:103–107; November, 1965.
202. Bush, Gerald. "Peace Corps Training: Trials, Tribulations, and Lessons," *Educational Leadership*, 22:577; May, 1965.
203. Butler, A.L. "Will Head Start Be A False Start?" *Childhood Education*, 42:163–166; November, 1965.
204. Byers, June. "Using Poetry to Help Educationally Deprived Children Learn Inductively," *Elementary English*, 42:275–279; March, 1965.
205. Campbell, Ronald F. "Public Decisions for Urban Education," *Elementary School Journal*, 66:168–173; January, 1966.
206. Cardereo, F.M., and J.G. Redd. "Summer Camp Education for Underprivileged Children," *School and Society*, 23:292–300; Summer, 1965.
207. Carleton, Charles S. "Head Start or False Start?" *American Education*, 2:20–22; September, 1966.
208. Carlton, Lessie, and Robert H. Moore. "Culturally Deprived Children Can Be Helped," *NEA Journal*, 55:13–14; September, 1966.
209. Carson, Arnold S., and A.I. Rabin. "Verbal Comprehension and Communication in Negro and White Children," *Journal of Educational Psychology*, 51:47–51; April, 1960.
210. Cary, Gene L. "Class Socialization Patterns and Their Relationship to Learning," *School and Society*, 94:349–352; October 29, 1966.
211. Chamberlain, J. "Project Head Start: Roanoke City and Country," *Virginia Journal of Education*, 59:32–33; November, 1965.
212. Chamberlain, L.J. "Teaching in the Large City," *Clearing House*, 39:483–486; April, 1965.
213. Chandler, B.J. "Institute for Teachers of Disadvantaged Youth," *Phi Delta Kappan*, 47:77–78; October, 1965.
214. Cherry-Peisach, Estelle. "Children's Comprehension of Teacher and Peer Speech," *Child Development*, 30, 2:467–480; 1965.
215. Chesler, M.A. "Tutors for Disadvantaged Youth," *Educational Leadership*, 22:559–563; May, 1965.
216. Cheyney, Arnold B. "Curricular Methods Used by Outstanding Teachers of Culturally Disadvantaged Elementary School Chil-

dren," *The Journal of Negro Education*, 35:174–177; Spring, 1966.

217. Clark, Edward T. "Culturally Disadvantaged Boys' and Girls' Aspirations to and Knowledge of White-Collar and Professional Occupations," *Urban Education*, I:3:164–174; Spring, 1965.

218. Clementine, Sister Marie. "Programs for the Culturally Deprived Youth with Academic Potential," *National Catholic Education Association Bulletin*, 62:377–378; August, 1965.

219. Clift, Virgil A. "Factors Relating to the Education of Culturally Deprived Negro Youth," *Educational Theory*, 14:76–82; April, 1964.

220. ————. "Curriculum Research in the Education of the Culturally Deprived," *Urban Education*, II:1:19–26; 1966.

221. ————. "What Can Education Do?" *Education Forum*, 30:147–151; January, 1966.

222. Cody, Wilmer S. Jr. "Control and Resistance in a Slum School," *Elementary School Journal*, 67:1–7; October, 1966.

223. Coffman, William E. "Developing Tests for the Culturally Deprived," *School and Society*, 93:430–433; November 13, 1965.

224. Coles, R. "What Migrant Farm Children Learn," *Saturday Review*, 48:73–74; May 15, 1965.

225. Conant, J.B. "Social Dynamite in our Large Cities," *Vital Speeches*, 27:554–560; July 1, 1961.

226. ————. "Dr. Conant Discusses Forced Integration of Schools," *U.S. News and World Report*, 51:63–65; October 30, 1961.

227. Cooper, E. "Program Aids Disadvantaged Preschool Child," *Pennsylvania School Journal*, 113:404–405; May, 1965.

228. Crosby, M. "Poverty and the School," *Educational Leadership*, 22:536–539; May, 1965.

229. ————. "Living Language: Three-year Experimental Project on Schools in Changing Neighborhoods," *Childhood Education*, 42:134–138; November, 1965.

230. Dale, E. "Vocabulary Development of the Underprivileged Child," *Elementary English*, 42:778–786; November, 1965.

231. Dalton, John L. "Teachers, I Say unto You, Teach Them to Live," *Clearing House*, 40:311; January, 1966.

232. Daniel, W.G. "Educational Planning for Socially Disadvantaged Children and Youth," *Journal of Negro Education*, 33:203–209; Summer, 1964.

233. ————. "Teachers for America's Disadvantaged with Special Reference to Race," *Journal of Negro Education*, 34:381–384; Fall, 1965.

234. ————. "New Focus on the American Student as a Learner," *Journal of Negro Education*, 34:1–4; Winter, 1965.

235. Darling, Richard L. "School Library Services for the Culturally Deprived Child," *School Life*, 46:18–20; October, 1963.

- 236. Daugherty, Louise. "Working with Disadvantaged Parents," *NEA Journal*, 52:18–20; December, 1963.
- 237. Daugherty, L.G. "Purposeful Language Arts Program," *Education*, 85:481–485; April, 1965.
- 238. Davis, A. "Teaching Language and Reading to Disadvantaged Negro Children," *Elementary English*, 42:791–797; November, 1965.
- 239. den Boer, J. Reply: "Pilot Lights — Educating the Underprivileged," *New Republic*, 150:5–6; January 18, 1964.
- 240. Deutsch, Cynthia P. "Auditory Discrimination and Learning: Social Factors," *Merrill-Palmer Quarterly of Behavior and Development*, 10:227–296; July, 1964.
- •241. ————. "Education for Disadvantaged Groups," *Review of Educational Research*, 35:140–146; April, 1965.
- 242. Deutsch, Martin. "Social and Psychological Perspectives on the Development of the Disadvantaged Learner," *Journal of Negro Education*, 33:232–244; Summer, 1964.
- •243. ————. "What We've Learned About Disadvantaged Children," *Nation's Schools*, 75:50–51; April, 1965.
- 244. ————. "Early Social Environment and School Adaptation," *Teachers College Record*, 66:699–706; May, 1965.
- •245. ————. "Some Psychosocial Aspects of Learning in the Disadvantaged," *Teachers College Record*, 67:260–265; January, 1966.
- •246. Dewar, J.A., and S. Grafton. "Teachers for the Disadvantaged," *Illinois Education*, 54:173–174; December, 1965.
- •247. Dickey, Frank G. "Frontal Attack on Cultural Deprivation," *Phi Delta Kappan*, 45:398–400; May, 1964.
- 248. ————. "Our Attacks on Ignorance," *National Association of Secondary School Principals Bulletin*, 49:267–276; March, 1965.
- 249. Doherty, James. "Pupil-Teacher Ratio in Head Start Centers," *Childhood Education*, 43:7–8; September, 1966.
- 250. Downing, Gertrude L. "Supervision Experiment with the Disadvantaged," *Educational Leadership*, 21:433–435, 445; April, 1964.
- •251. Drennan, H.T., ed. "War on Poverty. Symposium," *Library Journal*, 89:3239–3274; September 15, 1964.
- 252. Duncan, C.P. "Description of Learning to Learn in Human Subjects," *American Journal of Psychology*, 73:108–114; 1960.
- 253. Dunkley, M.E. "Some Number Concepts of Disadvantaged Children," *Arithmetic Teacher*, 12:359–361; May, 1965.
- 254. Durham, Joseph T. "Melting Pot: Minorities should strive for cultural pluralism but retain their identities," *Clearing House*, 39:547–550; May, 1965.
- 255. Edgar, R.W. "History, Reading and Human Relations," *Social Education*, 29:155–158; March, 1965.
- •256. Edgerton, W.D. "AV Helps Virginia's Deprived," *Audiovisual Instruction*, 10:18–23; January, 1965.

•257. —————. "AV Services for Schools in an Economically Depressed Community," *Educational Screen and Audiovisual Guide*, 44:18–19; March, 1965.

• 258. Education Policies Commission. "The Education of Teachers of Disadvantaged," *NEA Journal*, 54:12–13; September, 1965.

259. Edwards, T.J. "Language-Experience Attack on Cultural Deprivation," *Reading Teacher*, 18:546–551; April, 1965.

260. Eidlitz, Elizabeth Meigs. "Who Cares," *Independent School Bulletin*, 26:10–14; October, 1966.

261. Elam, S.M. "Is Compensatory Education Only Palliative?" *Phi Delta Kappan*, 47:65–66; October, 1965.

• 262. Ellis, Richard R. "Looking Toward Desired Behaviors in Teachers of the Disadvantaged," *Urban Education*, I:2:117–126; Winter, 1965.

263. Epperson, D.C. "Making Social Critics of Disadvantaged Children," *Social Studies*, 57:51–54; February, 1966.

• 264. Esser, G.H. "Widening the Horizons of the Culturally Deprived," *American Library Association Bulletin*, 60:175–178; February, 1966.

265. Etten, J.F. "Wanted: Inner-city Teachers," *Instructor*, 75:29; November, 1965.

266. Fantini, M., and G. Weinstein. "Stars, Smiles and the Hidden Curriculum," *Senior Scholastic*, 85:14; September 30, 1964.

267. Fisher, R.J. "Can We Categorize Children of Urban Poor?" *Educational Forum*, 29:285–290; March, 1965.

268. Fishman, Joshua A., and others. "Guidelines for Testing Minority Group Children," *Journal of Social Issues*, 20:127–145; April, 1964.

269. Flake, Tom. "Upward Bound: A Liftoff for Young Ego," *Southern Education Report*, 2:3–8; September, 1966.

270. Fleck, H. "Disadvantaged Students," *Practical Forecast for Home Economics*, 10:5; December, 1964.

271. Fleiss, B.H. "New Venture in New York City," *Young Children*, 20:140–142; January, 1965.

272. Foster, Florence P. "The Song Within," *Young Children*, 20:373–376; September, 1965.

273. —————. "Premature Independence in Preschools for the Disadvantaged," *Young Children*, 21:142–150; January, 1966.

274. —————. "The Impact of Early Intervention," *Young Children*, 21:354–360; September, 1966.

• 275. Foster, H.L. "Teaching the Disadvantaged Child: Individualized progress chart with student personnel plan," *Industrial Arts and Vocational Education*, 55:47–49; January, 1966.

276. Fowler, William. "Concept Learning in Early Childhood," *Young Children*, 21:81–91; November, 1965.

•277. Frazier, Alexander. "Broadening the Experience of the Culturally Disadvantaged," *American Library Association Bulletin*, 58:523–526; June, 1964.

278. French, Nathaniel S. "Values and the Sub-Culture," *Independent School Bulletin*, 26:9; October, 1966.

279. Frost, Joe L. "Effects of Enrichment Program on Personality Development of Disadvantaged Children," *Childhood Education*, 42:271–272; December, 1965.

280. Frymier, Jack, and James Thompson. "Motivation: The Learner's Mainspring," *Educational Leadership*, 22:567–570; May, 1965.

281. Fuller, William A. "A View of the Peace Corps," *The Educational Forum*, 30:95; November, 1965.

282. Fusco, G.C. "Preparing the City Child for His School," *School Life*, 46:5–8; May, 1964.

283. Furno, Orlando F., and Harry C. Hendrickson. "Pupil Mobility — Implications for Urban Education," *Urban Education*, I:3:134–148; Spring, 1965.

284. Gage, N.L. "Psychological Research on Teacher Education for the Great Cities," *Urban Education*, I:3:175–196; Spring, 1965.

285. Gamberg, A.W. "Lighthouse Day Camp Reading Experiment with Disadvantaged Children," *Reading Teacher*, 19:243–246; January, 1966.

286. Getzels, Jacob W. "Learning to Learn and the Education of the Lower-Class Urban Child," *American Journal of Orthopsychiatry*, 34:238–239; March, 1964.

287. Glatt, C.A. "Who Are the Deprived Children?" *Elementary School Journal*, 65:407–413; May, 1965.

288. Goff, Regina. "Promises Fulfilled: Progress Under Title I of the Elementary and Secondary Education Act of 1965," *American Education*, 2:10–17; February, 1966.

289. Gonzales, E. "Mexican-American in California," *California Education*, 3:19–22; November, 1965.

290. Goodlad, J.I., and M.C. Hunter. "Big City Schools: Problems and Prospects; a Custom Tailored Curriculum," *PTA Magazine*, 59:8–10; April, 1965.

291. Gordon, Edmund W. "A Review of Programs of Compensatory Education," *American Journal of Orthopsychiatry*, 35:640–651; July, 1965.

292. ————. "Characteristics of Socially Disadvantaged Children," *Review of Educational Research*, 35:377–388; December, 1965.

293. Gordon, Jessie. "Project Cause, the Federal Government Anti-Poverty Program, and Some Implications of Sub-Professional Training," *American Psychologist*, 20:334–343; May, 1965.

294. Grambs, Jean D. "Culturally Deprived Child: Achieving Adequacies Through Education," *National Elementary Principal Bulletin*, 44:8–15; November, 1964.

295. Gray, Susan W., and Rupert A. Klaus. "Experimental Preschool Program for Culturally Deprived Children," *Child Development*, 36:887–898; December, 1965.

296. Greenleigh, Arthur. "The Effect of Poverty on Personal Achievement," *American Journal of Orthopsychiatry*, 34:203–204; March, 1964.

297. Groff, Patrick J. "Culturally Deprived Children: Opinions of Teachers on the Views of Riessman," *Exceptional Child*, 31:61–65; October, 1964.

298. Grotberg, Edith H. "Learning Disabilities and Remediation in Disadvantaged Children," *Review of Educational Research*, 35:413–425; December, 1965.

•299. Gulo, E. Vaughn. "Attitudes of Rural School Children Toward Their Parents," *Journal of Educational Research*, 59:450–452; July-August, 1966.

300. Haberman, Martin. "Leadership in Schools Serving the Culturally Disadvantaged," *National Elementary Principal Bulletin*, 44:20–24; November, 1964.

301. Haney, George E. "Problems and Trends in Migrant Education," *School Life*, 45:5–9; July, 1963.

302. Harrison, E.C. "Working at Improving the Motivational and Achievement Levels of the Deprived," *Journal of Negro Education*, 32:301–307; Summer, 1963.

303. Hassell, E.S. "Cultural Enrichment Program Strengthened by Parents," *Chicago School Journal*, 46:363–369; May, 1965.

•304. Haubrich, Vernon F. "The Culturally Different: New Context for Teacher Education," *Journal of Teacher Education*, 14:163–167; June, 1963.

305. —————. "The Culturally Disadvantaged and Teacher Education," *Reading Teacher*, 18:499–505; March, 1965.

306. Havighurst, Robert J. "Who Are The Socially Disadvantaged?" *Journal of Negro Education*, 33:210–217; Summer, 1964.

•307. —————. "Educationally Difficult Student," *National Association of Secondary School Principals Bulletin*, 49:110–127; March, 1965.

308. —————. "Education for the Great Society," *Instructor*, 75:31; September, 1965.

•309. Hayes, Charles H. "Team Teaching in Culturally Deprived Areas," *National Elementary School Principals Bulletin*, 44:60–65; January, 1965.

•310. Hayes, Harry. "Some Ways To Teach Culturally Deprived Children," *Chicago School Journal*, 45:221–228; February, 1964.

311. —————. "Language Arts Program for Culturally Deprived," *Chicago School Journal*, 46:337–339; May, 1965.

312. Heald, Henry T. "The Right to Knowledge," *School and Society*, 91–92:376–380; December 12, 1964.

313. Henderson, George. "Quality and Integration," *Teachers College Record*, 67:276–281; January, 1966.

314. —————. "Poor Southern Whites: A Neglected Urban Problem," *Journal of Secondary Education*, 41:111–114; March, 1966.

315. Henle, R.J. "Collegiate Education for Modern Culture," *Educational Record*, 47:340–346; Summer, 1966.

316. Henry, Jules. "Reading For What?" *Teachers College Record*, 65:35–46; October, 1963.

• 317. Hersey, John. "Education: An Antidote to Poverty," *Young Children*, 21:66–72; November, 1965.

318. Herzog, Arthur. "Learn, Baby, Learn!" *American Education*, 2:4–6; September, 1966.

319. Hess, Robert D., and Virginia C. Shipman. "Early Experience and the Socialization of Cognitive Modes in Children," *Child Development*, 36:869–886; December, 1965.

320. Hines, R.H. "Social Expectations and Cultural Deprivation," *Journal of Negro Education*, 33:136–142; Spring, 1964.

321. Hockstein, R.A. "Tiger in Stephen's Jungle," *American Education*, 1:5–7, April, 1965.

• 322. Hott, Irving. "School Administrator and the 'Educationally Disadvantaged' Child," *National Association of Secondary School Principals Bulletin*, 48:85–98; March, 1964.

323. Howe, Harold II. "A View From Afar," *American Education*, 2:1; September, 1966.

324. Hughes, J.F. "Title I: Elementary and Secondary Education Act of 1965," *Audiovisual Instruction*, 10:620–625; October, 1965.

• 325. Hunt, David E. "Adolescence: Cultural Deprivation, Poverty, and the Dropout," *Review of Educational Research*, 36:463–473; October, 1966.

326. Hunt, J. McV. "The Psychological Basis for Using Preschool Enrichment as an Antidote for Cultural Deprivation," *Merrill-Palmer Quarterly*, 10:209–243; July, 1964.

327. Ingle, Dwight J. "Individuality as a Factor in Integration," *The School Review*, 73:339; Winter, 1965.

328. Jaffa, Neubert N. "Disadvantaged Child," *Instructor*, 74:29; November, 1964.

329. Jaffa, Neubert N., and R.M. Brandt. "Approach to the Problems of a Downtown School," *National Elementary Principals Bulletin*, 44:25–28; November, 1964.

330. Jainschigg, M. "Bibliography for the Teachers of the Culturally Estranged," *National Elementary Principals Bulletin*, 45:50–58; February, 1966.

331. John, Vera P. "The Intellectual Development of Slum Children: Some Preliminary Findings," *American Journal of Orthopsychiatry*, 33:813–822; October, 1963.

332. ——————. "A Brief Survey of Research on the Characteristics of Children from Low-Income Backgrounds," *Urban Education*, I:4:215–222; 1965.

333. Johnson, G. Orville. "Organizing Instruction and Curriculum Planning for the Socially Disadvantaged," *Journal of Negro Education*, 33:254–263; Summer, 1964.

• 334. Kaplan, Bernard A. "Issues in Educating the Disadvantaged," *Phi Delta Kappan*, 45:70–76; November, 1963.

• 335. Karp, Jean M., and Irving Sigel. "Psychoeducational Appraisal of Disadvantaged Children," *Review of Educational Research*, 35:401–412; December, 1965.

284 · *Deprivation and Compensatory Education*

★·336. Karraker, Cyrus H. "Education for Our Rural Slums," *School and Society*, 91:266–267; October 5, 1963.

·337. Keppel, F. "Poverty — Target for Education," *Vital Speeches*, 30:510–512; June 1, 1964.

338. Kerckhoff, Richard K. "Race and Social Class as Opportunities for Early Childhood Education," *Young Children*, 20:357–362; September, 1965.

339. Kessler, Jane. "Environmental Components of Measured Intelligence," *The School Review*, 73:339; Winter, 1965.

★· 340. Kirk, R. "Poverty of Condition and Poverty of Mind," *National Review*, 17:467; June 1, 1965.

341. Kirman, Joseph M. "Teacher Survival in Difficult Schools," *High Points*, 46:69–70; April, 1964.

342. —————. "A White Teacher in a Negro School," *Journal of Negro Education*, 35:178–179; Spring, 1966.

·343. Knapp, D.L. "Preparing Teachers of Disadvantaged Youth," *Journal of Teacher Education*, 16:188–192; June, 1965.

·344. Koenigsberg, S.P. "Teaching Disadvantaged Youth in Secondary School," *Journal of Secondary Education*, 41:17–24; January, 1966.

345. Koester, P.W. "Elementary Teacher and Disadvantaged Bug in a Tub," *Teachers College Journal*, 37:10; October, 1965.

346. Krugman, Morris. "The Culturally Deprived Child in School," *NEA Journal*, 50:23–24; April, 1961.

347. Kvaraceus, William C. "Alienated Youth Here and Abroad," *Phi Delta Kappan*, 45–46:87–90; November, 1963.

·348. —————. "Programs for the Disadvantaged: Promise or Pretense?" *National Elementary Principals Bulletin*, 45:59–64; February, 1966.

349. Landers, J., and C. Mercurio. "Improving Curriculum and Instruction for the Disadvantaged Minorities," *Journal of Negro Education*, 34:342–366; Summer, 1965.

350. Landowne, A. "Metropolitan Systems: AV and Culturally Disadvantaged," *Audiovisual Instruction*, 9:429–430; September, 1964.

351. Lane, Mary B. "Creative Thinking on Critical Needs of Children," *Childhood Education*, 43:30–39; September, 1966.

352. Law, Norma R. "Are the Public Schools Ready for Preschoolers?" *Young Children*, 21:322–328; September, 1966.

353. Lefevre, Carol. "Inner-City School — as the Children See It," *Elementary School Journal*, 67:8–15; October, 1966.

354. Leonard, G.B. "Big Trouble in Our City Schools," *Look*, 25:28–38; September 26, 1961.

355. LeShan, E.G., ed. "Your Stake in Better Schools for All," *Parent's Magazine*, 39:46; September, 1964.

356. Levine, Daniel U. "Integration: Reconstructing Academic Values of Youths in Deprived Areas," *Clearing House*, 39:159–162; November, 1964.

•357. —————. "Stereotypes Regarding Disadvantaged Students," *Journal of Secondary Education*, 40:102–104; March, 1965.

358. —————. "On the Popular Art of Teacher Baiting," *Clearing House*, 40:298–300; January, 1966.

•359. —————. "Differentiating Instruction for Disadvantaged Students," *Educational Forum*, 30:143–146; January, 1966.

360. —————. "Crisis in the Administration of Inner City Schools," *School and Society*, 94:322–324; October 15, 1966.

361. Lewis, Claudia. "Some Puerto Rican Viewpoints," *Childhood Education*, 43:82–84; October, 1966.

362. Lewis, P. "Elementary and Secondary Education Act of 1965," *Audiovisual Instruction*, 10:722–723; November, 1965.

363. Lieberman, E. James. "The Urban Adolescent," *Adolescence*, 1:45–53; Spring, 1966.

364. Lloyd, Helene M. "What's Ahead in Reading for the Disadvantaged?" *Reading Teacher*, 18:471–476; March, 1965.

365. Lloyd, J. "Developing Creativity with the Culturally Deprived," *Instructor*, 75:27; February, 1966.

366. Lockwood, J.D., and C.W. Hunnicutt. "Whither Project Head Start?" *Educational Digest*, 31:12–14; December, 1965.

•367. Lohman, J.D. "Expose. Don't Impose: Introducing Middle Class Values to Disadvantaged Children," *NEA Journal*, 55:24–26; January, 1966.

368. Love, R.B. "Counseling Disadvantaged Youth," *California Teachers Association Journal*, 61:32–34; March, 1965.

369. Lowrie, Jean., ed. "Providing School Library Services for the Culturally Disadvantaged," *American Library Association Bulletin*, 58:523; June-December, 1964; 59:49; January, 1965.

370. Lueptow, L.B. "Disadvantaged Child: Primary group training for secondary group life," *Teachers College Journal*, 37:5; October, 1965.

371. Lytle, L. "Even Before Kindergarten—City Council of Churches, Decatur, Illinois, experiments with a summer class for young children from deprived homes," *International Journal of Religious Education*, 41:10–11; June, 1965.

372. Mackintosh, Helen, and Gertrude Lewis. "Headstart for Children in the Slums," *American Education*, 1:30–31; January, 1965.

373. Mackler, Bernard, and M.G. Giddings. "Cultural Deprivation: A Study in Mythology," *Teachers College Record*, 66:608–613; April, 1965.

374. Marburger, Carl L. "The Economic Opportunity Act—and the Schools," *Educational Leadership*, 22:547–548; May, 1965.

375. Marie, Sister Clare. "Project: Love," *National Catholic Education Association Bulletin*, 62:508–513; August, 1965.

376. Marie, Sister Jean. "Summer School for Pre-First Grade for Mexican-American Children," *Catholic School Journal*, 65:34–35; June, 1965.

377. Martinson, W.D. "Summer Study-Skills Program for Minority Group Pupils," *School and Society*, 93:300–302; Summer, 1965.

378. Mayer, Frank C. "The Teacher from Appalachia," *School and Society*, 94:324–325; October 15, 1966.

379. Mayer, Martin. "Good Slum Schools," *Harper's*, 222:46–52; April, 1961.

380. McAteer, J.E. "Equality of Opportunity Must Be Real," *California Teachers Association Journal*, 60:14–15; March, 1964.

381. McCullers, J.C., and W.T. Plant. "Culturally Deprived Child," *Review of Educational Research*, 34:599–604; December, 1964.

382. McIntyre, E. "We Got A Head Start," *Kentucky School Journal*, 44:28; November, 1965.

383. McIntyre, J.P. "Education for the Culturally Different," *National Elementary Principals Bulletin*, 45:65–68; February, 1966.

384. McKendall, Benjamin W. Jr. "Breaking the Barriers of Cultural Disadvantage and Curriculum Imbalance," *Phi Delta Kappan*, 46:307–311; March, 1965.

385. Meckler, L. "Challenge of the Educationally Disadvantaged Child," *California Teachers Association Journal*, 60:31; March, 1964.

386. Metcalf, Lawrence E. "Poverty, Government and the Schools," *Educational Leadership*, 22:543–546; May, 1965.

387. Metz, F. Elizabeth. "Poverty, Early Language Deprivation, and Learning Ability," *Elementary English*, 43:129–133; February, 1966.

388. Mikula, Thomas M. "The Responsibility of the Independent School—Education of the Disadvantaged," *Independent School Bulletin*, 25:17–19; December, 1965.

389. Moore, W. Jr. "Time to Help This Child," *School and Community*, 51:14; November, 1964.

390. Moore, W.J., and M.B. Smith. "Two Curriculum Proposals for Programs for the Disadvantaged," *Teachers College Journal*, 37:6–7; October, 1965.

391. Mott, Betty. "What's N.E.W. in California," *Young Children*, 21:361–364; September, 1966.

392. Newton, Eunice S. "Planning for Language Development of Disadvantaged Children and Youth," *Journal of Negro Education*, 34:167–177; Spring, 1965.

393. Noar, Gertrude. "The Times Call for Courage," *Journal of Teacher Education*, 15:365–371; December, 1964.

394. Norris, C.G. "Attack on Poverty," *Hornbook Magazine*, 40:364–369; August, 1964.

395. Novak, D. "Counseling Culturally Disadvantaged Required Special Understanding," *Chicago School Journal*, 45:366–372; May, 1964.

396. Oberman, J.P., and R. Warshaw. "To Shape the Future," *New York State Education*, 52:12–14; June, 1965.

397. O'Hara, James M. "Disadvantaged Newcomers to the City," *NEA Journal*, 52:25–27; April, 1963.

398. Olsen, J. "Children of the Ghetto," *High Points*, 46:25–33; March, 1964.

399. —————. "Verbal Ability of the Culturally Different," *Reading Teacher*, 18:552–556; April, 1965.
400. —————. "Challenge of the Poor," *High Points*, 47:5–16; May, 1965.
401. —————. "Challenge of the Poor to the Schools," *Phi Delta Kappan*, 47:79–84; October, 1965.
402. Olson, James L., and Richard G. Larson. "Experimental Curriculum for Culturally Deprived Kindergarten Children," *Educational Leadership*, 22:553–558; May, 1965.
403. Ornstein, A.C. "Effective Schools for Disadvantaged Children," *Journal of Secondary Education*, 40:105–109; March, 1965.
404. Osborn, Keith. "Project Head Start: An Assessment," *Educational Leadership*, 23:98–102; November, 1965.
405. —————. "A Look at Child Development Centers — Operation Head Start," *Reading Teacher*, 19:332–334; February, 1966.
406. Overfield, R.M. "Early Childhood Education in California," *California Education*, 2:14–15; June, 1965.
407. Parsons, C. "Verna Learns to Read," *Michigan Education Journal*, 42:13; May, 1965.
408. Peters, R.M. "Teacher Looks at Culturally Deprived Children," *Chicago School Journal*, 45:22–25; October, 1963.
409. Ponder, E.G. "Understanding the Language of the Culturally Disadvantaged Child," *Elementary English*, 42:769–774; November, 1965.
410. Pope, L., and R. Crump. "School Drop-Outs as Assistant Teachers," *Young Children*, 21:13–23; October, 1965.
411. Powell, Adam C. "The Role of Education in the War Against Poverty," *National Association Elementary School Principals Bulletin*, 49:56–66; March, 1965.
412. Quinn, Paul F. "In-Service Training in Guidance for the Disadvantaged," *Clearing House*, 41:80–83; October, 1966.
413. Radin, N., and C.K. Kamii. "Child-rearing Attitudes of Disadvantaged Negro Mothers," *Journal of Negro Education*, 34:138–146; Spring, 1965.
414. Raph, Jane Beasley. "Language Development in Socially Disadvantaged Children," *Review of Educational Research*, 35:389–400; December, 1965.
415. Reid, William R., and Lowell A. Schoer. "Reading Achievement, Social-Class and Subtest Pattern on the WISC," *Journal of Educational Research*, 59:469–472; July–August, 1966.
416. Rice, A., ed. "How to Plan for Three and Four Year-Olds," *Nation's Schools*, 76:45–48; November, 1965.
417. Rice, Joseph P. Jr. "Education of Subcultural Groups," *School and Society*, 92:360–362; November 28, 1964.
418. Rich, Leslie. "It Takes Courage," *American Education*, 2:5–8; June, 1966.
419. Richard, F. "Giving Them a Head Start," *Illinois Education Journal*, 54:62–67; October, 1965.

420. Richmond, J.B. "Communities in Action; a Report on Project Head Start," *Reading Teacher*, 19:323–331; February, 1966.

•421. Riessman, Frank. "Teaching the Culturally Deprived," *NEA Journal*, 52:20–22; April, 1963.

422. ——————. "The Overlooked Positives of Disadvantaged Groups," *Journal of Negro Education*, 33:225–231; Summer, 1964.

•423. ——————. "The Lesson of Poverty," *American Education*, 1:21–24; February, 1965.

424. ——————. "Education of the Culturally Deprived Child," *The Science Teacher*, 32:14–16; November, 1965.

425. Riessman, Frank, and Martin Rein. "The Third Force: An Anti-Poverty Ideology," *American Child*, 47:10–14; November, 1965.

426. Rivlin, Harry N., ed. "Teaching and Teacher Education for Urban Disadvantaged Schools," *Journal Teacher Education*, 16:135–186; June, 1965.

427. Robison, H.F., and Rose Mukerji. "Language Concepts and the Disadvantaged," *Educational Leadership*, 23:133; November, 1965.

428. Ross, F.E. "For The Disadvantaged Student: A Program that Swings," *English Journal*, 54:280–283; April, 1965.

429. Ross, I. "Head Start is a Banner Project," *PTA Magazine*, 60:20–23; March, 1966.

430. Sacadat, E. "Arousing Parent Interest in a Program for the Culturally Deprived," *Journal of Negro Education*, 34:195–196; Spring, 1965.

431. ——————. "Helping Culturally Handicapped Children," *Educational Leadership*, 22:505; April, 1965.

432. Sacadet, E., and G. Liddle. "Culturally Disadvantaged," *Illinois Education*, 54:117–119; November, 1965.

•433. Savitzky, C. "Social Theory Advances on the Disadvantaged," *High Points*, 46:54–62; February, 1964.

434. Schoephoerster, Hugh, and others. "The Teaching of Prereading Skills in Kindergarten," *Reading Teacher*, 19:352–357; February, 1966.

435. Schrag, P. "Schools of Appalachia," *The Saturday Review*, 48:70–71; May 15, 1965.

436. Schwab, Rose L. "After-School Study Centers in New York City," *Reading Teacher*, 18:482–484; March, 1965.

437. Schwartzberg, Bernard, and Irving Sigel. "Mental Health Consultation and the Nursery School," *Young Children*, 21:329–334; September, 1966.

438. Schwebel, M. "Learning and the Socially Deprived," *Personnel and Guidance Journal*, 43:646–653; March, 1965.

439. Sebastian, Mother Mary. "Culturally Disadvantaged Student and the Science Fair," *American Biology Teacher*, 27:277–280; April, 1965.

440. Shaw, Frederick. "Educating Culturally Deprived Youth in Urban Centers," *Phi Delta Kappan*, 45:91–97; November, 1963.

441 Silberstein, Richard M., and others. "Can Head Start Help

Children Learn?" *Reading Teacher,* 19:347–351; February, 1966.

442. Silverman, Ronald H. "Watts, the Disadvantaged and Art Education," *Art Education,* 19:16–20; March, 1966.

443. ——————. "Art for the Disadvantaged," *NEA Journal,* 55:29–31; April, 1966.

444. Smiley, M.B. "Who Would Teach Here?" *PTA Magazine,* 58:16–19; September, 1963.

445. ——————. "Gateway English," *English Journal,* 54:265–274; April, 1965.

446. Smith, Louis M., and Paul F. Kleine. "The Adolescent and His Society," *Review of Educational Research,* 36:424–436; October, 1966.

447. Smith, M.B. "Reading for the Culturally Disadvantaged," *Educational Leadership,* 22:398–403; March, 1965.

448. Smith, R.W., and A.W. Van der Meer. "Media and Education of the Disadvantaged," *Audiovisual Instruction,* 10:8–9; January, 1965.

• 449. Snyder, E. "Self-Concept Theory: An Approach to Understanding the Behavior of Disadvantaged Pupils," *Clearing House,* 40:242–246; December, 1965.

450. Spacks, B. "How to Learn a Secret Name," *American Education,* 1:7–12; June, 1965.

451. Spears, Harold, and Isadore Pivnick. "How an Urban School System Identifies Its Disadvantaged," *Journal of Negro Education,* 34:47–56; Winter, 1965.

452. Spellman, C.L. "Psycho-social Retardation in Education," *School and Society,* 94:101–102; February 19, 1966.

453. Spodek, Bernard. "Poverty, Education, and the Young Child," *Young Children,* 21:2; October, 1965.

454. ——————. "Is Massive Intervention the Answer?" *Educational Leadership,* 23:108–112; November, 1965.

455. Staats, A.W., and W.H. Butterfield. "Treatment of Nonreading in a Culturally Deprived Juvenile Delinquent," *Child Development,* 36:925–942; December, 1965.

456. Stalnaker, J.M. "Scholarship Selection and Cultural Disadvantage," *Secondary School Principals Bulletin,* 49:142–150; March, 1965.

457. Steinberg, Erwin. "Middle-Class Schools for Lower-Class Children," *American Journal of Orthopsychiatry,* 34:212–213; March, 1964.

458. Stern, Carolyn. "Language Competency of Young Children," *Young Children,* 22:44–50; October, 1966.

459. Stevens, F.A. "Disadvantaged and School Library Service," *American School Board Journal,* 151:20–21; November, 1965.

460. Stewart, Charles E. "Racial Issues Confronting Large City School Administrators," *Urban Education,* I:4:202–214; 1965.

• 461. Storen, H.F. "Making up the Deficit — Special Problems Facing Those Who Teach in Culturally Deprived Areas," *Clearing House,* 39:495–498; April, 1965.

462. Strang, Ruth. "The Reading Ability of Disadvantaged Adolescents," *Adolescence*, 1:60–69; Spring, 1966.
463. Strang, Ruth, and W.J. Congreve. "Not All the Disadvantaged are Poor," *PTA Magazine*, 60:15–17; February, 1966.
464. Strang, Ruth, and Mary Frobisher. "Readily to School," *PTA Magazine*, 59:10–13; May, 1965.
465. Stratton, J. E. "Big City Schools: Problems, and Prospects," *PTA Magazine*, 59:16–18; January, 1965.
466. Stull, E.G. "Reading Materials for the Disadvantaged," *Reading Teacher*, 17:522–527; April, 1964.
467. Suchman, Edward A. "Social Factors in Medical Deprivation," *American Journal of Public Health*, 55:1725–1733; November, 1965.
468. Swanson, Bert E., and Sarah Lawrence. "Subcommunity Response to City-wide School Policies: Measuring White-Parent Decisions on School-Pairing," *School Review*, 73:392; Winter, 1965.
469. Tenenbaum, Samuel. "The Teacher, the Middle Class, the Lower Class," *Phi Delta Kappan*, 45:82–86; November, 1963.
470. Torrance, E.P. "Identifying the Creatively Gifted Among Disadvantaged Children," *Education Digest*, 30:8–11; March, 1965.
471. Townsend, A. "Disadvantaged Reader," *Reading Teacher*, 19:447; March, 1966.
472. Tumin, M. "Process of Integration," *National Elementary Principals Bulletin*, 45:6–14; February, 1966.
473. Van Egmond, E. "Social Policy and Education," *Review of Educational Research*, 34:89–91; February, 1964.
474. Velie, L. "Higher Horizons for Our Asphalt Jungles," *Reader's Digest*, 77:245–248; October, 1960.
475. Voinovich, M.J. "Parent-Teacher Relationship Contributes to Pupil Success," *Ohio Schools*, 42:42; March, 1964.
476. Wachner, C.W. "Detroit Great Cities Schools Improvement Program in Language Arts," *Elementary English*, 41:734–742; November, 1964.
477. Walker, Edith V. "In-Service Training of Teachers to Work with the Disadvantaged," *Reading Teacher*, 18:493–498; March, 1965.
478. Washington, Bennetta B. "Marshalling Our Resources: Cutting Poverty Cycle Through Creative Education," *National Association of Secondary School Principals Bulletin*, 49:79–88; May, 1965.
479. ————. "Books to Make Them Proud," *NEA Journal*, 55:20–21; May, 1966.
480. Wattenberg, W.W. "Education for Culturally Deprived," *National Elementary School Principals Bulletin*, 44:16–19; March, 1964.
481. Wayson, William W. "Expressed Motives of Teachers in Slum Schools," *Urban Education*, I:4:223–238; 1965.
482. West, E.H., and W.G. Daniel. "Programs in the South," *Journal of Negro Education*, 34:310–318; Summer, 1965.

483. Wheeler, S.H. "Deprived Child," *Wilson Library Bulletin*, 39:342; December, 1964.
484. Whipple, Gertrude. "Multi-cultural Primers for Today's Children," *Education Digest*, 29:26–29; February, 1964.
485. Wilkerson, Doxey A. "Programs and Practices in Compensatory Education for Disadvantaged Children," *Review of Educational Research*, 35:426–440; December, 1965.
486. Wilkowski, G. "Teachers of Culturally Disadvantaged Children," *Michigan Education Journal*, 42:14–16; May, 1965.
487. Williams, A. "Teacher Visits the Home of Disadvantaged Children," *Teachers College Journal*, 37:12–13; October, 1965.
488. Willie, Charles V. "Anti-Social Behavior Among Disadvantaged Youth," *Journal of Negro Education*, 33:175–181; Spring, 1964.
489. Wilson, T.M. "Helping the Disadvantaged Build Language," *National Elementary School Principals Bulletin*, 45:143–146; November, 1965.
490. Witham, A.P. "It Will Take Innovation, Teachers with Understanding, Seeking, Using Title I Funds," *Michigan Education Journal*, 43:16–20; February, 1966.
491. Wolman, Thelma A. "Preschool Program for Disadvantaged Children," *Young Children*, 21:98–111; November, 1965.
492. Yerby, Alonzo S. "The Disadvantaged and Health Care," *American Journal of Public Health*, 56:5–9; January, 1966.
493. Zeligs, Rose. "Children's Favorable Attitudes Toward Home and School," *Journal of Educational Research*, 60:13–21; September, 1966.

INDEX

293

91

AL